Longevity

Kathy Keeton

V I K I N G

*The
Science
of Staying
Young*

Longevity

VIKING
Published by the Penguin Group
Viking Penguin, a division of Penguin Books USA Inc.,
375 Hudson Street, New York, New York 10014, U.S.A.
Penguin Books Ltd, 27 Wrights Lane, London W8 5TZ, England
Penguin Books Australia Ltd, Ringwood, Victoria, Australia
Penguin Books Canada Ltd, 10 Alcorn Avenue, Suite 300,
Toronto, Ontario, Canada M4V 3B2
Penguin Books (N.Z.) Ltd, 182–190 Wairau Road,
Auckland 10, New Zealand

Penguin Books Ltd, Registered Offices:
Harmondsworth, Middlesex, England

First published in 1992 by Viking Penguin,
a division of Penguin Books USA Inc.

10   9   8   7   6   5   4   3   2   1

A Note to the Reader:
The ideas, procedures, and suggestions contained in this book are not
intended as a substitute for consulting with your physician.
All matters regarding your health require medical supervision.

Library of Congress Cataloging-in-Publication Data
Keeton, Kathy.
Longevity: the science of staying young / Kathy Keeton.
p.   cm.
ISBN 0-670-83961-2
1. Longevity.   I. Title.
RA776.75.K44   1992
612.6'8—dc20   91-36364

Printed in the United States of America
Set in Simoncini Garamond
Designed by Ann Gold

To my mother,
Queenie Keeton, with all my love,
and in sorrow that her life
could not be extended

Preface

My grandmother liked to say that middle age begins at seventy. She should have known: she was still riding horses well into her late seventies, didn't have to wear glasses until she was in her eighties, and lived the active, healthy life of a country lady until her peaceful death at ninety-eight. In fact, the very idea of aging was anathema to her. When any of us dared to ask her how old she was she would smile gently and say, "I'm the same age as my little finger and a little bit older than my teeth, dear." In her will she stipulated that the only date inscribed on her tombstone be the date of her death.

If we had questioned her about the source of her remarkable vigor, she would have replied that it was no accident. The truth was that she had developed a long list of personal strategies to keep her youthful looks and extend her life span to the maximum. She firmly believed in exercise and made a point of doing something physically strenuous almost every day. She rode late in life until, after she had suffered a bad fall, her doctor insisted she stop.

From then on she walked several miles a day, a habit she continued almost until the day she died.

Her ideas about diet were advanced too. Breakfast consisted of fruit and a cup of hot water with lemon. Lunch was always her main meal and was usually chicken or fish with plenty of salad and homegrown vegetables. (Gardening was both a passion and another of her exercise routines.) Dinner was confined to a light snack. She used alcohol for medicinal purposes only and maintained that smoking tobacco was something no respectable woman would ever do. She never went out in the sun without her parasol and a pair of long white gloves. Since she had lived all her life in a remote farming area in South Africa where nothing much was available except the bare essentials, she made all her own special creams and lotions of aloe, avocado, egg white, and other exotic native ingredients which she had learned from the local Xhosa women. (If only she had written down the recipes for those concoctions!) Despite raising five children and enduring the rigors of farm life under the searing African sun, she remained slim and lovely even when she was well into her eighties. I remember my dad carrying a picture of her taken at that age in his wallet.

Obviously, my grandmother was an inspiration to me, but it is to my mother, who never cared a fig about her appearance or health, that I owe my real inspiration. It was she who determined that I would become a ballerina and who continually warned me against the dietary evils of cakes, pies, candies, and fatty foods. In fact, it is more than likely that the loving care and attention she lavished on me as a child is a large part of the reason I have enjoyed such robust good health.

Like most young people, I thought of myself as immortal, and it wasn't until I was seven years old and my beloved dog, a Rhodesian Ridgeback called Rolfie, died that I began to ask those basic and sometimes terrifying questions that all of us must ask sooner or later: Why do we age? Why do our bodies ultimately deteriorate, no matter how well we take care of them? Why do we die? As time went on, the most daring question of all began to obsess me: Are these processes inevitable?

Eventually these questions began to merge with my own growing interest in science. It all started about 1945 when I was six years old and was taken to see *Tarzan, the Ape Man* (Weissmuller vintage, of course!). I fell madly in love with Tarzan and immediately dashed off to the local library to find the book by Edgar Rice Burroughs on which it was based. The book was checked out, but the librarian steered me to another book by Burroughs, called *Princess of Mars*. I read it in total fascination, and from that point on I was hooked. If science was going to get us to Burroughs's fabulous red planet, then science would be my route as well.

One of the things I found intriguing was Burroughs's notion of artificially created life. In fact, I became so interested that I desperately wanted to become a biologist so that I could solve for myself the eternal mystery of how life began. At the time, however, little girls were definitely not encouraged to think of careers in science; and besides, my mother had very different ideas. I had suffered through a bout with polio when I was five. Fortunately, it wasn't a bad one, but it had weakened my muscles. To help me regain strength in my back and legs, my doctor recommended ballet classes.

By this time we had moved from our sleepy little farming village to a gold-mining town near Johannesburg called Krugersdorp. Plenty of ballet classes were available, and, to my surprise, I actually showed a bit of talent for dancing. That, as far as my mother was concerned, was that. She had me take every ballet class I could, including two on Saturdays. She totally banned me from horseback riding (it would spread my behind), tennis (one arm would become too muscular), and every other activity she thought might ruin my body for ballet.

When I was thirteen I won a scholarship to the Royal Ballet School in London. My mother was thrilled. My dad wasn't quite sure, but he never contradicted my mother. A few months later my mother and I sailed on the *Winchester Castle* from Cape Town to Southampton. After settling me in a rooming house near the school, which at that time had no facility for boarders, she went home to South Africa, leaving me in London to become a ballerina.

You might think that this would be the answer to every young girl's dreams, but to me it was more like a nightmare. I enjoyed the ballet well enough, but I was thirteen years old, alone in a boardinghouse in a strange city thousands of miles from home, and perfectly miserable. Fortunately, I had not lost my fascination with science or my secret desire to become a biologist. In fact, it was probably the one thing that kept me sane, if not happy, during this difficult period of my life. I discovered London's wonderful museums, which I visited at every possible opportunity. Not only were the museums fascinating, they had a staff of experts who conducted free lectures on everything from astronomy to zoology, which I avidly attended. Another, more prosaic reason for my fondness for the museums was that they were centrally heated, a luxury few places in London had in those days. (I remember one summer keeping a calendar and marking the sunny days. From May to September, there were two and a half!)

Still, for the next six years I continued with my ballet training, passed my O levels, the British equivalent of high school, and danced for a while with the Royal Ballet. I was anything but happy and was barely able to survive on the pittance I was being paid. Then one day I saw an advertisement in a paper called *The Stage*, asking for dancers to audition for the Folies Bergère, which was coming to London. The Folies was offering twenty pounds a week for chorus girls. To me that sounded like an absolute fortune, and I decided it was at least worth investigating. By happenstance, the dance master who was conducting the auditions turned out to be a former ballet master from one of the famous Russian companies, and he thought I was just great. He offered me the role of principal dancer at the grand sum of fifty pounds a week. Without a moment's hesitation I took it. My family was scandalized. My mother was especially furious with me, but they were six thousand miles away, and I was eighteen and ready to kick up my heels.

I spent the next seven years dancing in a variety of theatrical productions. I tried my hand at modeling (which I hated), made a few commercials, was a hostess on a game show, and appeared in small roles in several movies. My career as a dancer was going well. I was making good money and having quite a bit of luck investing in the stock market, but life had an empty feeling and I was bored and restless.

One day, out of the blue, I got a call from my agent, who told me that a sensational new men's magazine called *Penthouse* had printed a rather snotty comment in its first issue about my performance in a small role I had played in the movie *The Spy Who Came in from the Cold*. He told me he had spoken to the publisher, who, after much pressure, had agreed to meet me.

One evening a few days later my agent brought Bob Guccione to see the show, and my life changed in yet another direction. After calmly telling me that I wasn't the right type for *Penthouse* (which made me furious), he went on to offer me a job selling "space." My first reaction was: Is this man mad? Space to me was, well, space, as in outer! He must have seen my expression, because he quickly went on to explain that he meant advertising space. I was intrigued. Here for the first time was someone who saw beyond the long blond hair and big blue eyes. Realizing that I could do *both* jobs, at least until I was sure I could succeed in business, I instantly made up my mind to accept his offer.

Leaving show business was a curious experience. Having spent my whole working life doing physical things, it was funny to think that I was actually getting paid to take people to lunch. Soon, though, I found I was enjoying the publishing business more and more. But trying to hold down both jobs was a real chore. Unfortunately, my contract with the Pigalle, a London supper club similar to the Lido in Paris, still had six months to run, and neither my agent nor the management at the Pigalle would allow me to break it. My agent was convinced I was crazy, as were most people I knew at the time. Deep down, though, I felt sure that I was making the right decision. Luckily for me, my doctor, who was a *Penthouse* fan, agreed to give me a letter stating that my knees were bad and I should take a rest from dancing for a while.

Suddenly, life was interesting and exciting. My relationship with Bob was gradually evolving from a business arrangement into a close friendship, and finally, after almost a year of working together, turned into a great love affair, which has endured ever since.

By its third year *Penthouse* had become a huge success, not only in Britain but all over Europe, where it began to outsell its rival, *Playboy*, substantially. When we found that it was actually outselling *Playboy* to the American troops stationed in Vietnam by more than two to one, Bob, who had always wanted to return home, decided to make his move. We scraped together every penny we had, took offices in Manhattan, and bought an advertisement on the back page of *The New York Times* announcing we were going "rabbit hunting." In September 1969 *Penthouse* hit the stands in the United States. It was an instant success. Ten years later that success allowed Bob and me to indulge our common fascination with science and launch *Omni*.

The very first issue of *Omni* contained an article entitled "Some of Us Will Never Die," which focused on scientific efforts to extend the human life span to what many experts think is its real biological limit of one hundred ten to one hundred twenty years. The overwhelmingly positive response to that article by *Omni* readers convinced me that the general public had been asking the same questions about life, aging, and death that I had been asking since childhood. They shared our tremendous enthusiasm for the subject of longevity, and they were fired by the same desire to remain young and healthy.

With that in mind, in 1986 we launched *Longevity*, first as a newsletter and then, in May 1989, as a full-fledged monthly magazine. *Longevity* was designed to keep its readers informed about the latest developments in the emerging science of life extension, from the role of diet and exercise to the possibility of tinkering with the biological clocks that determine when and how we age. Dramatic new experiments were being undertaken almost daily, with scientists following leads that could take us in promising new directions. But their results were usually published in widely scattered professional journals and written in the mysterious and all but inaccessible jargon of trained scientists.

The role of *Longevity* magazine has been to collect the promising news from the laboratories under one cover and to publish it in a form that's clear and understandable to all. So far, if the response from our readers and health-care professionals is any indication, *Longevity* is on the right track. In little more than three years it has grown to a circulation in excess of three hundred thousand and has won numerous awards from both the medical and the publishing communities.

But it soon became clear to me that we needed to do more, and that a book might be the answer. Although there have been a number of books on the subject of longevity, many have been of questionable scientific value, and a few have been downright irresponsible. Even the best of them often had a particular point of view or endorsed only a single limited approach toward life extension, ignoring other potentially fruitful ideas in a field that is still full of controversy. There has been no one book that could qualify as an industry standard, a thorough, encyclopedic, and responsible book that would reveal *all* the approaches toward reaching one's maximum life expectancy, from undereating and the reduction of body temperature to the role of diet, sex, and exercise in keeping us youthful beyond our years.

Thus the birth of this book. My underlying belief in writing it is that each and every one of us holds the power to lengthen his or her own life. To tap that power, it's crucial that we stay abreast of the incredibly important discoveries being made in laboratories all over the world. In this book I've done my best to assemble all the latest scientific trends in the study of longevity and life extension. In my search for the "right stuff" I've reviewed hundreds of books and articles on the subject and have interviewed scores of scientists and doctors. I've traveled from the National Institute on Aging (NIA) in Bethesda, Maryland, to research facilities across the country and even to the U.S.S.R. to look into the laboratories and over the shoulders of scientists as they manipulate the building blocks of life itself.

To ensure the book's accuracy and responsibility I've had each scientist review the section in which his or her work is mentioned. To produce a readable book written in clear, understandable prose, I've had considerable help from Bill Lawren, a veteran science reporter who writes for more than a dozen widely respected national magazines and who is a long-standing contributing editor to both *Longevity* and *Omni*. In addition, Richard Cutler of the National Institute on Aging read the manuscript in draft and made a number of helpful suggestions.

The average life expectancy for Americans born today is roughly seventy-five years. But, as I mentioned earlier, experts tell us that our maximum life span—the number of years our bodies are biologically capable of delivering—may be as high as one hundred twenty. That means there's a more-than-forty-year difference between what we're actually getting from our bodies and what we could be getting. This book is about how to improve our chances of retrieving those lost years, and about how to live those years in great and vigorous good health, with all the enthusiasm and vitality with which we lived our first forty-five years.

We're almost at the point now when middle age will truly begin at seventy. My fondest hope is that this book will make the reader aware that whether he or she is eighteen or eighty, it is neither too soon nor too late to take up the battle against aging.

Acknowledgments

A book of this complexity, had I done it alone, would probably have taken me twenty years to write, by which time the material would have been so old it would be irrelevant. Fortunately, I have had the best possible assistance, advice, support, and encouragement from numerous people. Rona Cherry, editor in chief of *Longevity*, let me "borrow" two of her best research assistants—Amy Butkus and Josie Fowler—and was always there, ready with help and advice whenever I needed her.

My thanks to Bill Lawren, my collaborator in chief, for his considerable contribution to the entire work; to Barbara Lowenstein, my agent, whose gentle prodding kept me on track; to Marcia Potash and Dick Teresi, whose persistence in the beginning got the whole thing started; and to Al Silverman, my editor at Viking, for nudging me to get the work done without seeming to.

My assistants, Bridget Sullivan, Mandy Lanoue, and Sharon Steinkemper, get a very special thank you for their patience at printing and duplicating discs, keeping track of everything and everybody, and generally doing all the donkey work. Many thanks also to Beverly Wardale, my best friend, for her much appreciated assistance in helping me with the tedious job of updating and correcting the final manuscript.

I also want to thank the hundreds of scientists, researchers, and other professionals whose brains we picked for their best advice on staying young and for the latest information about the fight against aging. Last but by no means least I want to thank my husband, Bob Guccione, for his encouragement, his help when I needed it, and his love and understanding when I felt it would never get done.

Contents

Longevity

1

Everything You Always Wanted to Know About Aging

(BUT WERE TOO YOUNG TO ASK)

All right, let's start with the truth. We all know that aging is no picnic. *But* it doesn't have to be a horror show, either. Believe it or not, there really is a lot of truth to the old adage that some things, including people, get better with age. The common picture of aging as a long, slow decline into doddering incapacity featuring, among other things, wasting diseases, senile dementia, and the occasional crippling accident, is in need of serious revision.

Listen to Dr. Richard Besdine, director of the Travelers Center on Aging at the University of Connecticut: "Aging doesn't necessarily mean that you must be sick, senile, sexless, spent, or sedentary." Or as Dr. T. Franklin Williams, former director of the National Institute on Aging (NIA) in Bethesda, Maryland, puts it: "In most ways, aging is a remarkably benign series of processes. People who lead reasonable life styles and who are spared some of the common diseases of aging can be phenomenally healthy and active in their late years."

To launch the battle against aging, then, it's important that we have an accurate and detailed picture of what really goes on as we

1

get older. So let's start out with a balance sheet—the minuses of aging arrayed against the pluses.

In general, there's little doubt that some of us will get sicker as we get older. But—and this may surprise you as much as it did me—the majority of us will stay remarkably healthy, even into advanced old age. Recent surveys show that at least half of all Americans between the ages of seventy-four and eighty-five remain free of health problems that would otherwise limit their lives or require special medical care. Even among the 3 million people who make up the very oldest segment of our population—people over eighty-five—more than one-third report that their lives are in no way compromised by bad health. In fact, in some ways overall health may actually improve a little in extreme old age.

Many of our major organs and systems—the heart, for example—have a kind of balance sheet. The accumulated damage of a lifetime of bad habits, alcohol, tobacco, a fatty diet, and lack of exercise makes the heart far more susceptible to disease and attacks. With age there is a decrease in the number of sinus node or "pacemaker" cells, which help keep the heart rate healthy and smooth. Increased deposits of calcium and collagen make the arterial walls thicker and stiffer, which can mean rising blood pressure.

But if it remains free of actual illness, the heart undergoes few age-related changes that compromise its ability to pump blood, which, of course, is what the heart is all about. In fact, with age our heartbeats are generally well maintained, so that a resting heart that pumps 5.6 quarts of blood a minute at age thirty would pump a similar amount at age seventy. And our resting heartbeat tends to stay about the same through life. In sum, our hearts have their own way of compensating for old age, at least partially.

This plus-and-minus balance seems to be true for many of our other organs as well. The eyes are a good case in point. The pupils do get smaller, meaning that less light gets in (the retina of an eighty-year-old woman in general receives only one-sixth the light that of a twenty-year-old does); and the lenses harden and cloud over, making it hard to focus properly on nearby objects. (This hardening and clouding of the lens often mean that cataracts have formed.) At the same time, though, the lenses of the eyes tend to thicken, meaning that people who have been far-sighted in youth may find their vision tending to self-correct as they age.

What about the skin? There's no denying that in some respects our skin tends to suffer as we get older. First of all, there are the wrinkles that we spend so much time trying to fight. More serious is the fact that the number of pigment cells that protect the skin from the sun's ultraviolet rays declines by 10 to 20 percent per decade, leaving us increasingly vulnerable to skin cancer no matter what the state of the ozone layer. The outside layer of the skin, the epidermis, gets drier, thinner, and baggier. The middle layer, the dermis, also gets thinner and drier, and because neighboring molecules tend to bind to one another, it also gets stiffer and less elastic. Underneath the dermis, in the subcutaneous layer, there's a loss of fat, which means that the skin loses some of its ability to regulate body temperature. That's why older people have a harder time keeping warm in the cold, and cooling off when it's hot.

Still, our skin is not entirely at the mercy of the ravages of time. For one thing, it tends to get tougher. That leathery look that we associate with men like John Wayne and Ronald Reagan actually has a function: it helps the skin resist some insults and injuries. And for those of us who don't accept wrinkles gracefully (I'm certainly one of them), there's now plenty of real help from the cosmeceutical industry, and I'm not just talking about Retin-A. We'll save the good news on skin care for Chapter 14.

In the meantime, let's have a look at the immune system, that biological marvel that helps protect us from disease. The immune system as a whole does lose vigor as we age. This decline begins at about age thirty and continues until by old age only one-quarter of a person's disease-fighting T-cells can proliferate as effectively as they did in youth. At the same time, the thymus, the immune system's master gland, shrinks to virtual invisibility by age fifty. The result? Older people are more susceptible to infectious diseases caused by bacteria and viruses, and have more trouble fighting off those diseases once they get them. The deteriorating immune system also leaves them more vulnerable to cancer (until, surprisingly, they reach their eighties, when the incidence of cancer seems to level off). In fact, many experts consider cancer to be a disease of aging.

But the story of the aging immune system is not simply a sad tale of unrelieved decline. Recent studies show that the bone marrow's ability to make B-cells, the cells that, in turn, manufacture disease-fighting antibodies, can be unaffected by aging. And although the proliferation of the T-cells which help govern the functioning of the immune system does decrease, there's new and exciting research to indicate that this tendency can be overcome in a number of ways.

Even at its most vigorous, though, the immune system will not entirely stop our bodies from deteriorating as we get older. The bones and joints certainly undergo changes as we age. They begin to get lighter, thinner, and more brittle. Bone mass reaches its peak around age thirty, then declines at a rate of about 1 percent a year. This gradual thinning and increasing brittleness of the bones is known as osteoporosis, and it strikes as many as 24 million Americans, both men *and* women. This means an increased rate of fractures, especially of the hip, and a slower recovery rate once fractures occur. The joints, battered by years of basketball, tennis, and pavement pounding, are more susceptible to degenerative arthritis, while worn cartilage and depleted lubricating fluid in the joints make us generally stiffer, slower, and less flexible.

So no matter how hard we work at it, the body inevitably loses some of its tone. Flab spreads, especially in the waist and chest; muscles stiffen as muscle fiber is gradually replaced by less flexible connective tissue; strength and stamina decline. Reflexes slow, although, surprisingly, by only about 10 percent during the forty years between thirty and seventy.

Does all this mean that as we age, our capacity for healthful physical exercise declines? No way. Conider Noel K. Johnson, author of the book *A Dud at 70, A Stud at 80*. Twenty years ago, when he was seventy, Johnson was fifty pounds overweight and a problem drinker. He had arthritis, gout, and heart trouble. He was so sick and sedentary, in fact, that his son suggested that he take up residence in a nursing home. Now over ninety, Johnson is down to a lithe 138 pounds. He works out at least three hours every day—running, lifting weights, jumping on a trampoline, doing speed work with a punching bag. He's run the New York Marathon seven times, with a personal best time of five hours, forty-two minutes, this when he was a lad of eighty-three. In fact, just after he completed the 1989 Marathon, he hopped a plane to the Soviet Caucasus, where, he told reporters, "There's a 110-year-old woman who wants to dance with me."

Johnson's story may be a bit of an exception to the rule. But the rule is stretched these days by what we now know about exercise. The fact is that older athletes, people in their sixties and seventies, actually have a greater aerobic capacity than much younger people who lead sedentary lifestyles. Muscles, according to Washington University physiologist John Holloszy, may lose a bit of mass and contractile speed, but overall they change surprisingly little with age. The message, which we'll explore in much greater detail in Chapter 11, is clear: don't surrender to preconceptions about age and physical activity.

There's another kind of physical activity that doesn't necessarily have to decline with age either, and it's some people's only form of exercise. Sex works for older people, and there's absolutely no age limit. The common picture that equates old age with sexlessness is just plain wrong. Men may take a little longer to get an erection, but their levels of the male hormone testosterone stay more or less constant throughout their lives; and most men still produce sperm well into their seventies. Impotence, when it strikes, is usually a function not of age but of disease, especially heart disease, diabetes, or chronic alcoholism. A study by Clyde Martin, Ph.D., one of the authors of the first Kinsey Report, showed that men who were sexually active in their later lives reported more active sex lives in their youth.

For women the sexual picture can be equally upbeat. Although older women may experience some physical difficulties, such as hot flashes or vaginal dryness, these problems can often be alleviated with hormone therapy. Basically, so long as a woman remains sexually active she can expect to be responsive well into old age. In many women, in fact, sexual desire actually increases after menopause.

So much for the body. Now on to the brain. Alas, the brain does shrink with age, gradually losing cells. (Unlike cells in most of the rest of the body, which are usually replaced when they die, a brain cell once lost is gone forever.) In old age the brain can actually weigh 10 to 15 percent less than it did in youth. With that shrinkage comes a certain slowdown: although older people can perform mental tasks just about as well as younger people, they can't do them as quickly. Geropsychiatrist Soo Borson of the University of Washington and Seattle Veterans' Hospital says that an older person facing a mental task may experience more stress in the sympathetic nervous system than a younger person facing the same task.

All this may not be as damaging as it may seem. "There is redundancy in the brain," explains neurologist David Drachman of the University of Massachusetts Medical Center in Worcester. "It's like the lights in Times Square. Suppose you turn off twenty percent of the bulbs: you'll still get the message." This redundancy allows our brains to continue functioning effectively even though a certain number of nerve cells have been lost.

For many of us—perhaps *most* of us—old age can be a time when the mind wants to go venturing. Despite the well-published ravages of Alzheimer's disease and other forms of age-related dementia, mental skills do not necessarily decline with age, and many mental capacities can be maintained as we get older. Take Stephen Powelson, an American business executive who lived for years in Paris. For ten years after his retirement at sixty, Powelson used his spare time to memorize all twenty-four books of Homer's *Iliad*! For those of us who may be slightly less ambitious, the news is still good. Studies among people sixty-five and older have revealed that more than 85 percent suffered little or no memory loss. And a number of researchers have shown that, in the words of Dr. John W. Rowe, director of the MacArthur Foundation Research Network on Successful Aging, "perhaps the most important type of change that occurs with aging is no change at all." (More about this in Chapter 12.)

If our brains can remain active, vigorous, and capable, so, apparently, can our spirits. While for some of us, especially those with general insecurities, old age can mean increased anxiety and depression, nationwide surveys by the Institute for Social Research show that a great many older people seem more carefree than younger adults, with fewer and less bothersome problems. According to University of Illinois psychologist Ed Diener, these surveys show "a slow rise in satisfaction with age . . . young persons appear to experience higher levels of joy but older persons tend to judge their lives in more positive ways." When stressful situations do arise, an inevitable feature of life at any age, the epic Baltimore Longitudinal Study, which was started in 1958, found that older people adapted to them as well as, if not better than, younger people.

Much of this emotional balance and well-being is no doubt due to the development of a kinder and more generous self-image with advancing years. "As persons age," says sociologist Walter R. Gove of Vanderbilt University, "their self-concepts . . . contain more positive attributes, fewer negative attributes, and become better integrated." In other words, we tend to judge ourselves less harshly, like ourselves better, and see our flaws as a good deal less tragic than they seemed in painful youth. "In middle age," as the writer Pete Hamill once put it, "you tend to forgive yourself." All in all, says University of Michigan psychologist Marion Perlmutter, "I think we get enough positive changes with age—especially wisdom—that the psychological outlook can actually be better than in middle age."

We still haven't quite exhausted our aging balance sheet. On the bad news side are certain detrimental changes in the lungs—they don't expand as well, so that a deep breath isn't as deep in old age as it was in youth. The kidneys' ability to filter waste out of the bloodstream decreases by as much as 50 percent between the ages of thirty and eighty. The bladder's capacity declines from two cups at age thirty to one cupful at seventy, making the need to urinate more frequent and urgent. The filtering power of the liver also seems to decline, so that alcohol and drugs remain in the body longer.

Less serious but possibly more annoying are the little things that show up not so much in the doctor's office as in the bathroom mirror. For men, hair appears in unwanted places—the ears, nose, and back, for example—and it either grays or disappears from the places they want it most. A woman's hair tends to thin and to lose some of its youthful sheen. Even the fingernails grow more slowly (0.6 millimeter a week at seventy, compared to 0.94 a week at twenty), which means less frequent need for grooming but more unsightliness because they're exposed to weathering for longer periods of time.

But like everything else we've talked about so far, there are compensations. For example, people become somewhat less sensitive to pain as they get older. They sweat less (sweat glands tend to dry up), sneeze less (fewer allergic reactions as the immune system slows down), and have fewer nightmares (no one knows why). Taste sensitivity remains relatively constant, while the skin is more resistant to insults from harsh chemicals and other irritants. Even the course of the day often improves for older people: since they need about two hours less sleep, the day is two hours longer, giving them extra time to exercise, socialize with friends and family, or even use their lives creatively.

So much for our balance sheet. It shows that while in many ways aging does mean slowdown and decline, in other and in some cases equally important ways, getting older actually does mean getting better. And the way to start this battle against aging is to have an optimistic and enthusiastic attitude. If we know that the second half of our lives can be a time of active good health, contentment, and genuine achievement, then the battle is already partially won.

Underlying much of our optimism and enthusiasm is a simple biological fact: there is an enormous difference between life *expectancy,* the number of years we actually live, and life *span,* the maximum number of years that we *could* live if nothing got in our way. Human life expectancy has increased impressively since the days of the Roman Empire, when people lived on average only about twenty-two years. (This probably represented no improvement on the life expectancies of Neanderthals and Cro-Magnons.) Today, with antibiotics, high-tech medicine, and especially modern sanitation, life expectancy, in the industrialized world, at least, has reached into the mid-seventies (experts estimate that more than two-thirds of the improvement in life expectancy has taken place in the twentieth century alone).

Perhaps even that improvement isn't good enough. Scientists think that the natural human life span, the number of years the human organism is biologically programmed to last, may be as long as one hundred and fifteen years, and perhaps even a bit longer. Jan Vijg, director of microbiology at the Institute of Experimental Gerontology near Delft, The Netherlands, believes that in the not so distant future many of us will live to be one hundred and thirty! That's a difference of at least forty years, forty extra years that we could be getting from life if we only knew how to do it.

What it comes down to, and what this book is all about, is, as anthropologist Ashley Montague put it, how to "die young, as late as possible." Can science show us how to slow down the aging process so that our life expectancy will more nearly match our potential life span? This is the question that lies at the heart of the vast and growing body of scientific research into the mysteries of aging and death.

For these *are* great mysteries, perhaps the greatest of all. Certainly they've drawn the fascinated attention of philosophers and fakirs, priests and pundits, since the dawn of human history. Now, in the midst of the restless unfolding of the age of biotechnology, we are witnessing the beginnings of an all-out scientific assault on these ancient questions. All over the world, in large national institutions like the NIA and in small, out-of-the-way laboratories at newborn biotechnology companies, researchers are attempting to coax from nature a set of solutions to the extremely complex problems posed by investigations into human longevity. What's more, they're going about it with an optimism that at times seems to border on hubris. Jan Vijg's attitude may be representative: "Growing old in the traditional sense," he says, "is not inevitable. We are already developing ways to counter it."

Throughout this book we'll become acquainted with many of the scores of scientists who are busily pushing at the very limits of human mortality. We'll go into their offices and laboratories, and peer over their shoulders as they probe and manipulate the stuff of life itself. We'll meet the men and women who are running some of the biggest anti-aging institutions in the country, places where a comprehensive, all-out attack is being mounted against the infirmities of old age, where, by implication and by stated objective, the curtains of death itself are being inexorably rolled back.

T. Franklin Williams is the former director of the National Institute on Aging in Bethesda, Maryland, one of the world's largest and most comprehensive centers for scientific research into the problems of aging. Under orders from Congress not only to delve into the sources of common aging diseases but to probe the biological mechanics of the aging process itself, the NIA currently sponsors state-of-the-art research projects in cellular aging, age-related hormonal changes, genetics, and the mysteries of the aging brain, all of which will be discussed in detail later on in this book.

While some researchers at the NIA are interested in the mechanics of aging, others are fascinated by the fact that aging occurs at different rates in different people. At one time or another, all of us have probably taken one of those tests that are supposed to tell us our real biological age—as opposed to the merely chronological age that appears on our driver's license and insurance policies. Well, we'll give you a smorgasbord of such tests, including the very latest, developed by *Longevity* magazine in collaboration with experts from the NIA. These tests appear in Chapter 7.

Getting a good score on these tests may be partially dependent on how one eats. Over the last twenty years scientists have focused as never before on the newly revealed relationship between diet and longevity. Several groups are busy investigating the intriguing notion that eating less can mean living longer. Those groups include teams headed by Edward J. Masoro of the University of Texas at San Antonio and Ronald S. Hart of the National Center for Toxicological Research in Jefferson, Arkansas. The best-known proponent of dietary restriction, though, is UCLA pathologist Roy L. Walford. Not satisfied with laboratory experiments that show that mice on restricted diets live a great deal longer, Walford has reduced his own food intake to around 1,650 calories a day. By doing so, Walford, who is now sixty-seven, hopes to live at least another fifty years.

This assumes, of course, that he isn't done in by free radicals. Perhaps the most chic of all the aging theories was first proposed by Denham Harman of the University of Nebraska and was popularized in the early 1980s by Durk Pearson and Sandy Shaw, the authors of *Life Extension*. Free radicals are atoms or molecules that have an extra electron. They stabilize themselves by finding other molecules that are willing to share electrons, and then combine with those molecules. The problem is that in combining, the free radicals may well destroy the donor molecules, cleaving them in half or playing havoc with their genetic information. Free-radical damage is thought by some scientists to be at the heart of the aging process. In Chapter 4 we'll look into the pros and cons of that idea with such experts as Lester Packer of the University of California at Berkeley and Simin Meydani of the USDA Human Nutrition Research Center on Aging at Tufts University, outside Boston.

While some scientists see aging as the result of too many free radicals, others have different theories. Dr. Leonard Sagan, a California epidemiologist, is the author of a controversial study called *The Health of Nations.* Sagan concludes that love at a very early age is the key to a longer, healthier life. Dr. Sagan has had a lot of help from Stanford University's Robert Sapolsky, who has done experiments involving rat pups that are handled just after they're born, and who thinks he may actually have found a biological mechanism that links love and longevity. More about this in Chapter 13.

Love, of course, is not the only emotion to figure in healthy aging. Relative freedom from stress and guilt, a feeling of control over one's life, satisfaction with one's past achievements, and a sense of a hopeful, active future all play a vital part in staying youthful beyond one's years. We will hear from experts like Sapolsky, Kenneth R. Pelletier, and Harvard's Ellen Langer on the subject. At the same time, psychologists like Marion Perlmutter and Harvard University's Jerome Kagan will assure us that an aging brain is not necessarily a deteriorating brain, not so long as we keep it stimulated with challenging tasks.

What's true for the mind should be true for the body as well. In Chapter 11 experts like Stanford's Ralph S. Paffenbarger, Jr., and John Meyer of Baylor will tell us why they think that physical exercise can lengthen our lives. Other experts will provide us with a sensible exercise program designed to keep the body strong and vigorous even into advanced old age. In Chapter 13 another group of scientists, including the author and researcher Alex Comfort, who wrote *The Joy of Sex* and *More Joy of Sex*, will tell us what to expect from their favored form of exercise.

As to sex and sex appeal, there's little doubt that looking good can help one feel good. This may be just as true for octogenarians as it is for blushing brides. In Chapter 14 we'll take a detailed look at the burgeoning list of tools, techniques, and tricks to help keep our faces and bodies lying about our age. This includes not only Dr. Albert M. Kligman's well-known wrinkle-eater, Retin-A, but other "cosmeceuticals" like the hair-growing Rogaine and the skin-rejuvenating Nayad. In Chapter 15 we'll talk about the seemingly magical techniques available to cosmetic surgeons with the advent of the laser, and we'll even include tips from one woman who actually went through plastic surgery.

Chapter 17 will be devoted to chemicals, both internal and external, and their still-controversial role in the aging process. In the 1970s W. Donner Denckla, an endocrinologist at Harvard University, proposed that as we age, the pituitary gland begins to release a specific hormone that turns on, or at least accelerates, human aging. Denckla spent much of his career trying to isolate that substance, which he called, chillingly enough, the "death hormone." At about the same time, the George Washington University biologist Allan Goldstein became fascinated with the thymus, the gland that plays such an important part in "training" the cells that keep our immune systems active and vigilant. Goldstein discovered *thymosin,* the first of a family of thymic hormones, and his subsequent experiments with the substances have turned up tantalizing clues to their role in biological aging.

Recently, Dr. Daniel Rudman of the Medical College of Wisconsin, in Milwaukee, has shown that human growth hormone, another important product of the pituitary gland, can help keep an aging body young. William Regelson of the Medical College of Virginia is among the scientists looking at the role of melatonin, the "light and dark" hormone that helps regulate the body's biological clock, as an important player in aging. And scientists at Alpha Biomedicals in Washington, D.C., are tinkering with hormones that could help bolster sagging immune systems, even in the elderly.

While Denckla, Goldstein, et al. think that aging may begin in the glands, other experts suspect that the major culprit is the brain. Dramatic operations have been performed in Sweden, Mexico, and the United States, in which patients with Parkinson's disease were given implants of fetal brain cells. There are a number of researchers who have even bolder ideas. Carl Cotman of the University of California at Irvine is studying the possibility that damaged brain and nervous system cells can be regenerated. There are at least some scientists who talk optimistically about a future in which surgeons will be able to combat aging by actually transplanting whole brains!

This is essentially the spare-parts approach to the attack on aging, and the brain is by no means the only spare part under consideration. A few years ago Eugene Bell, a former biology professor at the Massachusetts Institute of Technology, launched Organogenesis, a Cambridge, Massachusetts, biotech company whose labs are manufacturing replacement skin and blood vessels. Bell is now retired, but scientists at Organogenesis and elsewhere look forward to doing the same with bones, pancreases, and even thyroid glands. And there's more on the way. "A hundred years from now," says biomedical engineer Daniel Schneck of the Virginia Polytechnic Institute and State University in Blacksburg, "people will be able to walk into a department store, buy an organ off the shelf, and replace it themselves. With the appropriate prosthetic devices," concludes Schneck, who is currently president of the Biomedical Engineering Society, "we'll be able to extend life to a hundred and twenty-five years, and chances are it will be even longer than that."

Not everyone agrees that aging can be effectively combated or even defeated simply by replacing brain and body parts as they wear out. Many scientists are looking into what they see as the foundation of the aging matter: age-related changes that take place at the level of the cell, the chromosome, and even the individual gene. "How does the cell know when it's old?" asks Vincent Cristofalo of the University of Pennsylvania. "If the cells learn to time their life histories by some set of mechanisms, that will be a key to aging." Cristofalo and James R. Smith, a cellular geneticist at the Baylor College of Medicine in Houston, have found evidence for specific proteins that may be responsible for turning the process of cell division on and off. Marguerite M. B. Kay of the University of Arizona has found a single protein marker that may tag aging cells for destruction by the body's immune system. Meanwhile, J. Carl Barrett and his colleagues at the National Institute for Environmental Health Sciences in Research Triangle Park, North Carolina, have found a specific chromosome, called human chromosome 1, the absence of which appears to turn normal cells—that is, cells with normal cycles of growth, aging, and death—into cancerous "immortals." We'll go into all this in detail in Chapter 18.

In that same chapter we'll talk with the researchers who are launching an attack against aging at the place where it may well begin, in the genes. Jorge Yunis, a geneticist at Hahnemann College in Philadelphia, has identified as many as one hundred and ten "fragile sites," weak links in human chromosomes that can break when exposed to mutation-causing chemicals. J. Carl Barrett has isolated a chromosome that may help regulate normal aging in human cells; while Thomas E. Johnson, a molecular geneticist at the University of Colorado, has actually identified a single gene, called AGE-1, that may be one of the regulators of the aging process, in at least one species of worm.

So this is what we're up to in this book. First of all, we want everyone to know that there are techniques that can be applied *right now,* with a better than reasonable hope that they will actually have a positive effect on stretching out the years of our lives. And tomorrow? That's the truly exciting part. In the not so distant future, science may well unlock the biological keys to the aging process itself, providing each and every one of us with the chance to live out an extra forty years, and to live them in great good health.

That research, that fantastic scientific journey, is already under way; in fact, it's a good deal further along than most of us realize. So I encourage you to think of the rest of this book as a sort of travelogue, your personal guidebook to that most important of all destinations: living the longest, the healthiest, and the fullest life possible.

2

*The Quest
for the Fountain
of Youth*

On a brilliant fall day in 1889, the scholars of the august College
of France gathered in Paris to hear a lecture by a seventy-two-
year-old former Harvard professor named Charles Edouard
Brown-Sequard. Few of the Frenchmen had ever heard of Brown-
Sequard, but few would ever forget his startling announcement.
"I have recovered the strength and vigor of a young man," the
professor swore, "by drinking an extract of crushed dog testicles."
Brown-Sequard went on to claim that this concoction had so re-
newed him that he was able to sexually satisfy his new, and presumably ravenous, young bride.

For a year afterward, the elderly male population of France was
all astir, as doctors rushed to prescribe Brown-Sequard's promising
potion. The only problem was that it didn't work. A year later the
humbled Brown-Sequard was a public laughingstock, his disgrace
crowned when his young wife deserted him.

This story is one of my personal favorites. The battle against
aging tends to attract more than its share of wild-eyed loonies,
charlatans, and just plain quacks. Among the medieval alchemists,

for example, were a good many con men who were happy to sell immortality by the pound, in the guise of pieces of the "philosopher's stone." The same can be said of the medicine men who traveled around the country in the eighteenth and nineteenth centuries—usually just one step ahead of the local sheriff.

Still, for every snake-oil salesman who offered immortality in a jar there has been a scientist or philosopher whose intentions were honest and whose interest was genuine. The subject of longevity is lodged in earliest human history. The Book of Genesis, for example, declares that before the great Flood, everyone lived much longer. So Methuselah, the grandest of all great-grandfathers, supposedly lived to be 969 (at 950, Noah wasn't far behind), while poor postdiluvian Jacob only made it to 147.

The poetry and mythology of the Greeks was likewise full of yearnings for long life. The Greek poet Hesiod painted a lovely and wistful picture of an Arcadian past in which members of the "Golden Race" lived a century or more without aging; then, when their time came, they lay down to a calm and peaceful death, "as though they were overcome with sleep." Next in Hesiod's "history" came the "Silver Race," whose childhood lasted a hundred years. But when the long-lived children of the Silver Age failed to show proper appreciation to the gods, Zeus had them all whisked off to the underworld, where their very longevity became an especially cruel form of punishment. Still, the Greeks believed that in Hyperboreas—the Land Beyond the North Wind—and in the mythical Isles of the Blest, located somewhere in the Atlantic, were a perfect people who lived a thousand years. "Their hair crowned with golden bay leaves," wrote the poet Pindar, "they hold glad revelry; and know neither sickness nor baneful old age."

Even while some Greeks were reveling in their myths of eternal life, others were developing an attitude toward longevity that even today can be called scientific. Both the philosopher Aristotle and the second-century Greek physician Galen saw life as a function of body temperature. They believed that each of us is endowed with a certain amount of "innate heat" (Galen, who was evidently a bit of a sexist, thought this "heat" was ignited at conception by the man's sperm), and that aging occurs when that heat starts to dissipate and the body turns cold and dry. Although neither Aristotle nor Galen ever stated this explicitly, their ideas left room for the hopeful to conclude that to enjoy a long life all one had to do was stay warm and wet. (Maybe this is why the great Greek mathematician and inventor Archimedes seemed to spend so much of his time in bathtubs.)

The semi-scientific ideas of Aristotle and Galen were definitely in the minority in ancient times. Most peoples in most places seemed to prefer fantasy to science. In fact, many cultures have had myths involving elixirs that could keep one young forever: the Hindu Pool of Youth; the Hebraic River of Immortality, with its source in Eden; and the Greek Fountain of Youth in the jungles of Jupiter, where the nymph Juventas had been transformed into a clear, sweet stream whose waters would restore youth and health to anyone lucky enough to swim in them.

The Arabs also had their fountain of youth, which they called the "Well of the Water of Life." The well was supposed to have been discovered accidentally when El Khidr, a popular figure of Arabic legend, washed a dried fish in it and saw the fish come back to life before his eyes. Not one to pass up a good thing, El Khidr immediately jumped into the well himself, and, sure enough, became immortal.

Two thousand years later, the Spanish explorer Juan Ponce de León set off in search of the island of Bimini, supposedly the site of another Fountain of Youth. Ponce de León was said to be a sentimental old man who was aging so poorly that he could no longer satisfy his gorgeous young wife (I wonder how many dreams of eternal life have been ignited by May-December romances). Hoping to find a magical way to keep himself youthful and vigorous, the Spaniard bravely set sail into the unknown. Poor Juan: There was no Fountain of Youth—the best he could do was discover Florida.

While Ponce de León and others looked for immortality in far-off islands and bubbling streams, others sought long life through right living and spiritual discipline. The goal of the Chinese Taoist, for example, was to find the "way" (the Tao), to actualize himself so thoroughly that he became a *hsien*—an exalted being who would live so long as to become virtually immortal. To do this, the Taoists tried to conserve their vital energies so that life became essentially effortless. They learned how to reduce their breathing rate while at the same time "guiding" their inhalations directly to the brain, keeping it nourished with oxygen. They ate little but fruit and roots—no meat, no grains, certainly no alcohol—and tried to achieve a state in which they could live on nothing but their own breath and saliva. They practiced t'ai chi to keep their insides clean, and a peculiar (to us, anyway) form of sex in which ejaculation was replaced by meditation. The idea of all this conservation of energy was to cheat death for as long as possible.

Actually, the Taoist search for long life through right living had something in common with medieval alchemy. Although some alchemists were undoubtedly charlatans, most were serious, respectable types whose quest for the philosopher's stone can be seen as an allegory for the search for immortality. The idea of turning lead to gold can be viewed metaphorically: the "lead" is the ordinary human soul, the "gold" is that soul in its perfect, immortal state, and the philosopher's stone, a concoction that blended oil of antimony with a number of herbs in a secret, coded recipe, was supposed to effect the magical transformation from ignorance to perfect wisdom—and, more important, from mortal to immortal.

Sounds like mumbo-jumbo, doesn't it? Yet, curiously enough, the truly scientific struggle against aging may have had its beginnings with such alchemists as the sixteenth-century German scholar Paracelsus, the Englishman Basil Valentine, and particularly the medieval Franciscan monk, philosopher, and scientist Roger Bacon. Like the Greek philosophers before him, Bacon used reason as a tool to attack the fear of death. "The possibility of the prolongation of life is confirmed," he wrote, "by the consideration that the soul naturally is immortal and capable of not dying. So, after the Fall, a man might live for a thousand years; and since that time the length of life has been gradually shortened. Therefore it follows," Bacon concluded, "that this shortening is accidental and may be remedied wholly or in part."

Like Aristotle, Bacon argued that aging resulted from a gradual loss of "innate heat." But the combination of a righteous lifestyle and the right medicines, Bacon asserted, could overcome this gradual loss. In particular he advocated drugs made from serpent's flesh and stag's heart (both snakes and deer were thought to be long-lived animals), from gold, coral, and pearl (these shiny objects were presumed to generate heat), and from sweet-smelling ambergris, aloe, and rosemary. His favorite, though, was a sort of medieval version of inhalation therapy: rejuvenating oneself by inhaling the breath of a young virgin. By rigorously practicing a combination of these techniques, Bacon thought, one might be able to extend the human life span by as much as a hundred years.

Bacon's practical ideas soon inspired a number of his fellow immortalists to come up with anti-aging prescriptions of their own. The Italian Renaissance nobleman Luigi Cornaro used himself as a sort of living laboratory for his ideas on extending life. In his *Discorsi della vita sobria* (*Discourses on the Sober Life*), Cornaro tells us that a lifetime of riotous good living had left him prematurely old at forty-five. He had gout, fever, pains in his stomach, and an insatiable thirst; was so bad off, in fact, that his doctors gave him only a few months to live. This scared Luigi so completely that he immediately swore off his old and evil ways, and became a model of temperance.

To conserve his "innate moisture," Cornaro developed a special, restricted diet: small portions of bread, meat, egg broth, and spring wine. This diet made him feel so good that "I feel when I leave the table that I must sing." Whether it was the diet itself or Luigi's basic good nature no one can say, but the fact is that he was still writing merrily away in his nineties, and ultimately lived to the age of 103.

Over the next two hundred years, Cornaro's ideas attracted a number of disciples. Probably the greatest of these was the eighteenth-century German clinician Christopher Hufeland. A friend of Goethe and Schiller, Hufeland was the first German doctor to practice the art of vaccination, which he learned from its English inventor, Edward Jenner. More interesting to us, he developed a scientific-sounding formula for determining the maximum life span: animals, he calculated—humans included—lived roughly eight times longer than their period of childhood growth. So dogs, who reached full growth in a year to a year and a half, lived eight to twelve years. Humans, who in what Hufeland called their "natural state" took twenty-five years to reach full growth, would then have a maximum life span of two hundred years!

To reach that maximum, Hufeland, like Cornaro, prescribed moderation in all things, especially diet. (He also gave advice on how to avoid two of the great enemies of long life: suicide and mad dogs.) Hufeland wrote all this up in a collection of explicit diet and lifestyle recipes, which anticipated modern hippies and New Agers not only in its content but in its title: *Makrobiotik.*

The idea that scientific techniques could help extend life was enthusiastically supported by a number of the best-known philosophers of the seventeenth and eighteenth centuries. Descartes, for one, believed that practical medicine could find "many very sound precepts for the cure of diseases and for their prevention, and also even for the retardation of aging." (Unfortunately, this wasn't much help to Descartes himself—he died at fifty-four.) In his *New Atlantis*, Francis Bacon called for experiments to determine the feasibility of removing and replacing vital organs, thus anticipating modern transplantation medicine by more than three hundred years! And Benjamin Franklin, who had a burning ambition to see how the new country he had helped to build would look in a hundred years, wrote that he would like to be "immersed with a few friends in a cask of madeira wine until that time, to be then recalled to life by the solar warmth of my dear country." Like Descartes and Bacon, Franklin was sure that old age and even death itself would eventually succumb to the march of scientific progress.

The real father of practical aging research was probably the nineteenth-century French physician Jean Martin Charcot. Charcot, a dashing, man-about-Paris intellectual whose impeccable social connections were the result of an excellent marriage, was a physician at the Saltpetrière Hospital, an old saltpeter factory that had been converted into a huge medical institution for the aging and indigent. His vast hands-on experience with the elderly led him to publish in 1867 *Clinical Lectures on Senile and Chronic Diseases*, probably the first truly scientific treatise in the new field of gerontology.

Charcot wanted nothing to do with the search for immortality or what he called "the nonsense of innate heat." Instead, he outlined the goals of what to him would be the only useful way to study aging: "to search for central themes and causes of aging; and to describe the facts of aging, the organ changes, the physiology—in short, to define the aging process as it actually appears." The sound of Charcot's work is so contemporary that many modern researchers still consider it a sort of field guide to the practical study of aging.

By the turn of the twentieth century, then, the battle against aging was beginning to take scientific shape. At the same time, the new century saw the emergence of a new bunch of life-extension crackpots—inspired, perhaps, by Brown-Sequard and his crushed dog testicles. There was Elie Metchnikoff, a serious scientist whose demonstration that the body defends itself against bacterial infection by mounting an army of bug-eating cells won him a shared Nobel Prize for Medicine in 1908.

Metchnikoff went off the deep end, however, when he proposed that human aging was the result of poisons released by a gradually putrefying large intestine. His remedy? Liberal portions of sour milk and yogurt, which he thought was responsible for the famed longevity of the Bulgarians. (That longevity, by the way, has since been found to be largely a myth.) Still, Metchnikoff's "colonic theory" had its devotees, among them the musician Louis Armstrong, who took strong laxatives every night; and the actress Mae West, who attributed her longevity (she died at eighty-seven) to a lifelong regime of daily enemas.

According to some—and there is much disagreement about this—the most modern version of the old snake-oil routine is Gerovital, a much-touted life-prolonger promoted for the most part by the Rumanian physician Dr. Ana Aslan. The Rumanian version of Gerovital is actually a modified version of the painkiller novocaine, plus, some say, a secret ingredient. I am both a believer and a user of Rumanian procaine hydrochloride myself, having seen the positive effects it had on my dad, who was given the Aslan version of the drug for his arthritis in the late sixties. Not only did it stop the progress of his arthritis but to some extent it actually reversed the damage to his hip and shoulder joints. A noticeable effect the drug had on him, and the main reason I take it now, was the dramatic improvement in his skin tone. During the 1950s, more than 5,000 elderly patients, including Konrad Adenauer, W. Somerset Maugham, and Charles de Gaulle, were treated by Aslan. To date no one in the West has been able to verify her assertions, except in the case of arthritis and some forms of depression. A comprehensive study of all the evidence conducted in 1975 by the Veterans Administration Hospital in Los Angeles using an American-made version of the drug concluded that there was little scientific basis for Aslan's claims. Sadly, we will probably never know how effective Dr. Aslan's Gerovital really is, because no drug company will undertake the enormous expense necessary to prove the worth of the drug.

Still, Gerovital looks almost respectable when compared with some of the other recent "remedies" for old age. Just after World War I, the Russian physician Serge Veronoff, who had emigrated to France, undertook to revive flagging sexual energies by transplanting ape testicles into old men. A few years later an American witch doctor named John Romulus Brinkley tried the same trick using goat testicles, and made so much money that he was able to buy a radio station, which he used as a launching pad for his campaign for governor of Kansas.

At about the same time that Gerovital was circulating, the Swiss physician Paul Niehans injected a number of patients—including Adenauer, Sir Winston Churchill, Pope Pius XII, and Charlie Chaplin—with fresh cells from unborn lambs. Needless to say, none of these "therapies" benefited anyone but their inventors.

As loony as some of these remedies seem, there's another school that has gone a great deal further. Members of this group call themselves "immortalists." For them the goal is the ultimate defeat of death itself. What's more, they think they have the means: freeze a dying human body into a state of suspended animation, wait until science comes up with a treatment for whatever's ailing that body, then thaw it out, cure it, and send it on its way until it's ready to die again. Then repeat the process *ad infinitum.* The result? Life becomes a combination of hotel and bionic meat locker, with people checking in and out of one or the other as necessary, and thus achieving a sort of staggered immortality.

Known as *cryonics,* this freeze-thaw technique was dreamed up in the 1950s by physicist Robert Ettinger and has subsequently gained enough proponents to qualify as a minor movement. Not only are there cryonics societies all over the world, there are a number of facilities in which the faithful dead—at this writing several dozen of them—lie frozen, awaiting the glorious day when science will be able to thaw them out and restore them to life.

One of those facilities, the Alcor Life Extension Foundation Laboratory in Riverside, California, was the site of a spectacular and widely publicized flap in 1988. The decapitated head of Dora Kent, mother of foundation head and cryonics guru Saul Kent, was found frozen in a vat of liquid nitrogen. Kent had allegedly transferred his mother from a local convalescent home to the lab as she lay near death (she was eighty-three years old), then had her decapitated and frozen without the benefit of a doctor's help. The central question in this bizarre case was whether or not Mrs. Kent was still alive when she was decapitated. Police later found four more frozen heads and a frozen body on the Alcor premises, and the findings generated a grand jury investigation and a number of civil cases. If nothing else, the incident has subjected the entire cryonics movement to grisly suspicions.

The machinations of a Saul Kent are not the only, or even the major, problem with cryonic immortality. The real problem is the technique itself. Most of us remember from our elementary-school biology courses that the cells of our bodies are made up largely of water, and we may remember from high-school physics what water does when it freezes. It expands, of course, and therein lies the rub. As the water inside our cells hardens and expands, it does tremendous and probably irreparable damage to cell tissues. No one knows how to freeze a human body without causing this damage, which occurs in every cell of the body, and very few respectable scientists can see a way around the problem, although some are trying various cold-protective agents to see if the barrier can be overcome. In effect, this means that in freezing the human body, the immortalists—who undoubtedly mean well—are, in effect, killing it cell by cell, a death so thoroughgoing that not even cancer can compare.

So beware the magic potion, the quick fix, and the freezer. But such wrong turns do *not* mean that the search for maximum longevity has been illegitimate. Like Roger Bacon, like the Taoists, like Christopher Hufeland, the vast majority of the scientists who have engaged in the battle against aging in the twentieth century have been sober, cautious, and respectable—intellectual descendants not of Brown-Sequard but of Charcot.

There was Dr. Ignatz Leo Nascher, who coined the term "geriatrics" and who fought—unsuccessfully, for the most part—to have the study of aging take an honorable and independent part in the curricula of the world's medical schools. (Suitably enough, Nascher published one of his most important works, *The Aging Mind*, when he was eighty-one years old.) There was Raymond Pearl, whose experiments led him to conclude that slowing down the rate of metabolism could retard aging; Charles Sedgwick

Minot, who saw the decline and death of whole organisms as reflections of the aging of individual cells; and Sir Peter Medawar and Sir MacFarlane Burnet, who were among the first to focus on the role of genetics in the aging process.

Slowly but surely, the work of these scientists helped make the study of aging respectable. With the end of World War II research on aging got its biggest boost to date. The first issue of the *Journal of Gerontology* appeared in 1946. Twelve years later, in 1958, Dr. Nathan Shock, director of the Gerontology Research Center, launched the Baltimore Longitudinal Study on Aging, perhaps the first research project to scientifically track a large number of people (660 at the study's outset) from young adulthood to death, looking for biological factors, called "biomarkers," that seemed to predict lifelong good health and long-term survival.

By the 1970s, scientists had allied themselves with politicians to push for even more government support for research on aging. Some of these politicians, especially California Senator Alan Cranston, supported the creation of a National Institute on Aging within the National Institutes of Health, a research facility which would focus not simply on the diseases associated with aging, but on the mechanics—biological, social, and behavioral—of the aging process itself. There was considerable opposition from the NIH, as many administrators thought the multifaceted approach of the NIA was inappropriate to a group of institutions which were supposed to be doing purely biological research. In the end, the Cranston faction won, and in 1976 the National Institute on Aging was founded, with psychiatrist Robert N. Butler as its first director.

Today, as the proportion of older people in our population continues to grow—from 18 million in 1965 to 28 million in 1987—support for aging research is increasing dramatically: the $15.8 million allotted in 1975 swelled to as much as $323.8 million, a growth rate, before inflation, of over 1,000 percent. And it's not just government that is spearheading the charge—private industry and business are getting into the anti-aging act as well. A number of huge corporations, including AT&T, Saatchi and Saatchi, and

Tenneco have established wellness programs for their workers, while Johnson & Johnson, a pioneer in this area, with a comprehensive health and education program that is more than ten years old, is so enthusiastic that in 1987 it created a subsidiary company to supply fitness and education programs to other firms.

Still, few experts are satisfied with today's level of funding. "We could certainly use more money," says former NIA director T. Franklin Williams. "Ten years ago, the NIH was funding about 50 percent of approved applications for research grants. This year [1990], we can fund only one in six of the approved applications. This is devastating, because at least half of those applications are very high quality." At the same time, Williams says, "interest and scientific capability has grown rapidly, and it really is a historic time in the aging field."

This brings us to the real question: Given enough money to make the interest and expertise pay off, what are the chances that we can make our limited life expectancies more nearly match our maximum life spans? "I think they're reasonably good enough to move in that direction," says Williams. "There are always going to be circumstances that will cut short some lives: accidents, acts of nature, some diseases that we may not be able to get completely on top of. But I think we'll continue to see a rise in the life expectancy—probably to a hundred or beyond."

Heady talk. But if we're going to make such exciting speculations a reality, we're going to have to know a lot more about the process of aging, about the mechanics of our bodies and the ticking of our biological clocks. In other words, we're going to have to be able to answer what is probably the central question in the whole vast mystery of life:

Why do we age?

3

How
We Age:

THE DAMAGE THEORY

In a museum in Munich, Germany, sits the first automobile ever built—the original 1886 Benz. Although she has been in splendid, frozen retirement for over a hundred years, the Benz still looks as if she were ready to roll out of the carriage house for the first time. Her body gleams with wax; her leather seats are still soft and supple; even her tires seem to shine. I have to admit that there are days when I wish I looked that good.

Most amazing, though—and most interesting for our purposes—is the fact that although the Benz has been motionless and silent for nearly a century, she's still in perfect running condition. The museum staff has primped and preened her like a movie star, and such loving care has kept this wonderful machine in what amounts to a state of perpetual youth. In fact, given the same fussy and knowledgeable attention over the very long run, the Benz could—theoretically, at least—become immortal.

The question, of course, is: Why can't this be true for us? Why can't we run forever like that grand old automobile? Now that twentieth-century science and technology have given us the tools to peer into the heart of the life process, to watch aging as it takes place, not only in large biosystems like the heart and the skin but on a microscopic level, in the cells and even in the DNA, a number of theories have emerged to try to answer these ancient, and perhaps most important of all, questions.

Essentially, there are two kinds of informed speculation about aging: "damage" theories and "clock," or "program," theories. The damage theories hold that aging and death are basically accidental: in the course of our lifetimes our bodies and brains get bumped, nicked, pinged, and bruised until the sum total of these tiny accidents cripple and finally kill us. It's death by exposure—like rocks in the wind or cars left out in the sun and rain, we are eroded, rusted, simply chipped away by the elements, some of which, in an ultimately cruel paradox, we actually carry within us.

According to the "program," or "clock," theories, we all carry the seeds of aging and death in our genes, and no matter how good we become at avoiding damage, no matter how well we care for ourselves, we are still biologically programmed to grow old and die at roughly similar rates and in a roughly similar number of years. As UCLA's Roy Walford puts it, "Aging is part of development, like childhood, adolescence, and mid-adulthood. These are all genetically controlled. Somehow the genes turn on which are appropriate to whatever period in life comes next, and others turn off, until next is now." It might be helpful to think of this idea as "biosuicide"—we are killed, in the end, not so much by outside forces as by our own bodies.

Damage theories come in many varieties. Some are general, whole-body sorts of ideas; others concentrate on specific kinds of damage or damage to specific systems. Probably the oldest of the damage theories is known as the *stochastic* theory, although I prefer to think of it as the "tired refrigerator" hypothesis. It is, as I stated earlier, that our bodies simply wear out, get tired beyond repair, and finally quit on the job.

The tired refrigerator is an old refrain and has a number of variations. One of the best known is what Nobel Prize–winning biologist Sir Peter Medawar liked to call the "broken test tube" theory. This idea asks us to consider what happens to test tubes as they live out their "lives" in scientific laboratories. Some of the test tubes might have "birth defects": manufacturing flaws that cause them to break easily, or, to pursue our metaphor, to die premature deaths. (Actually, this sounds a lot like the kinds of defects that produce Down's syndrome or progeria in humans, both diseases marked by an acceleration of the aging process and early, untimely death.) Those test tubes that were more nearly "normal"—that is, manufactured exactly according to specifications and without flaws—would still be subject to damage or breakage in the hands of butterfingered graduate students. Others would be chipped, scratched, or corroded by the very materials they were made to hold—acids, say, or scratchy abrasives like silicon.

The point is that even the strongest of the tubes, those that could best and longest withstand all these damaging forces, would eventually break. Sooner or later all the test tubes, every single one of them, would age, wear out, and ultimately "die." Theoretically, one could study these "deaths," plot them on a graph, and come up with numbers that represent the average life expectancy and maximum life span for test tubes—much as scientists have done for fruit flies, Galápagos tortoises, and *Homo sapiens.*

A second and somewhat more dynamic variation on the tired refrigerator hypothesis is what's known as the "rate of living" theory, which was proposed by Raymond Pearl in 1928. To explain this one, let's leave the refrigerator for a moment and return to our other mechanical metaphor, the car. Obviously, a car driven at an average speed of 40 miles per hour is going to last a good deal longer than one driven at an average speed of 70 miles per hour. The same is true, the rate of living argument goes, of all animals, including ourselves: the slower the metabolic rate—the rate at which an animal converts food to energy—the longer the animal, or person, lives.

On the face of it, the rate-of-living hypothesis sounds perfectly reasonable. The only problem is that it may be wrong. At Washington University in St. Louis, the biologist John O. Holloszy and the veterinarian E. Kaye Smith took a group of rats and raised their metabolic rates by immersing them in cool water for four hours a day, five days a week. If the rate-of-living theory were correct, the rats with accelerated metabolisms should have died earlier than normal rats with slower metabolic rates. But they didn't—on average they lived just about as long, or even a little longer. So much, at this writing, at least, for the rate-of-living theory. "In the context of current biological knowledge," concludes Holloszy, "it makes little sense."

So much, too, for the tired-refrigerator hypothesis. Among scientists, its appeal as an overall theory of aging is declining fast. After all, we are not refrigerators or toasters or automobiles. Unlike us, automobiles do not have cells that replicate over and over again. If humans were really like machines, if the reason we age were simply that we wear out, then taking perfect care of ourselves would solve the problem and make us potentially immortal. Remember that 1886 Benz in the Munich museum: immaculate maintenance has allowed it to live almost fifteen times its normal life expectancy. If human beings could benefit from good maintenance in the same way as the Benz—or any purely mechanical machine—we'd have people walking around who were over a thousand years old. Obviously, no amount of exercise and no special diet can accomplish that—not yet, anyway.

Before we dispose entirely of the tired-refrigerator hypothesis, though, we should look at one of its more interesting stepchildren. Some scientists think that what wears us out as individuals is exactly the same thing that keeps us going as a species: reproduction. Evolution, says this argument, is interested in the individual only as a piece of reproductive machinery. Once we're through passing on our genes in the form of children—in other words, once we pass the reproductive phase of our lives—we become, for nature's purposes, yesterday's news. We've done our job and are no longer of much use. So nature trashes us.

Skeptical? Listen to this: A British research team led by Valerie

Beral, director of the Cancer Epidemiology Unit of the Imperial Cancer Research Fund in Oxford, recently analyzed health statistics of one hundred thousand Englishwomen aged sixteen to fifty-nine. In general, the researchers found that the more children a woman bore, the greater her risk of getting potentially deadly diseases like diabetes, heart disease, hypertension, and some kinds of cancer. The diabetes findings were especially dramatic: women who had had five children, the study found, had five times the chance of developing diabetes as women who had had only one child. Although the study did not focus on the ages of the women when they bore their children, the conclusion is obvious, and it's a plain, folksy truth that every mother knows in her bones: the more kids, the faster the body wears out.

But what if we could pull a fast one on nature and put her off by postponing reproduction until later on in life? Would we then live longer? Over the past ten years, the biologist Michael Rose of the University of California at Irvine has tried to answer that question by playing God (or nature) with the life cycles of fruit flies. Rose delayed their reproduction until later in their lives simply by throwing away all the eggs they laid earlier on. Then, when they reached the desired (old) age, he let their eggs hatch.

He kept postponing reproduction through fifty generations of fruit flies. The result? After ten generations, the late-reproducing flies were living 10 percent longer than their normal counterparts. After thirty generations, they were living 30 percent longer. After fifty generations, they were living 50 percent longer. "Not only did they live longer," Rose says; "they resisted starvation better, and they flew and ran around more at later ages. The only price," he concludes, "was that they didn't reproduce as much as they would have when they were younger."

Does this mean that we humans could increase our life expectancy, and even our life span, if we put off childbearing until we were in, say, our mid-thirties? It's a fascinating question, but at the moment it simply can't be answered. For now, let's just think of Rose's work as an interesting revival of the tired-refrigerator hypothesis, a theory that without the "Methuselah flies" would probably be ready for burial.

The tired-refrigerator hypothesis views aging as basically passive; the poor old human body just sort of sits there running down while the cruel world helps beat it into submission. Most of the other damage theories describe a more active, dynamic process: a beating, yes, but one in which the body itself participates.

Take the "blurred-Xerox" theory. This is an interesting belief put forth by Alex Comfort, who is probably best known for his book *The Joy of Sex*, but who is first and foremost a respected gerontologist. The blurred-Xerox theory starts with the observation that many varieties of human cells, when maintained in nutrient solutions in a laboratory, seem to replicate about fifty times, then stop. (Brain and muscle cells are exceptions—they have only one life, not fifty). Each time the cells replicate, Comfort has proposed, the new copy is just a little bit off. To visualize this, take a page out of a magazine and copy it. Then copy the copy, and so on, for fifty times. Each copy is a bit smearier than the previous one, so that by the time you get to the fiftieth copy, you've got a blurry, illegible mess. Something similar, Comfort has maintained, happens to the cells in our bodies as we age: copy number fifty is a poor version of the original and probably doesn't work anywhere near as well, if it works at all. In Comfort's theory, then, death is actually little more than a smudged copy.

There's a variation on this one, too, a theory that sees aging as a series of "error catastrophes." Originally proposed by Leslie E. Orgel of the Salk Institute in La Jolla, California, this theory looks deep inside the cell itself. To understand error catastrophe theory, think of the cell as a factory that manufactures the proteins and enzymes that keep life humming along. The chief executive officer of this factory is DNA (deoxyribonucleic acid). She's got the specifications and blueprints for the proteins and enzymes in her head, but she's bound to her desk, and needs another nucleic acid, RNA (ribonucleic acid), to carry the orders down to the assembly line. The error catastrophe theory suggests that while the cells are young, the RNA transmits its orders faithfully, without making serious mistakes. But as cells age, there's a greater and greater chance that the RNA will misread the order from the DNA, or will miscommunicate it to the assembly line. If the order's wrong, then the product—the protein or enzyme—will turn out wrong, and won't be able to do its job. Once the factory starts producing faulty products—that is, once proteins or enzymes start doing the wrong thing—then parts of the "economy," the body as a whole, start to deteriorate. The sum of these many small error catastrophes is aging and death.

The error catastrophe theory, then, sees aging as the result of unavoidable mistakes on the part of DNA's chief lieutenant and cellular messenger boy, RNA. But others prefer to look at damage to the chief executive officer herself—the DNA, which is actually giving the orders. An early version of the "battered DNA" theory, known to scientists as "somatic mutation," was proposed in the early 1960s by Leo Szilard, the brilliant and cantankerous Hungarian physicist who had been one of the key figures in the birth of the atomic bomb, and who later recoiled from weapons work to become a biophysicist.

Szilard suggested that radiation in many forms made direct hits on the DNA in cells, causing changes, or mutations, that scrambled the DNA's instructions. With their blueprints battered, the cells themselves were damaged, and ultimately killed, one at a time. As life went on, Szilard thought, more and more DNA was victimized by "hits" from radiation until so many cells were wounded or killed outright that the body itself went more and more haywire until it finally aged and died.

The somatic mutation theory in its original form had too many problems to survive. First of all, there are a number of vital cell types—especially brain cells and muscle cells—that never replicate at all. In those cells DNA is essentially inactive, so even if a direct hit from a cosmic ray destroyed the DNA entirely, the cell would go right on doing its job. Thus, if the sole cause of aging were somatic mutation, brain and muscle cells would never age. But they do, they do—we know it all too well.

Another problem with the somatic mutation theory, as proposed by Szilard, is that it requires a tremendous number of radiation hits on individual cells before enough of them are damaged or killed to begin to produce the symptoms of aging. Yet more recent work has determined that these mutations occur far less often than Szilard thought. Something that Szilard did not take into account at all is that the nuclei of cells have the ability to *repair* damage to DNA. In 1960, Ruth Hill of Columbia University discovered a group of enzymes in cells whose sole job it is to fix DNA when it gets hurt. Since mutations are changes that persist to act in the next generation (or next replication of a cell), these enzymes are, in effect, neutralizing or even eliminating mutations as they occur.

These "DNA repairmen" are specialists—they work only on the DNA found in the nucleus of the cell. But there's DNA elsewhere: in the cytoplasm that surrounds the nucleus, and especially in the *mitochondria,* the parts of the cell that convert food to energy. The DNA in mitochondria get hit by mutations ten times as much as the DNA in cell nuclei. When mitochondrial DNA mutates, it doesn't get fixed—there are no enzyme "repairmen" running around the mitochondria the way there are in the cell nucleus. Anthony Linnane, a molecular biologist at Monash University in Clayton, Australia, thinks that as these mutations accumulate over the course of life, the mitochondria lose some of their pep—their ability to convert food into energy—and so do we. This, Linnane concludes, may become "an important contributor to the aging process."

DNA repair is a shining example of what appears to be nature's preference for biological systems that feature built-in flexibility. Stated simply, nature's rule seems to be "Stiff is bad." This appears to hold true for everything from athletics (we stretch before we run) and economics (we try to keep our investment portfolios varied) to the survival of the species. Many evolutionary biologists argue that the key to our success as a species is our amazing and exquisite adaptability. So it should come as no surprise that one of the more interesting damage theories holds that aging is due at least in part to an ongoing increase in what might be called "molecular stiffness."

In the early 1940s, a young chemist, Johann Bjorksten, noticed an odd similarity between the duplication films he was working with and aging human tissue. The molecules of both, he saw, were characterized by a large degree of "cross-linking," or adjacent molecules that had been bound together by other chemicals. Bjorksten went on to propose that this cross-linking was an important feature of the aging process, that it may, more than any other single process, define aging.

Why is cross-linking so damaging? Think of a childhood game, the three-legged race. Two people running side by side, each using both legs freely, can run a competent fity-yard dash. Take those same two people and tie one of their legs together, and not only are they substantially slowed, but they become so stiff that they may not be able to run at all. According to Bjorksten's theory, much the same thing happens when molecules inside cells become cross-linked: the molecules, be they proteins or what have you, stiffen to the point that they eventually lose their ability to do their jobs. The result? Our now-familiar enemies, aging and death.

At one point, the cross-linking theory had so much appeal that an expert said that it was "likely to be of equal importance to biology as were Albert Einstein's contributions to physics." That was in 1968. By the mid-1970s, though, cross-linking had lost much of its glow. Although everyone agreed that cross-linking occurred and that it increased with age, it came to be seen by the majority of the gerontological community as a result, rather than a cause, of aging.

Lately, though, the idea has been picking up steam again. The biologist Anthony Cerami of the Picower Institute for Medical Research in New York has long been interested in glucose, the body's most abundant sugar. (A significant amount of the food we eat is converted in the body to glucose.) The conventional wisdom had it that glucose is mostly inert, but Cerami discovered in the mid-1970s that this sugar was actually the trigger in a chain of chemical events that produced substances called AGEs (advanced glycosylation end products). In some cases, Cerami found, these AGEs caused cross-linking. In other words, AGEs were the ropes that bound neighboring protein molecules together.

Here's another damage hypothesis—the "congested brain" theory. In the 1970s William Bondareff and Robert Narotzky of the Northwestern University Medical School in Chicago looked inside the brains of rats, at the spaces between the cells. When they measured those spaces, they found that they were only about half as wide in older rats as they were in their younger counterparts. It may be that these spaces are akin to Los Angeles freeways, in that they are the "roads" along which travel the vital chemicals that are the brain's messengers. As anyone who lives in Los Angeles knows, when you narrow the freeway, even by one lane, you get horrible traffic jams, and everybody's late to work. It could be that just this sort of thing is going on in the aging brain. And if the messengers—the neurochemicals—get bogged down because of congestion, so does the brain. Since much of the rest of the body needs the brain to tell it what to do, when the brain gets jammed, the body has a rough time processing its workload.

If the congested-brain theory sounds like the workings of a big city, so does a damage hypothesis that we'll call the "cellular garbage" theory. During the middle and late 1950s, a number of researchers noticed that many cells, especially the nonreplicating cells of the brain and muscles, tend as they age to build up piles of chemical garbage, in particular, a pigmented fat called *lipofuscin*. In some of those cells the lipofuscin piles got so big that they took up as much as 30 percent of the cell's room.

Anyone who's ever been in New York City during a garbage strike can instantly see the power of both the analogy and the theory: garbage can indeed be paralyzing. On the level of the cell, it can cause cross-linking and other kinds of malfunctions that are among the signposts of aging. As science writer Albert Rosenfeld puts it: "One can see how the cell might choke on its own pollutants. It would be as if, on an increasingly crowded dance floor, the mere taking up of the physical space made it harder and harder for anyone with purposeful activities (say, waiters carrying food or drinks) to get through."

Many experts now see lipofuscin buildup, like cross-linking, as a result, rather than a cause, of aging. But the cellular garbage theory has generated a couple of interesting new twists. The physiologist J. Fred Dice of the Tufts University School of Medicine has discovered that just as cells have "repairmen" chemicals that go around fixing up battered DNA, they also have "garbagemen"—substances, some of which are known as *lysosomes*—that dispose of old, damaged, or discarded cellular proteins. Furthermore, Dice says, this vital garbage service tends to slow with age. In old cells, it can drop to as little as one-fifth of the original rate. This means, first of all, that the trash proteins start to pile up—it's the garbage strike all over again.

But it also means that other garbagemen—researchers have uncovered as many as twelve distinct mechanisms for disposing of old proteins—rush in to help out. These other garbagemen may mistake good proteins for trash and indiscriminately destroy them as well. It's as if they were scabs who, because they did not have the same training as the experienced garbagemen they were replacing, couldn't help making these potentially lethal mistakes.

Dice hopes to test this notion by genetically sculpting more durable lysosomes—creating tougher garbagemen, as it were—and putting them to work in newborn mice. If these new, improved lysosomes do manage to help keep cells acting youthful, we'll know that cellular garbage is an important aspect of the aging process.

In the meantime, Marguerite Kay has another idea. Kay, an immunologist and physician at the University of Arizona in Tucson, began in the 1970s to look at a garbage disposal system that operates on a different level: she wanted to know how the body gets rid of red blood cells when they become old and worn out. This question eventually took her far beyond mere garbage disposal systems to an elegant and perhaps all-encompassing theory of cellular aging as a whole.

Kay's work in the laboratory has revealed that as red blood cells age, they begin to produce a protein that she calls *senescent cell antigen,* or SCA. Once produced, the SCA appears on the edge of the cell, where it becomes, for all practical purposes, a flag that bears the legend I'M OLD. TAKE ME AWAY. Specific antibodies that circulate in the bloodstream see the flag, zero in on the cell, and destroy it—much as they would destroy an invading bacterium or virus.

Kay has found SCAs not only on red blood cells, but on virtually every cell and membrane in the body. She now thinks that the appearance of these antigens—these flags—may be a crucial aspect of cellular aging. Even more intriguing, she thinks that aging may result when SCAs start to appear on too many of the body's most vital cells, which are then destroyed, or turned to garbage, by the circulating antibodies that are the body's patrolmen.

Among the damage theories, SCAs should certainly win the prize for cruel irony: the body as its own worst enemy, producing the substances that ultimately age and kill it. But there's another version of the damage-from-inside theory, one that's been around a good deal longer than SCAs and has a growing amount of evidence—and a growing number of scientists—on its side. That theory has an irony of its own: it says that we're killed by the element that above all others keeps us alive in the first place.

That element is oxygen.

4

Free Radical Chic

Picture a henpecked husband suddenly turned loose at a business convention. He's on the prowl, looking for a good time and someone to share it with. He meets a woman in the hotel bar, and as they talk he finds that she's got exactly what he's looking for—in fact, she's so perfect for him that it's almost as if she had somehow gotten hold of a missing piece of his own flesh. He wants that piece *back*. At the end of the evening, in the king-size bed in his hotel room, he gets what he's after: she shares that missing piece with him. And how does he thank her? He ties her to the bed, then cuts her in half.

This grisly little metaphor is inspired by Alex Comfort, the eminent gerontologist who wrote *The Joy of Sex*. Comfort uses a version of this metaphor to vivify an aging theory that has attracted the attention of a growing number of scientists. It's known as the "free radical" theory, but it has nothing to do with Jerry Rubin or any of the other former poitical renegades of the 1960s.

Free radicals are a variety of oxygen atoms that are either lacking an electron or have one electron too many. They can be produced in a bewildering variety of ways: by heat, radiation, air pollution, smoking, pesticides, asbestos, cured meats, dietary fats, even otherwise healthful sources like sunlight and heavy exercise.

The imbalance in their electrons makes these atoms highly unstable, and since nature dislikes this kind of instability, free radicals go racing wildly around the cells of the body looking for other atoms or molecules that are willing to share electrons. Once it finds a friendly, stable counterpart that's willing to cooperate, the free radical combines with the "helper" atom or molecule. Like a convention delegate away from his wife, says Comfort, free radicals are "highly reactive, and they'll combine with anything that's around."

Once the free radical combines with the "helper," it adds injury to insult by committing what might be thought of as the ultimate molecular treachery: it "thanks" its consenting, electron-sharing partner by damaging or even destroying it. (One expert has actually compared free radicals not to mere adulterers but to rapists.) In one kind of free radical damage, the perpetrator incapacitates the cell in which the "helping" molecule resides. In another kind of damage it tears large pieces from the victim molecule's "body"; in still another it actually cuts the cell in half.

In grabbing an electron from a victim molecule, the free radical renders the helper molecule unstable, so that it has to go off looking for yet another molecule with which to share an electron and restore its balance. But this leaves that next molecule unstable, and so on and so on, forming a chain reaction, a sort of cascade of little disasters that ultimately cripple the cell. When enough cells have been put out of commission by this molecular carnage, so the theory goes, one begins to get age-related diseaes like atherosclerosis (narrowing and hardening of the arteries), cancer, and Alzheimer's disease. Eventually, there's so much free radical damage that the whole body simply gives up the ghost.

Free radical theory has been developed over the last thirty years or so, originally by the chemist-turned-physician Denham Harman of the University of Nebraska. It was popularized in the early 1980s by Durk Pearson and Sandy Shaw in their best-selling book *Life Extension*. But even though some scientists think that Pearson and Shaw oversold the free radical notion, there is little doubt that it has become the most chic and hippest of all theories of aging.

The thing that makes free radical theory exciting and attention-worthy is its ubiquity. Theoretically, free radicals and free radical damage occur virtually all over the body. Just about every type of cell is vulnerable to free radicals, which can attack everything from the cell's membrane to its DNA. This means that free radical damage may account for an astonishingly broad range of debilitating and life-threatening diseases.

In the eyes, for example, free radical damage to proteins in the lenses is thought to contribute to the formation of cataracts, the leading cause of blindness in Americans over sixty-five. In the lungs, free radicals may cause inflammation and may trigger the production of an enzyme that attacks connective tissue, leading to emphysema. In the blood vessels, research suggests that "evil" LDL cholesterol turns bad and forms artery-clogging plaques only after being oxidized by free radicals. And free radicals may be responsible for the damage to heart muscles that takes place during heart attacks.

That's not all. Free radical damage to cells in the brain is thought by many scientists to start the chain of tiny disasters that can eventually bring on Parkinson's and Alzheimer's disease. Some kinds of cancers, especially cancers of the dietary tract, may be caused by free radicals racing out of control. Put all these diseases together, and add the general wear and tear to the body's cell population caused by free radical damage, and the sum, so the theory goes, is aging.

If there were no brake on free radicals and the damage they do, the human life span would probably be a good deal shorter than it is. Luckily, in the case of free radicals, nature seems to be on the side of balance, providing us with an extensive menu of substances that either counteract free radical damage or prevent it from occurring in the first place. These substances are known as *antioxidants* or *free radical scavengers*—they combine with free radicals and turn them into harmless chemicals before they can do their dirty work.

Some of these antioxidants seem to occur naturally in the human body, although in some cases we don't know whether we're born with them or whether we ingest them from outside. One of these is an enzyme called *superoxide dismutase,* or SOD, which combines with oxygen radicals to form harmless hydrogen peroxide. It was the discovery in the late 1960s of hydrogen peroxide in the body that helped prove that free radicals do penetrate the structure of living tissue. Another is *glutathione,* a tiny protein made up of three amino acids. And researchers at the University of California at Berkeley have recently shown that bilirubin, a so-called waste product of hemoglobin in red blood cells, is actually an energetic free radical scavenger.

Superoxide dismutase et al. do their good deeds by sopping up free radicals before they can do their damage. Other substances move in the aftermath of free radical attacks. The enzyme *macroxyproteinase* (appropriately shortened to the acronym MOP) hauls away the cellular debris—damaged amino acids, to be specific—left in the wake of free radical invasions. Another class of enzymes, the *phospholipases,* clean up free radical damage in cell membranes. In the meantime, the *nucleases* and *glycolases* actually move into the cell's "control room" and help repair free radical damage to its DNA.

These are some of the endogenous "good" substances that help battle free radicals. As time goes on, scientists will undoubtedly discover new antioxidants in the body, or find that substances thought to have one function, like bilirubin, also do service as free radical scavengers. Luckily the body doesn't have to depend solely on its own resources in the ongoing fight against oxidation. There are a number of potent antioxidants in nature just waiting for us to swallow them. One example is beta carotene, a vitamin A precursor found in carrots, spinach, kale, Swiss chard, pumpkins, sweet potatoes, apricots, peaches, papayas, and cantaloupe. Another is vitamin C (ascorbic acid), found in a wide variety of fruits (especially citrus) and vegetables. Still another is vitamin E, which is found in small amounts in vegetable oils like safflower and sunflower. Some experts think that *quinones,* a class of substances that occur not only in fruits and vegetables but even in drinking water, may turn out to be antioxidants as well.

Scientists have recently begun to find that, either singly or in combination, these free radical scavengers can fight a wide range of diseases. At the University of Western Ontario, for example, the epidemiologist James McDonald Robertson found that people who took 300 to 600 milligrams of vitamin C and 400 international units of vitamin E every day were up to 70 percent less likely to develop cataracts than people who didn't take the vitamins. Similar findings were reported in 1990 by a research team from the USDA Human Nutrition Research Center on Aging at Tufts University.

Antioxidants can also help reduce the damage done by smoking. It's been known for years that inhaled smoke creates bursts of free radicals, which in combining with other molecules tear tiny holes in the membranes of the heart and lungs. The gastroenterologist Khursheed Jeejeebhoy of the University of Toronto wondered if some of that destruction might be mitigated by free radical scavengers. So he gave daily doses of 800 IUs of vitamin E to a group of thirteen one-pack-a-day smokers for two weeks. Then he monitored the smokers' breath for pentane, a gas released when free radicals destroy membranes. He found that pentane levels decreased as much as 40 percent, an indication that vitamin E really was reducing the damage done by free radicals. When you think about it, it's really not surprising that smoking should produce a lot of free radical damage. But it *is* surprising—to the point of irony, actually—that free radical damage can also result from what we normally think of as among the healthiest of all activities: heavy exercise. Nevertheless, the increased burning of energy brought on by strenuous running or lifting can indeed produce bursts of free radicals. To counteract the damage those free radicals might do, Lester Packer, director of the Membrane Bioenergetics Group at the University of California at Berkeley has a remedy: after exercise he takes an antioxidant "cocktail" consisting of 400 IUs of vitamin E, 1,000 milligrams of vitamin C, and 10 milligrams of beta carotene.

If the theorists are right, free radicals can attack the brain as well. Many scientists suspect that free radical damage is implicated in the development of Parkinson's disease, a debilitating illness marked by tremors and loss of balance. Traditionally the symptoms of the disease have been treated with the powerful drug L-dopa. But following the free radical trail, Stanley Fahn, director of the Parkinsonism and Movement Disorder Research Program at the Columbia University College of Physicians and Surgeons, took fourteen patients who were beginning to show early signs of Parkinson's and gave them 3,000 milligrams of vitamin C and 3,200 IUs of vitamin E a day. The heavy doses of antioxidants were thought to have delayed the need for L-dopa treatment in those patients for as long as two and a half years, suggesting that the disease may well be brought on, or at least exacerbated, by free radical damage.

Few of us will develop Parkinson's disease, but all of us will undergo age-related changes in our brains: the membranes surrounding our brain cells will dry out and stiffen, impairing to a greater or lesser extent their ability to do the brain's work. Some of that drying and stiffening of the membranes is thought to be due to that now familiar villain, the free radical. Recently, researchers at the Hungarian-Italian Verzar International Laboratory for Experimental Gerontology gave doses of an antioxidant drug called Centrophenoxine to a number of elderly patients with medium-level Alzheimer's disease. The antioxidant to a large degree restored the fluidity of their brain cell membranes, and the patients scored significantly better on mental performance tests. In the wake of these encouraging results, Imre Zs-Nagy, scientific coordinator of the laboratory, thinks that free radical scavengers may actually slow down the normal process of aging in the brain.

There's also growing evidence to suggest that free radicals are implicated in some kinds of cancer, and that free radical scavengers can actually provide a degree of protection against those cancers. A recent Finnish study looked at over 36,000 men and women, and found that people with high blood levels of vitamin E had less cancer overall and a lower rate of death from cancer. (The dark side of this study was that women with low blood levels of vitamin E had one and a half times the risk of developing breast cancer, while men with low vitamin E levels were twice as likely to get cancer of the stomach.) A number of other studies show that vitamin E can protect against cancers of the dietary tract by preventing common food preservatives like nitrates and nitrites from turning into cancer-causing nitrosamines.

Free radicals may also play an important role in clogging up the plumbing of the circulatory system and bringing on heart attacks. It may be that free radicals are the real bad guys in the cholesterol story. Scientists at the University of Southern California have shown that low-density cholesterol in its normal form in the blood is relatively harmless. Once it is oxidized by the free radicals in fats—especially, ironically enough, the polyunsaturated fats long thought to be "healthful"—the LDL cholesterol oxides scar the tissue in the linings of blood vessels, and these scarred areas become "traps" where deposits of plaque are set down.

At the same time, experiments in Austria have shown that free radicals may be implicated in the formation of the plaque itself: once low-density cholesterol is oxidized by free radicals, it attracts the attention of macrophages, the cells that do garbage collection for the immune system. As far as the macrophages are concerned, LDL in its oxidized form is toxic waste—when the macrophages try to ingest it and carry it away, they're "poisoned" and killed. The dead macrophages then pile up along arterial walls, forming one of the elements of artery-choking plaques.

The Austrian researchers found that the first step in this potentially deadly process of oxidation of LDL was partially prevented by the free radical scavengers vitamin E and beta carotene.

Going a step further, scientists at the Pasteur Institute in Lille, France, tested "antioxidant therapy" on a group of twenty men with elevated blood cholesterol. Some of these men were given a cholesterol-lowering drug, others 1,000 IUs of vitamin E daily, and others a combination of the drug and vitamin E. The rest of the men got only a placebo. After two months, the men who took both the cholesterol-lowering drug and vitamin E had the largest reduction in blood cholesterol levels.

All in all, these are exciting indications that antioxidants can provide at least some degree of protection against a wide range of deadly diseasees. At least one of the antioxidants, vitamin E, may boost the immune systems of the elderly. Simin Meydani, an associate professor of nutrition at Tufts University, gave 800 IUs of vitamin E a day for thirty days to eighteen healthy men and women aged sixty or over. At the end of the thirty days she evaluated the function of their immune system T-cells, and found that the vigor of the T-cells was significantly greater in the people who got vitamin E than in those who did not take the vitamin.

This raises a fascinating and vitally important question. If antioxidants like vitamin E can energize the immune system so that it affords better protection against disease, does that mean that they can actually prolong life? There's at least one tantalizing piece of evidence from the laboratory to suggest that this may be so. At the University of Louisville, the biochemist John P. Richie gave the antioxidant *nordihydroguaiaretic acid* (NDGA), which is found in creosote bushes, to a group of female mosquitoes. The NDGA almost doubled their life spans—from twenty-nine to forty-five days. Of course, it's a long way from mosquitoes to man, and it will take a number of human generations—as well as many human volunteers—to see if free radical scavengers have the same kind of impact.

Still, experiments like Richie's have many experts excited. Imre Zs-Nagy talks of free radical scavengers raising "hopes for a successful attempt at life prolongation." Denham Harman, who has lived long enough to see the free radical resarch he pioneered move from the fringes of respectable science to a position near the center of the anti-aging stage, is even more emphatic: "There's no question in my mind that free radical reactions are the basic cause of aging. Once we fully comprehend their mechanisms," he concludes, "our life span will dramatically increase."

5

The Clock of Aging

Every spring, the Pacific salmon plays out its furious drama of love and death. We all know about the spawning runs of this majestic fish, the hundreds of miles of nonstop upstream swimming, the leaping of waterfalls, the sheer, raw muscle of the mating drive. The salmon's story is often used to illustrate the overwhelming power that nature invests in the urge to reproduce.

Something equally powerful and, for our purposes, even more interesting switches on in the salmon when the spawning run is over. During the mating drive, the salmon's adrenal and pituitary glands become grossly enlarged. The control function of the pituitary, in particular, gets turned off, so that the gland pours out a cascade of powerful hormones. That cascade, which may be the chemical fuel that powers the mating drive, also turns out to be a fountain of death. Within hours of spawning, the salmon begins to grow suddenly old. In a grotesquely accelerated version of the aging process, its bones soften, its scales lose their color, and its flesh starts to rot—all virtually overnight. Within two weeks, the magnificent fish is dead.

What happened? What turned on that cascade of poisonous hormones that transformed the salmon so quickly from a muscular leaper of waterfalls to a dried-out hulk? It's hard to imagine that the hormone cascade could be the result of a random accident. Something else must be at work here.

To many scientists, that something else is a biological clock, an internal program that gets turned on when it's time for the salmon to age and die. The scientists who subscribe to this idea believe that all of us—salmon, fruit flies, and human beings—carry our death sentences in our genes. Put it another way: the "clock" or "program" theories attribute death and aging not to "murder," as the damage theories do, but to the presence in each and every one of us of what amounts to a genetic time bomb. Or put it yet another way: death, when all is said and done, is nothing more than a birth defect.

There are a number of indications that these program theories may have a lot going for them. In the first place, it's been known for a long time that many of our body's cells are dying off even when the body itself is still young and vigorous. More cells die before birth, when we're still floating around in the womb, than at death! Most of us are aware that we lose a great many brain cells—the actual number is still controversial, but it ranges from ten thousand to one hundred thousand cells every day of our lives. To many scientists, it seems obvious that all this is no accident, that no amount of random damage due to outside causes could explain such regular, methodical, and massive cellular slaughter. It could only be the result of an ongoing genetic mandate—a computer specialist might call it a "resident program"—that calls for certain cells to die according to a more or less fixed schedule.

Like the damage notions that we have talked about, program or clock-of-aging hypotheses are not one theory, but many. Like damage theories, the program ideas can be divided into two camps: one that sees the program as residing in larger systems—the brain, for example, or the immune system, or certain specific glands— and a second, which looks for the programs in smaller units—in cells, in chromosomes, or in the complex chemicals that make up the genetic code.

Let's start with the program theories that look at large systems. The salmon's sad story is a perfect illustration of one of the most interesting of these, a large-system program theory that we'll call "death by hormone." Essentially, this idea has it that aging and death are the result of a predetermined biological plan that calls for us to be poisoned by our own glands. This theory has had, and continues to have, a great number of proponents in the scientific community, each of whom focuses on a different set of glands, or *endocrine systems.*

One of these glands is the *thymus,* a pinkish-gray mass of tissue that lives in the chest cavity, below the breastbone and just above the heart. The thymus has been called the immune system's master gland, and its job seems to be to function as a sort of boarding school for the immune system's young T-cells, taking them when they're immature and don't know what they're doing and training them to do specific jobs in either fighting certain kinds of diseases or regulating and controlling the immune system. Interestingly enough, the thymus starts life at about the size of a walnut, shrinks by puberty to the size of a pea, and then, in old age, all but disappears. As the thymus shrinks, our resistance to many kinds of diseases shrinks with it.

Some scientists have used this fact to argue that aging and death are at least in part the result of an internal program that calls for the thymus to shrink. But shrinkage alone is not the whole story. Experiments at the National Cancer Institute in the early 1960s showed that mice who had no thymus gland at all could still be stimulated to produce functioning T-cells simply by implanting *tissue* from the thymus gland. To some researchers, this meant that the thymus had to be producing a substance that was keeping the T-cell factory humming. By 1966, Alan Goldstein, a young endocrinologist then at the Albert Einstein Medical College in New York, had isolated that substance: a hormone that he called *thymosin.*

Since then, Goldstein, who is now at the George Washington University School of Medicine in Washington, D.C., and other scientists have discovered that thymosin is not one hormone but many. As a family of hormones, the thymosins seem to be implicated in the aging process, in that their levels in the body decline as we get older; and so, as we all know, does our resistance to disease. That's not all. Goldstein and his colleagues have found that the thymosins are directly linked to important hormone systems in the brain: they stimulate the brain's pituitary gland to produce hormones that help regulate the reproductive endocrine system. They also help stimulate "fight or flight" hormones like ACTH (adrenocorticotrophic hormone), growth hormones, prolactin, and even the "feel-good" hormone, beta-endorphin.

As far as Goldstein is concerned, this "brain-thymus loop" may hold the key to the entire aging process. "As we grow older," he says, "there are changes in brain chemistry. These changes alter hormone levels, causing deterioration throughout the body. Our studies place the thymosins at the center of this process. The suggestion is that it's the deterioration of the endocrine thymus that leads to deterioration of the brain—and ultimately of the body itself."

In Chapter 17 we'll have much more to say about thymosins and their potential promise as anti-aging drugs. For the moment, though, let's continue our tour of the body's glands to see which of them—in addition to the thymus—might be important players in the aging process.

Let's start with the thyroid. This gland produces a hormone called *thyroxine,* which helps govern the basal metabolism rate— the rate at which the body's cells convert food to energy. Without this conversion there would be no life at all, so it's not surprising that thyroxine acts on virtually every cell in the body. Scientists have long been tempted to see it as a sort of master hormone, one that influences, or controls outright, all sorts of bodily processes that are related to aging—everything from the vigor of the immune system to the development of heart disease.

Lately, much of the attention formerly given to the thyroid has shifted to the pituitary, the little gland that dangles from the base of the brain. A good deal of this interest has been due to the work of W. Donner Denckla, an endocrinologist formerly at Harvard University. In the 1970s, Denckla found that when he removed the pituitary glands of rats, remarkable changes took place: the immune system was revitalized, the rate of cross-linking in cells decreased, and cardiovascular function was restored to the levels of flaming youth. Denckla went on to speculate that as we age, the pituitary begins to release a hormone that inhibits the ability of cells to use thyroxine, and that the resulting changes in metabolic rate bring on and accelerate the process of aging. Isolate this "death hormone," Denckla believes, find a way to block its action on the body's cells, and we'll have, if not an antidote to aging, at least a way of significantly extending our life expectancy.

Denckla called this death hormone DECO, for "decreasing oxygen consumption." Unfortunately, although he was very close to finding it, his research money was cut, and the last we heard he was building boats in Woods Hole, on Cape Cod.

Some scientists now think that aging may be due not so much to the *presence* of death hormones as to the *absence* of certain "life hormones." That's the idea of William Regelson of the Medical College of Virginia. Regelson has his eye on melatonin, a hormone secreted by the pineal gland. Melatonin is involved in regulating the internal biological clocks that govern sleeping and waking patterns and the way our bodies respond to seasonal changes. Regelson thinks it's significant, even crucial, that melatonin levels decline with age. When Regelson transplanted pineal glands from young mice into the thymus glands of older mice, he saw "dramatic prolongation of survival" in the older mice, some of whom lived more than 50 percent longer than they might have without the transplant.

Another candidate for a life hormone may be DHEA (dehydroepiandrosterone), a substance secreted by the adrenal gland. In the early 1970s, a British researcher, Dr. Richard Bulbrook, discovered that many women who had breast cancer also had low levels of DHEA. Other researchers went on to find that DHEA was involved in converting the body's excess glucose to energy—without DHEA, the glucose turned to fat. Too much fat can lead to obesity, and obesity can be a key factor in premature death. Recently, DHEA has been proven to play a role in protecting the thymus gland so that it can do its job in fighting disease. Put them all together—protection against obesity, infectious disease, and many forms of cancer (in laboratory animals)—and you have a hormone and a gland that are obviously very important in the ongoing internal battle against aging. Significantly, levels of both melatonin and DHEA decline markedly with age.

The question now is: Who's in charge? Is there any single gland or organ or system whose job it is to regulate all the others? Is there one place in the body, one engine room or mission central, where the aging process is controlled?

If there is one such control room—and you still get plenty of arguments that there isn't, that aging is not only distributed among, but is also regulated by, a large number of systems—many scientists would locate it somewhere in the brain. One candidate for the control room itself is the *hippocampus,* a large, thick band of cells buried deep within the brain. The hippocampus seems to be in charge of the adrenal gland, which, in turn, is in charge of stress. When we're challenged by something in our environment—anything from a charging bull to an overwrought boss—the adrenal gland pours out a stream of powerful hormones, called *glucocorticoids,* which give the muscles the extra energy they need to either do battle or run from it—the familiar "fight or flight" response that is so essential to pure survival. The hippocampus tells the adrenal gland to turn on this response; then, when the stress has been dealt with (when the bull is gone or the boss soothed), tells the adrenal gland to turn it off.

But as we get older, says Stanford biologist Robert Sapolsky, a vicious circle sets in. Cells in the hippocampus start to die, killed by the very glucocorticoids that it is supposed to be in charge of.

As its cells die off, the hippocampus itself becomes less and less able to shut off the adrenal gland. So the glucocorticoids pile up, and, with nothing better to do, kill off more cells in the hippocampus. And so on. It's mutiny, and like most mutinies, it leaves no one in command. The glucocorticoids rise in the body, causing ulcers, loss of muscle mass and bone calcium, even impotence— symptoms not only of chronic stress but of aging. As far as Sapolsky is concerned, this hormonal mutiny, this crippling of the hippocampus, may be crucial to the process of getting old—in rats, at any rate.

Many researchers—Sapolsky included—suspect that a pea-sized area of the midbrain known as the *hypothalamus* is as important as, and perhaps even more important than, the hippocampus. For such a small area, the hypothalamus has a great deal to do: it's known to regulate such basic biological functions as hunger, sleep, and sexual desire, and it also seems to be the seat of one of the most powerful of all emotions—rage. (Maybe that's why we get so angry when we're deprived of food, sleep, or sex.)

Equally interesting for our purposes is the fact that the hypothalamus also regulates the thyroid and pituitary, two glands that, as we've already seen, may be deeply implicated in the aging process. It sends its instructions to these glands via a set of chemical messengers known as *neurotransmitters*—the brain's own Western Union system. At the University of Southern California, the gerontologist Caleb Finch has found that as we age, the level of neurotransmitters declines significantly; or, to stick with our Western Union metaphor, the volume of telegrams goes down. This decline sets off what Finch calls an "endocrine cascade"—a bevy of changes in hormone secretion patterns that starts to play havoc with our bodies. (One example of this havoc is Parkinson's disease, a nervous system affliction that is triggered by an extreme loss of the neurotransmitter dopamine.) Over time, the theory goes, various versions of a biologically programmed endocrine cascade— perhaps triggered by a progressively weaker and wearier hypothalamus—increase our risk of dying.

Evidently, then, the hypothalamus plays a crucial role as the control center for a number of vital endocrine systems, the faucet for the hormone bath that may help to age and kill us. The hypothalamus may also play a part in regulating another system that has been centrally implicated in the aging process: the immune system. It's been shown over and over again that as we age, the immune system becomes less vigorous. (Conversely, a recent study of 102 centenarians in Japan showed that most of these ancients had very strong immune systems.) Its B-cells make fewer antibodies and make them at a slower rate, while its disease-fighting T-cells are more likely to get confused, "go blind"—that is, lose their ability to recognize invading bacteria and viruses—or simply lie down on the job. In general, the immune system's response to the presence of foreign invaders or to the onslaught of cancer cells is increasingly sluggish. Like a tired and demoralized army after a long campaign, it seems to simply lose its will to fight. The result? We are with age increasingly susceptible to infectious diseases and cancer.

There is another, equally disastrous side to this decline. It seems that while some of the immune system's soldiers are either losing their aim or putting down their weapons entirely, others are becoming actively rebellious. In a phenomenon known as *auto-immunity,* many of the immune system's cells turn against the body. They start treating our own cells as if they were foreign spies, grimly hunting them out and executing them. As a result, we are more likely to be afflicted with such autoimmune diseases as lupus, multiple sclerosis, and rheumatoid arthritis. It's not just the official autoimmune diseases that haunt us; autoimmunity has also been implicated in the development of atherosclerosis, high blood pressure (hypertension), and other classic diseases of aging.

As we get older, then, the immune system can go haywire in two different and equally destructive ways. As Albert Rosenfeld puts it, "It's as if the armed forces of a constantly beleaguered community (which fairly describes a human body in the real world) were to grow increasingly careless about keeping out or hunting down invading forces, who were thus free to destroy and despoil at will and, at the same time, began to attack their own fellow citizens. In that event, the formerly secure population suddenly finds itself set upon simultaneously by both the cops and the robbers!"

What's behind this combination of sit-down strike and armed rebellion? Apparently the endocrine system plays a part, in that some of its hormones—the thymosins, for example—are an integral part of the immune system's mechanics. If the brain (the hypothalamus or the hippocampus) loses its ability to control those hormones, or if it turns them on or off at the wrong times, then the immune system suffers, and so do we.

But the hormones are probably not the whole story. Much, if not all, of what happens in the aging immune system seems to be under the control, whether direct or indirect, of the genes. Many scientists think that the "program," or "biological clock," that regulates aging as a whole is to be found not so much in the larger systems (immune system, endocrine system) as in the cells that make up those systems and, ultimately, in the genes that regulate what goes on in the cells.

This cellular-genetic branch of the clock-of-aging theory owes much to the work of Leonard Hayflick, a biologist at the University of California at San Francisco. Like many imaginative scientists, Hayflick launched his career—and his fame—by challenging what had been the common wisdom. In Hayflick's field, that wisdom had been established by the Nobel laureate Alexis Carrel, a colorful scientist who was so convinced of the mystic nobility of his pursuits that he made his lab technicians perform their experiments dressed in black robes and hoods. Carrel's theory was that human cells— all human cells—are "immortal," and if nothing gets in their way, they'll go on happily dividing and replicating themselves forever.

In the 1950s Hayflick, then at the Wistar Institute in Philadelphia, began to wonder if that was really true. In the laboratory, he put a batch of human cells in a nutrient broth and watched them carefully as they began to divide. As the cells approached fifty divisions, he saw, they began to divide more slowly. At the same time, they became increasingly suffocated by a buildup of lipofuscins, the yellowish fatty pigments that make up the cells' garbage piles. In other words, the cells aged. Not only did they age, but after about fifty divisions, they stopped replicating themselves entirely; there was no cellular immortality (with the exception of cancer cells).

Not satisfied with this evidence, Hayflick went on to try to clinch his case. He found that if he stopped cell division by freezing the cells after, say, twenty doublings, then thawed them out again, they doubled about thirty more times, then aged and stopped dividing right on schedule. As far as Hayflick was concerned, this indicated that they were under the control of an internal clock that was preset to have a fairly precise number of ticks.

Hayflick called these experiments "aging under glass." He became convinced that what he had seen in the laboratory was not only a duplicate of what happened in the human body, but the process that underlay all the other processes that we call aging. So what regulated cellular aging? Where was the control room, and what was keeping time? Hayflick suspected that the answer to both could be found in the heart of the cell, the nucleus.

At Stanford, Hayflick and his colleague Woodring Wright, along with the University of Colorado's David Prescott, developed a technique that enabled them to extract the nuclei from some cells and transplant them into others. When they transplanted nuclei from old cells—cells that had divided, say, forty times—into much younger cells, the younger cells would divide about ten more times, then stop dividing, even if before transplantation they had had forty divisions left. The same was true, Hayflick found, if he transplanted young nuclei into old cells: the old cells would be given a new lease on life, and would divide as many more times as allowed by the age of the young cells whose nuclei they had received.

This seemed to indicate that the control room for cellular aging is indeed to be found in the nucleus of the cell. Now, the nucleus is where the genes live. To be more precise, it's the engine room where the genetic machinery—the DNA and the various forms of

RNA—start the process of protein manufacture that keeps life ticking. (Actually, DNA has recently been found in the cytoplasm that surrounds the cell nucleus, but no one is yet sure what that DNA's job is.) To Hayflick, it all seemed clear: aging is essentially a cellular process, and the cell's "clock of death" is embedded in the genes.

Unfortunately, the picture is not as clear as Hayflick might like. First of all, if Hayflick was entirely correct, cells that divide (remember that brain and muscle cells do not) should have a limit of about fifty divisions (this is now known as the "Hayflick limit"), no matter what kind of cells they are or in what individual they happen to be. But there are some indications that cells in the immune system, known as *lymphocytes,* may have a limit of only twenty to thirty divisions. On the other hand, it seems that when cells from old animals are transplanted into successive generations of younger animals, the Hayflick limit no longer applies—in some cases, those "serially transplanted" cells have exceeded the Hayflick limit by as much as three times! It's also been shown that adding various substances—cortisone, for example, or vitamin E —to the nutrient cultures that sustain the cell in lab tests can almost double the number of times the cells are able to divide. Finally, one of Hayflick's co-workers found that even when cells in a culture stopped dividing, they didn't actually die—their DNA remained active and went merrily along giving orders to make proteins.

Scientists are still arguing about what all this means. Does the Hayflick limit apply to only some cells in some situations? Is it a fiction, a laboratory artifact, a false trail? Or is there some sort of "youth factor"—cortisone and vitamin E might be examples— that allows transplanted or souped-up cells to go on dividing far beyond the Hayflick limit? At this point, we just don't know. To Hayflick the real point has already been made: most cells do have finite lifetimes (no matter what those lifetimes might be); they do age and stop dividing; and that process of cellular aging is the biological foundation for our own mortality.

Perhaps more important, the controversy over the Hayflick limit doesn't really put much of a dent in the notion that when all is said and done, aging is controlled at the level of the genes. In the past few years, this "genetic clock" theory of aging has been given a significant boost by the emergence of two new and exciting pieces of evidence. At a National Institutes of Health laboratory in Research Triangle Park, North Carolina, the molecular biologist J. Carl Barrett and his colleagues were trying to determine what made normal cells that age and die different from "immortal" cancer cells. To do that, they fused a line of normal human cells with immortal cells from hamsters to engineer a line of hybrid cells. Most of those hybrids acted like normal cells—they grew old and ultimately stopped dividing. But a few remained immortal. When they looked closely at the immortal cells, Barrett and his colleagues found that they were all missing a specific chromosome, known as human chromosome 1. When the scientists inserted copies of human chromosome 1 into the immortal cells, they turned mortal again: they aged and stopped dividing just like their hybrid cousins. Apparently, the process of cellular aging had been turned on by the genes in one single chromosome.

Scientists have found that in at least one animal, life expectancy is affected by a single gene. The molecular geneticist Thomas E. Johnson of the University of Colorado at Boulder isolated that gene in a worm called *C. elegans.* When he removed the gene, Johnson found that the worms lived as much as 70 percent longer than normal. (Interestingly, the apparent price for this increase in longevity was a reduced reproductive rate—the long-lived worms produced 25 percent fewer offspring than their normal counterparts. This recalls Michel Rose's findings that the life spans of fruit flies could be extended by selection for late reproduction, and adds fuel to the argument that life span and reproduction are related in some important ways.) Johnson gave this gene what seems an absolutely appropriate name: he calls it AGE-1.

Of course, human beings are not worms or fruit flies. But even though few scientists think that there's an AGE-1 gene in humans—that is, a single gene that helps regulate the entire aging process—the majority opinion is that aging may well be under the control of a relatively small number of "longevity determinant" genes, perhaps fewer than one hundred. The big question is: Which ones? That question is now occupying the minds and the labor of hundreds of scientists at dozens of laboratories, many of whom hope ultimately to be able at least to influence the rate of aging, and possibly to control it entirely, by manipulating nothing more than one small cluster of genes. In the meantime, Thomas Johnson has sounded the call: "We will," he declares, "identify the genes for longevity in mammals, including humans."

We've now had a close look at all the major theories of aging—the wear-and-tear theories, the damage theories, the clock, or program, theories. Few scientists think that any one of these is the ultimate answer to the aging puzzle; most likely, aging is the result of an interplay among all these forces. Our genes, for example, may determine how susceptible we are to the various kinds of damage that age us. At the same time, aging may result from damage to the genes themselves or to the systems that repair the genes. In any case, it's obvious that we know a great deal more about all this than we used to. As Roy Walford says, "We are no longer wandering around in the dark of total guesswork which surrounded gerontologists until quite recent times. The theories are beginning to coalesce, to make sense as parts of a whole process."

Biology
Versus
Chronology

Most of us remember the spring day in 1981 when President Ronald Reagan was nearly assassinated by an emotionally disturbed young loner named John W. Hinckley, Jr. Much of Reagan's tremendous popularity had been due to his youthful and vital image (one must admire his dedication to chopping wood, walking, and working out, if not his politics), but with the bullet from Hinckley's gun in his chest, that image was put to its most severe test. Well, Reagan's body passed that test in presidential fashion. The surgeons who removed the bullet remarked that Reagan's internal organs seemed to be those of a much younger man.

We all admire and envy those fortunate people who, like Ronald Reagan, somehow always seem to be younger than their years. Even in their sixties and seventies, actors like William Shatner and Kirk Douglas still seem to retain their youthfulness. Martha Graham was still performing even in her seventies, and directed her dance company until her death at ninety-six. Grandma Moses was doing brilliant work well into her eighties. Verdi composed *Falstaff* at seventy-nine and Winston Churchill was at retirement age when he began to lead Britain through World War II. The historian Will Durant was still writing when he died in his mid-nineties, and former ambassador George F. Kennan, now in his eighties, continues to give new meaning to the term "elder statesman." How often have you heard someone say (about you, I hope), "She's thirty-five, but she has the body of a twenty-year-old"?

There's no denying it: although everyone ages, some people do it much more slowly and much more gracefully than others. "You just can't generalize," says John W. Rowe, president of New York City's Mount Sinai Medical Center, and director of the MacArthur Foundation Research Program on Successful Aging. "I can describe to you a seventy-five-year-old man with a history of heart disease and diabetes, and you can't tell me with any confidence whether he will be sitting in a nursing home or on the Supreme Court."

The question is, of course, why? Why is it that some people seem prematurely old—their bodies depleted, minds fatigued, and spirits sagging—even in middle age, while others cruise through their sixties, seventies, and beyond, bright-eyed and eager, still in charge of businesses and running marathons with the enthusiasm of a teenager?

There are a lot of answers to this question. One easy one is that it helps to be a woman. In just about every respect, men seem to be at greater risk of aging faster and dying at a younger age than women. Men, for instance, die from coronary heart and liver disease at twice the rate women do, at twice the rate from accidents, and at four times the rate from suicide. They also have a 50 percent higher death rate from cancer.

The experts are still arguing over why this should be so, but many think that in our society, at least, men have traditionally been the breadwinners, and so have had to deal with more stress—jobs, bosses, and the like. Biologically, one of the culprits may be the male hormone testosterone. For one thing, testosterone seems to make men more vulnerable to blood vessel damage caused by hormones that are released in response to stress. It also seems to increase the blood levels of "bad" cholesterol (LDL) while dimin-ishing the levels of "good" cholesterol (HDL). Testosterone is implicated in so much overall bodily damage that in the long run, according to Georgetown University physiologist Estelle Ramey, "males actually destroy themselves."

As to women, many studies (for example, the Health in Detroit Study of 1978) have suggested that we feel sick more often than men, and we do seem to have a higher rate of arthritis and osteo-porosis. However, a number of studies show that we seem to have greater resistance to such serious conditions as rheumatism, hem-orrhages, and a number of varieties of cancer. We tend to have better blood circulation to the brain, which can mean less memory loss and clearer eyesight as we get older. In later life our hands stay somewhat more dextrous and our legs somewhat stronger. All this adds up to the greatest payoff of all: we live longer—an average of 78.3 years for an American woman born today, as opposed to 71.5 years for a man.

There's some evidence, though, that men are starting to catch up. Recent studies in Britain have shown that between 1974 and 1984, men's mortality rate from heart attacks declined by 22 per-cent as compared with only 17 percent for women. Between 1979 and 1987, the number of men who died from alcohol-related cir-rhosis of the liver increased by 11 percent, but the number of women who drank themselves to death went up by a startling 37 percent. Young women were more likely to take up smoking (one in three teenage girls as opposed to one in five teenage boys) and less likely to give it up later on (a 24 percent decline in smoking among men, only 18 percent among women). This may be the down side of women's liberation: as we come closer and closer to living our lives as the equals of men, we come closer and closer to equality in death as well.

As the longevity scales tip slightly in favor of women, they also tip toward those who maintain ideal weight. It's been known for many years that being greatly overweight increases one's risk of heart disease, which remains the number one killer in the United

States. People who are overweight also run a higher risk of having strokes and diabetes. A large body of recent research indicates strongly that the tendency to overweight is inherited. Scientists now seem to be narrowing in on identifying the "fat genes" themselves. One of these may be a gene that instructs fat cells to produce a protein called *adipsin*. Bruce Spiegelman of the Dana Farber Cancer Institute in Boston has found that obese mice have one hundred times "lower expression," that is, "turning on," of adipsin genes than normal mice. He thinks that lowered expression of adipsin could contribute to the development of obesity or obesity-linked dysfunctions such as diabetes.

While thin people do seem to have an advantage when it comes to living long and living well, being overweight is not necessarily a death sentence. It may be more important to find a weight that works for you and to keep it relatively constant. A recent study in Houston indicates that a pattern of gaining and losing large amounts of weight may be an even greater problem than being consistently overweight. Peggy Hamm and her co-workers at the University of Texas School of Public Health in Houston looked at the weight patterns of 339 men who had died of heart disease. Predictably enough, the lowest percentage (14 percent) were men who had not gained weight in middle age. Surprisingly, though, men who had gained weight in middle age and never lost it came in a close second (15 percent). The losers (26 percent) were men who had a tendency to gain weight, lose it, and then gain it back again. (Hamm thinks this may have had something to do with cholesterol levels. "These men probably regained weight quickly by eating fatty foods," she says. "Their cholesterol levels would have soared, leaving plaque deposits on their arteries.")

If weight is an important factor in longevity, it may be that resistance to disease is even more significant. We've all known people who can truthfully and thankfully boast that they've never been sick a day in their lives. Their toughness and extraordinary good health is probably due to the vigor of their immune systems, and that vigor may be inherited. A study of people in Japan who lived to be a hundred seems to bear this out. When the immunologist Hajime Takata of the Keio University School of Medicine in Japan looked at the immune systems of 102 centenarians, he found that most of them carried an extremely rare cell marker called DR1, and were lacking a cell marker known as DRw9, which has been linked to diabetes, colitis, and liver disease. "We are not certain," Takata concluded, "but it seems that there is some genetic control over human survival."

So we know that gender, weight, and resistance to disease are all important factors in longevity and aging. While gender is obviously something we're born with, many experts think that's also true of body build and disease resistance. A lot of scientists are tempted to believe that longevity and aging rates are all in the genes. Look at your parents and grandparents (if you've got living great-grandparents, that in itself could be a powerful sign in your favor). Did they age early and die relatively young? Were their later years compromised by ongoing bad health? Or were they, like my grandmother, still riding horses and running the farm even in their eighties? (This reminds me of a friend whose grandfather was never sick a day in his life, and was still playing eighteen holes of golf a day even in his mid-eighties. The only time my friend's grandfather was ever hospitalized was when he was in his late eighties, when he sustained a hernia carrying his son's suitcases to an airplane!) If it's the latter, the genetic determinists will tell you, then you yourself have an excellent chance of repeating the family performance of living to a healthy and vigorous old age.

This is the folk version of the genetic argument. But it turns out that genetic determinism also seems to have some scientific weight on its side. The Danish researcher Thorkild Sorenson looked at the life histories and the disease and death rates of adopted children and their natural parents. If adopted children tended to get the same diseases and die at more or less the same age as their biological parents, Sorenson reasoned, that would be strong evidence that nature was more important than nurture in determining how well we age and how long we live.

For their study, Sorenson and his co-workers at Hvidovre University Hospital in Copenhagen selected from the Danish Adoption Registry almost one thousand adopted children who were born between 1924 and 1926. Like a team of detectives, the researchers went to local population registries to hunt down both the children and their biological parents. By looking at death certificates, Sorenson's team was able to find out not only when both parents and children died, but how. The researchers could then compare the ages and causes of death of the children and their natural parents to see if the genetic connection held up.

The results were astonishing. Adopted children whose natural parents had died early of natural causes were twice as likely to die early from natural causes themselves. If one of the parents had died early of heart disease, the child was four times as likely to be struck down by an early heart attack. If one of the parents had died prematurely from an infectious disease, the adopted child was *five* times as likely to die early in the same way. The important exception to this pattern was cancer: while there was no correlation between cancer deaths among adopted children and those among their natural parents, adopted children whose *adoptive* parents had died of early cancer were five times more likely to die of early cancer themselves. (This may be a strong argument for cancer's being primarily either a lifestyle or a psychosomatic disease, brought on by stress, diet, environmental toxins, or smoking.) Sorenson's conclusion was that premature death in adults has a "strong genetic background."

The results of Sorenson's study would have been no surprise to Jorge Yunis. A medical researcher at Hahnemann College in Philadelphia, Yunis has for the past thirty years been looking at the role genes play in making a person susceptible to certain diseases—especially cancer. But instead of looking at census figures and death certificates, Yunis has turned his microscope on what may be the living heart of the problem: human chromosomes and the genes they carry. In doing so, Yunis may eventually be able to tell whether or not a person's life will be shadowed with cancer and, if so, whether or not that person might be expected to survive a bout with the killer disease.

When Yunis and his wife, Mary, were first married, he took a sample of her blood to his lab so he could check for signs of impending cancer in her chromosomes. The result? "I took out more life insurance for her," he says. "I wasn't surprised," says Mary calmly. "There's cancer in my family, so I already had a good idea of what my genetic Achilles' heel might be."

The key to Yunis's biological crystal ball is what he calls "fragile sites" on human chromosomes. These are weak points on the chromosomes vulnerable to attack by certain chemicals, viruses, or radiation. To find the fragile sites, Yunis puts cells in a nutrient soup, then does something that no good cook would ever do to a broth: he stirs in a dollop of caffeine. The caffeine, it turns out, reveals the fragile sites as effectively as a police technician's powder brings out a criminal's fingerprints. So far Yunis's "caffeine soup" technique has turned up at least fifty-one fragile sites where chromosomes can be nicked or broken. On average, these nicks and breaks show up in about 6 percent of the cells Yunis has tested. But in some cases they've appeared in as many as 30 percent of the cells. These are the cases, Yunis believes, where the cells are most likely to break down and start the mad, out-of-control division that spells cancer.

Obviously, early testing for fragile sites could alert people to danger and encourage them to take preventive measures to keep their chromosomes from breaking—to stop smoking, for example, or avoid exposure to radiation and toxic chemicals. In general, fragile site testing could become a sort of early warning system, alerting people to the presence of danger and prompting them to take heed and make changes.

In the meantime, researchers at the University of Texas M. D. Anderson Cancer Center in Houston have developed a test that helps determine how good a job a person's cells do of repairing damaged chromosomes, which in turn may tell how susceptible that person will be to cancer. The researchers mix a sample of the individual's blood with the drug bleomycin, which is known to cause chromosome damage. Three days later, a lab technician looks at the cells under a microscope and simply counts the broken chromosomes. The more breaks, the higher the implied risk of cancer. In early testing, only about 24 percent of healthy people showed high rates of chromosome breakage, compared with as many as 64 percent of cancer patients.

The point of all this is that if Yunis and the Texas researchers are right, if looking at people's genes and chromosomes can help predict whether or not they will get cancer and how well they will respond if they do, then similar tests might reveal their genetic susceptibility to any number of ailments—heart disease, for example, or infectious diseases—that could cut their life short. They could then make changes in lifestyle, in diet, exercise, even the kind of job they have, that would help them live their maximum number of years. In other words, if you have an unfortunate array of "bad" genes, you could take the kind of preventive measures that might help you defy your own heredity. If your parents gave you "good" genes, you could take extra care to maintain your lucky endowment with a healthy lifestyle.

So heredity *is* obviously a powerful factor in determining how long and how well we'll live. But it's certainly not the whole story. If it were, we might expect the range of changes that occur with age to look pretty much the same around the world, no matter what the country or culture. But they don't. For many Americans, for example, the percentage of body fat tends to increase as they get older. Their blood pressure rises, and so does their cholesterol count. Yet people in most primitive cultures—from the Kwaio of the Solomon Islands to the ¡Kung San (Bushmen) of the Kalahari Desert—tend to become leaner in old age. Among the Yanomamo of Venezuela and the Yiwara aborigines of Australia, blood pressure is low in young people and stays low in the old. The average cholesterol count of the Hadza of Tanzania, the Mbouti of Zaire, and the Tarahumara of Mexico stays at about 150, no matter what the individual's age, while the American average rises to about 210 in adulthood. There are cultural differences, too, in the kinds of diseases people tend to get. In America, heart disease and cancer are by far the biggest killers, while people in more primitive cultures, where antibiotics may not be readily available, tend to be struck down by infectious diseases like pneumonia.

To many experts, this says that longevity and rates of aging are not just a matter of heredity, that environmental factors can be equally important. Lifestyle, diet, psychological makeup, family life, even geography can be as significant as genetics in helping us live long and age well. As S. Boyd Eaton, a radiologist and co-author of *The Paleolithic Prescription*, puts it: "It isn't our inherent biological nature alone that determines how we age, but the interaction between our genes and the way we live."

It also may be that where we live has something to do with the way we live—and thus our aging rate and life expectancy. In the village of Vilcabamba, high in the Ecuadoran Andes, American researchers found that people who survive to old age remain admirably vigorous. Although stories of Vilcabamba elders living to be as old as 134 have been shown to be fabrications, no one can deny what these scientists saw: very old people, some of them in their nineties, riding horses, chopping wood, and continuing active work lives.

American scientists have seen similarly remarkable populations of older people among the Hunza of Pakistan and the people of Abkhazia in Soviet Georgia. According to Kenneth R. Pelletier, a senior clinical fellow at the Center for Disease Prevention of the Stanford University School of Medicine, older people in these communities tend to enjoy excellent cardiovascular and musculoskeletal health, and their life expectancy may be as much as twenty years longer than ours!

Much of this is probably due to lifestyle, to purer environments. In general these exotic cultures are cleaner than ours—no smog, no nuclear dumps, no toxic waste. The people may also be relatively free of the stresses that trouble those of us who live in more complex, industrialized societies. The semiprimitive quality of life tends to keep people physically active even in advanced old age, while close-knit families provide the kind of social and emotional support that can help maintain mental health. There's tantalizing evidence that their low-calorie diets, punctuated by periods of semistarvation when wintertime food stores run low, may actually be helping them to live longer.

But one doesn't have to live in an isolated mountaintop culture to take advantage of geographical differences in aging and longevity. Even in the United States, it's apparent that where one lives can be an important factor in determining how well and how long one lives. According to the National Center for Health Statistics, people in Hawaii live an average of seven years longer (to age 77.02) than people in the last-place District of Columbia (69.20). No one quite knows why there's such a pronounced difference, but it's apparently not a matter of climate: in second place, just after balmy Hawaii, is frigid Minnesota. (In fact, eighteen of the top twenty are cold-weather states, while five of the last six states are in the Sun Belt.)

There also seem to be major differences in longevity between people who live in the city and those who live in the country. A classic study of two thousand healthy men by C. L. Rose and M. L. Cohen concluded that out of sixty-nine possible factors influencing health and longevity, living in a rural area was the fifth most important. At least one set of available statistics tends to bear this out: people from LaCrosse, Wisconsin, where the population is only about 50,000, live an average of four years longer than people in Milwaukee (population 740,000), and seven years longer than Chicagoans, where the population is 3 million.

It's certainly not hard to figure out why this is so. City air is dirtier, meaning a higher rate of respiratory diseases. There's likely to be more contact with toxic chemicals, meaning higher rates of cancer—6 percent higher in Los Angeles and Houston, for example, where petroleum refineries emit carcinogens into the atmosphere—and a uniquely modern condition known as multiple chemical sensitivities, or MCS. The constant noise of the city is also a health hazard: a 1981 study showed that children in a class-room close to a jet airport had higher blood pressure and were more likely to make errors in their schoolwork than children in quieter neighborhoods—even a year after the airport noise had been reduced by special insulation.

The classic response to all this has been to move to the suburbs. But even suburban living has its drawbacks, many of them related to commuting. For the last ten years, psychologist Raymond Novaco of the University of California at Irvine has been studying the effects of commuting on scientific samples of drivers in suburban Orange County, California. He found that the longer the commuting distance, the higher the drivers' blood pressure. The more congested the route, the more absences from work because of illness. And the more a driver had to switch among freeways, the more likely he or she was to come down with colds or flu. Furthermore, Novaco's studies showed that a negative mood at home in the evening is strongly related to commuting on congested roadways.

Novaco's work is one piece of evidence that helps bear out what many people have suspected all along: that suburban living may not be much healthier than life in the metropolis. Does this mean that if you want to live a long and healthy life you should put on a pair of overalls and get out to the country? Maybe. The Northwestern National Life Insurance Company of Minneapolis did a study recently in which they examined a long list of health statistics in a search for the "healthiest" states in America. The winners: Utah, North Dakota, Idaho, Vermont, Nebraska, Colorado, Wyoming, and Montana—all of them predominantly rural states.

For the majority of us, who remain tied to cities because that's where the jobs are, it may be a relief to know that some cities are more healthful than others. Recently, psychology professor Robert Levine and his colleagues at the California State University at Fresno studied the style and quality of life in thirty-six small, medium, and large cities across the United States. They looked for telltale clues of stressful environments by measuring such things as the speed at which people walk, how quickly bank tellers counted out change, and even the number of people who didn't wear watches. Not surprisingly, the highest levels of stress were found in the Northeast, where cities like Buffalo, Boston, and New York won the dubious distinction of being designated "Type A" cities—those whose residents have a greater risk of developing heart disease. The laid-back West, on the other hand, had the slowest rates of living and the lowest rate of death from heart disease. Among cities, Houston was the winner, showing the lowest rate of death from heart disease of all the thirty-six cities in the study.

Of course, no one's going to tell you that living in Houston— or, for that matter, on a tropical island or on a midwestern farm —will guarantee you a long and healthy life. Scientists are beginning to wonder if *personality*—how you relate to yourself and to the people around you—may not play as important a role in longevity as genetics and geography. The question is: Do healthy attitudes help one live a long and vigorous life?

Experts are beginning to come up with an answer to this question. For more than fifty years a team of researchers, now led by the psychiatrist George Vaillant of Dartmouth Medical School, has been looking at the link between attitude and health in a group of Harvard graduates. When they were twenty-five, the ninety-nine Harvard volunteers filled out questionnaires designed to assess whether they were optimists or pessimists. For the next thirty-five years, the volunteers got medical examinations at five-year intervals. Vaillant and his colleagues then correlated the volunteers' attitudes with the state of their health in middle age and beyond. The results? "Pessimism in early adulthood," the researchers concluded, "appears to be a risk factor for poor health in middle and late adulthood."

Evidently, then, personality can play an important role in determining how well we age. This is hopeful news, because while our genetic heritage is outside our control—we can be aware of it and work with it, but we can't really change it, not yet anyway—we *can,* by working hard, change our personality in a healthy direction. This is also true of a number of other factors that are part of the aging equation. Education is one. When the nutrition and anthropology professor Stanley M. Garn and his colleagues at the University of Michigan studied 1,017 married couples, they found that the more years a woman went to school, the more likely she was to be slender, and thus to avoid some of the health risks—heart disease, high blood pressure, and diabetes—that go with being overweight.

If being well educated can help you live longer, so, evidently, can sharing your life at home. It seems to be true: married people have substantially lower death rates than single people. To prove it, the researchers Yuanreng Hu and Noreen Goldman of Princeton University looked at statistics from sixteen industrialized countries—not only the United States and Western European countries, but Asian countries like Japan and Taiwan as well— over the last thirty years. In every country, single people had higher death rates than married people—an average of twice as high for single men and one and a half times as high for single women. Divorced and widowed people seemed especially woeful: ten times as many of them died in their twenties and thirties as did married people of the same age.

Goldman offers two possible explanations for these differences. On the one hand, she says, healthier people may be more likely to marry in the first place. On the other hand, having a partner with whom to share the ups and downs of one's life may make a person better able to cope with disease. "No one has the ultimate answer," Goldman concludes, "but clearly both these factors play a part."

If being married can have an effect on how long you'll live, *whom* you marry can be equally important—especially if you're a woman. Here again, education can be a factor. Garn's study showed that women who married high-school dropouts ended up as much as twelve pounds heavier than women who married college graduates. Strangely enough, though, this didn't seem to work for men. In fact, regardless of the education level of the women they married, male college graduates tended to be two to three pounds heavier than men who attended high school only.

If marrying smarter men has a positive influence on a woman's longevity, so, apparently, does marrying younger men. Looking at data from the U.S. Census, the psychologists Laural Klinger-Vartabedian and Lauren Wispe of the University of Oklahoma found that women in their late fifties who were married to men one to nine years younger had a death rate only one-third as high as all women in that age group. And women in their seventies who were married to younger men had only half the death rate of their peers. In contrast, the death rate for women who were married to older men was higher than that of women in general.

Genes, gender, geography, health, weight, personality, love life—that's a fairly comprehensive list of the factors that help determine who will remain biologically younger as they get chronologically older. Obviously, even those who are less fortunate in the heredity department can still exercise a powerful influence over the other factors, and this, to a large degree, is what this book is all about.

Later on, I will give you a list of specific prescriptions that could help you to live long and live well. First, though, you might find it interesting and informative to see if you've got a head start on the clock of aging. In the next chapter, I will give you a number of tests that can help you answer what could be one of your most important questions: Am I biologically older or younger than my actual years?

7

How Old Are You Really:

LONGEVITY POTENTIAL TESTS

All of us have two ages: the official, chronological age that appears on our birth certificates, and our *biological* age, which reflects the rate at which we're getting older. If you're like me, your biological age is probably more important to you than the number of candles on your birthday cake—you want to look, act, and feel younger than your actual years. You say to yourself: "I feel like a kid," or "She looks like a teenager," and these impressions may hint at the difference between chronology and biology. But in the end, they're only impressions, and you may want to know: Is there any way I can scientifically determine my biological age?

The answer is a qualified yes. In recent years scientists have devised a number of potentially instructive tests to help you estimate how old you might be inside. Some of these tests can even be done at home on your own. For example, the longevity pioneer Roy Walford has developed a test that allows you to measure four distinct "biomarkers"—physical functions that may be key indicators of how fast you're aging. The first of these is skin elasticity. To measure this, pinch the skin on the back of one hand between your other thumb and forefinger for five seconds. Then let it go and time how long it takes to return to normal. If it takes five seconds or less, your biological age is less than fifty. It it takes ten to fifteen seconds, you're in the range of sixty to sixty-nine. Above that means a biological age of seventy or more. A declining score over time reflects deterioration of the connective tissue under the surface of the skin, which in turns leads to wrinkles.

Next text your reaction time. To do this, get a thin, eighteen-inch ruler and ask a friend to dangle it vertically in front of you, holding it from the top. Now hold the thumb and middle finger of your right hand three and a half inches apart at the bottom end of the ruler. Have your friend drop the ruler between your out-stretched thumb and finger, and catch it as quickly as you can. Look at the inch mark where you caught the ruler—that's your score. Repeat the test twice more and take the average. If you averaged eleven inches or more, that gives you a functional age of twenty. At nine and three quarters you're around thirty, eight and a half is about forty, seven and a quarter equals fifty, and six or less means sixty or more.

Next, Walford asks you to test your visual capacity. To do this, hold a newspaper at arm's length. If you're nearsighted you can leave your glasses on, but take them off it you're farsighted. Now bring the newspaper toward you until the print—not the head-lines, but the regular-sized print in the articles—starts to blur. Measure the distance between your face and the newspaper at that point. At about thirty-nine inches, you've got a functional age of sixty. Fifteen inches brings the functional age down to fifty, nine inches to forty, five and a half to thirty, and four inches to about twenty-one.

Finally, you'll want to assess what's known as your *static balance*. Stand on a hard surface with your shoes off. Put both feet together, close your eyes, lift one foot—the left foot if you're right-handed, the right foot it you're left-handed—about six inches off the ground, and bend that knee at a 45-degree angle. Time how long you can hold that stance without opening your eyes or lowering your foot to avoid falling. Repeat the test twice more and take the average time. Four seconds gives you a functional age of between sixty and seventy, ten seconds is between fifty and sixty, eighteen seconds is between forty and fifty, twenty-two seconds is between thirty and forty, and twenty-eight seconds equals a functional age of between twenty and thirty. Add up the total of your functional ages on each test and divide by four. This will give you an overall functional age on the Walford test.

If you want something a little more comprehensive, try the test developed by the researchers Richard Earle and David Imrie for the Canadian Institute of Stress in Toronto. This is a three-step test that estimates your "body age" by asking detailed questions not only about your physical biomarkers but also about your heredity, lifestyle, personality, and response to stress. Like the Walford test, you can take this one without setting foot in a doctor's office or laboratory.

The first stage of the Earle and Imrie test is similar to Walford's in that it gives you a quick way of estimating your body age. The Canadians call it the Near-Vision Blurring Test, and, like Walford's, it measures how closely you can see printed material without any blurring. "Since you use your eyes all the time," explain Earle and Imrie, "aging (lost elasticity in the lens) shows up here early."

To take the test, you'll need a partner, a roll-up tape meaure, and a three-by-five-inch index card. Using a typewriter with a normal-size typeface, type the phrase "Vitality Is Bodily Efficiency" on the index card. Now tape the card to the end of the tape measure. If you wear glasses or contact lenses, take them off. Now hold the fat part of the tape measure (the casing) next to your head at eye level. Have your partner hold the end of the tap measure with the index card six feet away from your face. Now have them walk toward you, rolling up the tape as they do. Have them stop at the point where the letters on the index card begin to blur. Record that distance as your near-vision blur point.

Now look at the Body Age Score Sheet to determine your "body age." If your body age is more than three years older than your actual age, you may want to consider making some changes in your lifestyle and health habits. You'll find plenty of tips on how to make positive lifestyle changes in the next section of this book. If your body age is more than three years younger than your actual age, you're obviously doing some important things right, so keep up the good work.

Body Age Score Sheet

NEAR VISION IN INCHES	BODY AGE IN YEARS	NEAR VISION IN INCHES	BODY AGE IN YEARS
0.0–3.9	19		
4.0–4.1	20		
4.2	21		
4.3	22		
4.4–4.5	23		
4.6–4.7	24		
4.8	25		
4.9–5.0	26		
5.1	27		
5.2–5.3	28		
5.4	29		
5.5–5.7	30		
5.8–6.1	31		
6.2–6.5	32		
6.6–6.8	33		
6.9–7.1	34		
7.2–7.5	35		
7.6–7.9	36		
8.0–8.2	37		
8.3–8.5	38		
8.6–8.9	39		
9.0–9.5	40		

NEAR VISION IN INCHES	BODY AGE IN YEARS	NEAR VISION IN INCHES	BODY AGE IN YEARS
9.6–10.1	41		
10.2–10.7	42		
10.8–11.3	43		
11.4–11.9	44		
12.0–12.5	45		
12.6–13.1	46		
13.2–13.7	47		
13.8–14.3	48		
14.4–14.9	49		
15.0–17.3	50		
17.4–19.7	51		
19.8–22.1	52		
22.2–24.5	53		
24.6–26.9	54		
27.0–29.3	55		
29.4–31.7	56		
31.8–34.1	57		
34.2–36.5	58		
36.6–38.9	59		
39.0–41.3	60		
41.4–43.7	61		
43.8–46.1	62		
46.2–48.5	63		
48.6–50.9	64		
51.0–53.3	65		
53.4–55.7	66		
55.8–58.1	67		
58.2–60.5	68		
60.6–62.9	69		
63.0–65.3	70		
65.3 +	71		

Now that you've estimated your body age, the next step is to determine the rate at which you're aging. To do this, first answer all the questions in the Aging Potential Test (below). For the first eleven items, score yourself according to the formula given at the end of each list. Following question 11, there's another formula that tells you how to score your answers to items 12 to 61.

Aging Potential Test

1. Medication profile
(add up how many of the following you use one or more times during a typical week)

- aspirin
- antacids
- laxatives
- antihistamines
- cough syrups
- decongestants
- diuretics
- nonprescription sleeping pills
- nonprescription stimulants

Score:
0 if one or none   3 if four
1 if two   4 if five
2 if three   5 if six or more

2. Alcohol use
(1.25 oz. liquor = 1 beer or 1 glass of wine)

Score:
0 if nondrinker–1 oz./day   5 if 4–6 oz./day
1 if 1–2.5 oz./day   6 if 6–9 oz./day
3 if 2.5–4 oz./day   8 if 10+ oz./day

3. Exercise frequency
(more than 20 minutes at training heart rate)

Score:
0 if 3 or more times/week   4 if once/week
2 if twice/week   7 if rarely or never

4. Sugar intake
(count 1 for each food you use more than once per week)

- tea/coffee/cocoa
- colas/sodas
- ice cream
- doughnuts
- candy/sweets
- chocolate
- sweetened cereal
- honey
- dried fruits
- canned or frozen fruits
- baked desserts
- cookies/cakes
- jam/jelly
- raw fruits more than twice/day
- alcohol
- sweet wines/liqueurs
- canned fruit juices

Score:
0 if none   2 if 5–8
1 if 1–4   3 if 9+

5. Fat intake
(score 1 for each food eaten at least once per week)

- steak/roast
- beef or veal
- butter
- margarine
- hard cheeses
- processed cheeses
- fried/sautéed foods
- nuts
- canned meats
- bologna/salami/hot dogs
- fast-food chicken
- bacon/sausage
- ham
- tuna/sardines (in oil)
- pork
- avocado
- French fries
- pastries/doughnuts
- hamburger
- ice cream
- eggs
- whole or 2% milk
- chocolate
- peanut butter
- salmon
- poultry skin
- cream
- TV dinners

6. Salt intake
(score 1 for each food you eat at least once per week)

- salt in cooking
- salt in food at the table
- salt in foods before tasting
- pickles

- salty foods
- cheese
- pizza
- bologna/salami/hot dogs
- salted nuts
- potato or corn chips/puffs
- anchovies
- olives
- saltines/crackers
- sauerkraut
- fast-food hamburger
- canned vegetables
- soy sauce
- ketchup
- Worcestershire sauce
- powdered soup/gravy mixes
- corned or smoked meat/fish
- pretzels
- TV dinners
- commercial salad dressings
- frozen vegetables
- bacon
- fast-food chicken

Score:
0 if none   2 if 7–12
1 if 1–6   3 if 13 +

7. Refined or processed foods
(estimate the percentage of your diet made up of these foods, including ham, bacon, sausage, smoked fish or meat, all canned foods and beverages, all white or enriched flours, breads and cookies, pies, candy, ice cream, chocolate, and all protein powders)

Score:
0 if less than 20%   2 if 50–75%
1 if 20–50%   3 if 75%

8. Smoking
Score:
0 if nonsmoker
1 if nonsmoker exposed to
   smokers
2 if smoke 1–8 cigarettes/day

4 if smoke 8–20/day
7 if smoke 20 +/day
   (1 pipe = 2 cigarettes;
   1 cigar = 3 cigarettes)

9. Caffeine
(add up the cups of coffee, tea, and cola you drink per day)

Score:
0 if none   2 if 4–7
1 if 1–3   3 if 8+

10. Heart disease
(put a checkmark next to any relative who has, or has had, this disorder)

• father _____   • grandfathers _____
• mother _____   • grandmothers _____
• siblings _____

Score = total number of checks up to a maximum of 4

11. Hypertension
(high blood pressure; put a checkmark next to any relative who has, or has had, this disorder)

• father _____   • grandfathers _____
• mother _____   • grandmothers _____
• siblings _____

Score = total number of checks up to a maximum of 4

How frequently has each of the following statements been true about you during the last year?
(For questions 12–61, enter the number from 0–10 that best describes how you relate to each statement: 0 = never; 2 = rarely; 4 = infrequently; 6 = occasionally; 8 = frequently; 10 = very frequently.)

_____ 12. I feel used up at the end of the day.
_____ 13. I'm callous about a lot of things.
_____ 14. I'm critical of others.

_____ 15. I blame myself for things.

_____ 16. I feel uncomfortable about the way I treat people.

_____ 17. I tire quickly.

_____ 18. I wish I could be as happy as other people seem to be.

_____ 19. I get annoyed and irritated easily.

_____ 20. I can't turn my thoughts off long enough at nights/on weekends to feel relaxed the next day.

_____ 21. I find that long periods of time around people are a strain.

_____ 22. I feel exhausted, tired, or unable to get things done.

_____ 23. I feel sad, depressed, down in the dumps, or hopeless.

_____ 24. I find I'm waking up earlier than I planned to.

_____ 25. When something stressful comes up, I think about all the ways something can go wrong.

_____ 26. I'm not able to give what I would like to the people close to me.

_____ 27. I get a lot of tension headaches.

_____ 28. I feel blocked in getting things done.

_____ 29. My sleep is restless or disturbed.

_____ 30. It takes me a long time to get over distressful situations.

_____ 31. I don't feel really close to or accepted by my family or friends.

_____ 32. My lower back is a problem.

_____ 33. There are a lot of people who would take advantage of me if I let them.

_____ 34. I get into arguments.

_____ 35. My friends would worry about me if I weren't worrying about something.

_____ 36. I feel lonely.

_____ 37. Allergy problems bother me more than other people.

_____ 38. The way I use time isn't a very accurate reflection of my interests.

_____ 39. I sweat easily, even on cool days.

_____ 40. Worrying a lot seems to be part of the price of success.

_____ 41. I feel self-conscious with others.

_____ 42. I have migraine or tension headaches.

_____ 43. Other people have made a lot more out of their talents than I have.

_____ 44. I anticipate others in conversation (interrupting sentences).

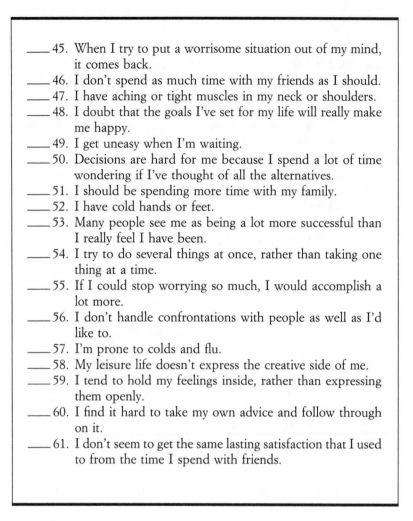

____ 45. When I try to put a worrisome situation out of my mind, it comes back.

____ 46. I don't spend as much time with my friends as I should.

____ 47. I have aching or tight muscles in my neck or shoulders.

____ 48. I doubt that the goals I've set for my life will really make me happy.

____ 49. I get uneasy when I'm waiting.

____ 50. Decisions are hard for me because I spend a lot of time wondering if I've thought of all the alternatives.

____ 51. I should be spending more time with my family.

____ 52. I have cold hands or feet.

____ 53. Many people see me as being a lot more successful than I really feel I have been.

____ 54. I try to do several things at once, rather than taking one thing at a time.

____ 55. If I could stop worrying so much, I would accomplish a lot more.

____ 56. I don't handle confrontations with people as well as I'd like to.

____ 57. I'm prone to colds and flu.

____ 58. My leisure life doesn't express the creative side of me.

____ 59. I tend to hold my feelings inside, rather than expressing them openly.

____ 60. I find it hard to take my own advice and follow through on it.

____ 61. I don't seem to get the same lasting satisfaction that I used to from the time I spend with friends.

When you have your Aging Potential Test scores, follow the instructions for the Which Stress Type Are You? quiz and factor in your scores according to those instructions. The following are explanations of stress types:

Cliff Walkers: Cliff walkers have a cavalier, what-me-worry? attitude toward their own health. They tend to smoke and drink to excess, be overweight and out of shape. To fight stress they rely on drugs: tranquilizers, antacids, alcohol. These people are prime candidates to die of heart failure while still in middle age.

Basket Cases: These people are lacking in basic vitality. They're always tired, even just after they've gotten up in the morning. Their diet is really poor—low in vital nutrients and high in stress enhancers like caffeine and sugar—and so are their exercise habits.

Drifters: Drifters lack a sense of direction and purpose in life. They go passively and almost mindlessly from job to job and lover to lover, never settling into anything with any sort of dedication. This category also includes the victims of midlife crisis—otherwise focused people who suddenly start to drift in middle age. Some of the symptoms: chronic fatigue, inability to sleep, depression, minor and mysterious illnesses.

Speed Freaks: These are workaholics who seem to thrive on abnormally high levels of stress. Often very successful, they're also frequently victimized by stress-related illnesses: ulcers, fatigue, and heart disease.

Worry Warts: A more or less constant concern with the negative side of life characterizes worry warts. Generally low in self-esteem, these people suffer from chronic guilt and frequent anxiety attacks. Their common illnesses—headaches, insomnia, lower back pain —are usually brought on by their constant state of tension.

Loners: Loners are overly controlled, locked-in people who don't like revealing or even dealing with their own feelings. Consequently, they tend to shun other people and are especially afraid of anything that smacks of intimacy. Since they get little feedback from others, they're usually uncertain about themselves, and this uncertainty in itself becomes an unhealthy form of stress.

Which Stress Type Are You?

1. Write the numerical answer you gave each question in the Aging Potential Test in the appropriate space below.

2. Add up the numbers across each row. You'll end up with a total score for each, which becomes your score on that particular stress type.
   Scoring:
   0–30—you bear no resemblance
   31–36—you're borderline; take preventive measures
   37 up—you're a classic textbook example; you should get going on your prescription right away

3. Now add up your six scores. Enter the total in the space provided. Subtract this from 600. This is your personal "vitality quotient," reflecting your current rate of aging.
   Scoring:
   420 and up—you're a slow ager; keep up the good work
   382–419—early warning signs; take preventive measures
   0–381—you're aging too quickly; slow things down by taking corrective action right away

Type	*Stress Type Score*
Cliff Walker	
Items _ _ _ _ _ _ _ _ _ _ _	_____
1 2 3 4 5 6 7 8 9 10 11	(This total × 2)
Basket Case	
Items _ _ _ _ _ _ _ _ _ _	_____
12 17 22 27 32 37 42 47 52 57	
Drifter	
Items _ _ _ _ _ _ _ _ _ _	_____
13 18 23 28 33 38 43 48 53 58	
Speed Freak	
Items _ _ _ _ _ _ _ _ _ _	_____
14 19 24 29 34 39 44 49 54 59	

Worry Wart

Items __ __ __ __ __ __ __ __ __ __   _____
      15 20 25 30 35 40 45 50 55 60

Loner

Items __ __ __ __ __ __ __ __ __ __   _____
      16 21 26 31 36 41 46 51 56 61

If I have whetted your appetite for aging rate tests, here's one that's even more comprehensive than the previous two. This test was developed by the staff of *Longevity* magazine in collaboration with experts at the National Institute on Aging and others in the field of gerontology. The test lists seventeen key factors, divided into six general categories. Simply add or subtract the numbers next to each factor. At the end of the test are instructions on how to calculate your score and find out what your chances might be of living a longer-than-average life.

The Longevity Potential Test

A. CHANGEABLE LIFESTYLE FACTORS

1. Tobacco
(1 pipe = 2 cigarettes; 1 cigar = 3 cigarettes)

Never smoked   + 20

Quit smoking   + 10

Smoke up to 1 pack per day	− 10
Smoke 1 to 2 packs per day	− 20
Smoke over 2 packs per day	− 30
Pack-years smoked (number of packs smoked per day × number of years smoked):	
7–15	− 5
16–25	− 10
over 25	− 20

2. Alcohol
(1 beer or 1 glass of wine = 1.25 oz. alcohol)

1.25 oz. per day or less	+ 10
Between 1.25 and 2.5 oz. per day	− 4
− 1 more for each additional 1.25 oz. per day	− ___

3. Exercise
(20 minutes or more moderate aerobic exercise)

3 or more times per week	+ 20
2 times per week	+ 10
No regular aerobic activity	− 10
Work requires regular physical exertion or at least 2 miles walking per day	+ 3
+ 1 more for each additional mile walked per day	+ ___

4. Weight

Maintain ideal weight for height	+ 5
5–10 lbs. over ideal	− 1
11–20 lbs. over ideal	− 2

21–30 lbs. over ideal		− 3
− 1 more for each additional 10 lbs. over ideal		− ___
Yo-yo dieting		− 10

5. Nutrition

Eat well-balanced diet	+ 3	
Do not eat well-balanced diet		− 3
Regularly eat meals at consistent times	+ 2	
Do not regularly eat meals at consistent times		− 2
Snack or eat meals late at night		− 2
Eat a balanced breakfast	+ 2	
Eat fish or poultry as primary protein source (totally replacing red meat)	+ 5	
Do not eat grains and fish as primary protein source		− 2
Eat at least 5 servings of green leafy vegetables per week	+ 3	
Eat at least 5 servings of fresh fruit or juice	+ 3	
Try to avoid fats	+ 5	
Do not try to avoid fats		− 5

Score as indicated for each of the following
foods eaten 2 or more times per week:

Beef, veal, or pork		− 1
Bacon or sausage		− 1
Luncheon meat or hot dogs		− 1
Fast food		− 1
Fried food		− 1
Processed food/TV dinners		− 1

Eggs	−	1
Cheese	−	1
Butter	−	1
Whole milk or cream	−	1
Pastries, doughnuts, muffins	−	1
Candy, chocolate	−	1
Pretzels, potato chips	−	1
Ice cream	−	1
Eat some food every day that is high in fiber (whole-grain bread, fresh fruits and vegetables)	+	3
Do not eat some food every day that is high in fiber	−	3
Take a daily multivitamin/mineral supplement	+	10
(Women) take a calcium supplement	+	5
Subscribe to health-related periodicals	+	2
SUBTOTAL A:	+	—
SUBTOTAL G:	−	—

B. FIXED FACTORS

1. Gender

Male	−	5
Female	+	10

2. Heredity

Any grandparent lived to be over 80	+	5
Average age all four grandparents lived to:		
60–70	+	5
71–80	+	10
Over 80	+	20

3. Family history

Either parent had stroke or heart attack before age 50   − 10

−5 for each family member (grandparent, parent, sibling) who prior to age 65 has had any of the following:

Hypertension   − __

Cancer   − __

Heart disease   − __

Stroke   − __

Diabetes   − __

Other genetic diseases   − __

SUBTOTAL B: + __   − __

C. PARTIALLY FIXED FACTORS

1. Family income

$0–$5,000   − 10

$5,001–$14,000   − 5

$14,001–$20,000   + 1

+1 for each additional $10,000 up to $200,000   + __

2. Education

Some high school (or less)   − 7

High-school graduate   + 2

College graduate   + 5

Postgraduate or professional degree   + 7

3. Occupation

Professional	+ 5	
Self-employed	+ 6	
In health-care field	+ 3	
Over 65 and still working	+ 5	
Clerical or support		− 3
Shift work		− 5
Unemployed		− 7
Possibility for career advancement	+ 5	
Regularly in direct contact with pollutants, toxic waste, chemicals, radiation		− 10

4. Where you live

Large urban area		− 5
Near an industrial center		− 7
Rural or farm area	+ 5	
Area with air-pollution alerts		− 5
Area where air pollution has curtailed normal daily activities		− 7
High crime area		− 3
Area with little or no crime	+ 3	
Home has tested positive for radon		− 7
Total commuting time to and from work:		
0–½ hour	+ 3	
½–1 hour	+ 0	
− 1 for each ½ hour over 1 hour		− ___

94

Within 30 miles of major medical/trauma center	+ 3	
No major medical/trauma center in area		− 3
SUBTOTAL C:	+ __	**+** − __

D. CHANGEABLE HEALTH STATUS AND MAINTENANCE FACTORS

1. Health status

Present overall physical health:		
Excellent	+ 15	
Good	+ 12	
Fair	+ 5	
Poor		− 10
Normal or low blood pressure	+ 5	
High blood pressure		− 10
Don't know blood pressure		− 5
Low cholesterol (under 200)	+ 10	
Moderate cholesterol (200–240)	+ 5	
High cholesterol (over 240)		− 10
Don't know cholesterol count		− 5
HDL cholesterol 29 or less		− 25
30–36		− 20
37–40		− 5
41–45	+ 5	
Over 45	+ 10	
Don't know		− 5
Have medical insurance coverage	+ 10	
Able to use physicians of your choice	+ 5	

2. Preventive and therapeutic measures

WOMEN:

Yearly gynecological exam and Pap smear	+	2
Monthly breast self-examination	+	2
Mammogram (35–50, every 3 years; over 50, every year)	+	2
Smoke and use oral contraceptives	−	5

MEN:

Genital self-examination every 3 months	+	2
Rectal or prostate exam (yearly after age 30)	+	2

ALL:

Physical exams (every 3 to 4 years before 50, every 1 to 2 years over 50)	+	3
Current on mumps, measles, rubella, diphtheria, and tetanus immunizations	+	2
Tested for hidden blood in stool (over 40, every 2 years; over 50, every year)	+	2
If over 50, yearly sigmoidoscopy of the lower bowel	+	2
Regularly use sunscreen and avoid excessive exposure to sun	+	2
Actively involved in a life-extension, disease prevention or comprehensive wellness program	+	10

3. Accident control

Always wear seat belt as driver and passenger	+	7
Do not always wear seat belt as driver and passenger	−	5
Never drink and drive or ride with a driver who has been drinking	+	2
− 10 for each arrest for driving while under the influence of alcohol in the past 5 years	−	___

−2 for every speeding ticket or accident in the past year		− __
For each 10,000 miles per year driven over 10,000 (national average)		− 1
Primary car weighs over 3,500 lbs.	+ 10	
Subcompact		− 5
Motorcycle		− 10
−2 for every fight or attack you were involved in, or witness to, in the past year		− __
Smoke alarms in home	+ 1	
SUBTOTAL D:	+ __	**+** − __

E. CHANGEABLE PSYCHOSOCIAL FACTORS

Married or in long-term committed relationship	+ 5	
Satisfying sex life	+ 3	
Children under 18 living at home	+ 3	
For each 5-year period living alone		− 1
No close friends		− 10
+ 1 for each close friend (up to 5)	+ __	
+2 for each active membership in a religious community or volunteer organization (up to 4)	+ __	
Have a pet	+ 2	
Maintain regular daily routine	+ 10	
No regular daily routine		− 10
Hours of uninterrupted sleep per night: Less than 5		− 5

5–8	+ 5	
8–10		− 7
− 1 for each additional hour over 10		− __
Not consistent		− 7

Maintain regular work routine	+ 5	
No regular work routine		− 5
− 2 for every 5 hours worked over 40 in a week		− __
Take a yearly vacation from work (at least 6 days)	+ 5	
Regularly use a stress-management technique (yoga, meditation, music, etc.)	+ 3	
SUBTOTAL E:	+ __ **+** − __	

F. CHANGEABLE EMOTIONAL STRESS FACTORS
(N = never; R = rarely; S = sometimes; A = always or as much as possible)

	N	R	S	A
Generally happy	−2	−1	+1	+2
Have and enjoy time with family and friends	−2	−1	+1	+2
Feel in control of personal life and career	−2	−1	+1	+2
Live within financial means	−2	−1	+1	+2
Set goals and look for new challenges	−2	−1	+1	+2
Participate in creative outlet or hobby	−2	−1	+1	+2
Have and enjoy leisure time	−2	−1	+1	+2
Express feelings easily	−2	−1	+1	+2
Laugh easily	−2	−1	+1	+2

Expect good things to happen	-2	-1	$+1$	$+2$
Anger easily	$+2$	$+1$	-1	-2
Critical of self	$+2$	$+1$	-1	-2
Critical of others	$+2$	$+1$	-1	-2
Lonely, even with others	$+2$	$+1$	-1	-2
Worry about things out of your control	$+2$	$+1$	-1	-2
Regret sacrifices made in life	$+2$	$+1$	-1	-2

— + — + — + —

SUBTOTAL F: = __

SCORING

$A + B + C + D + E + F =$ _____ (subtotal, up to 200*)

Subtotal + G = Total
Divide total by 2. This gives your chance (expressed as a percent) of living to or beyond the average life expectancy of a person your age.

Total: _____ Divided by 2 = _____ percent

If you scored 100 percent, congratulations. But don't rest on your laurels. Keep looking for ways to improve your good health. And if you didn't score as well as you would have liked, remember that it's never too late to begin improving your longevity potential.

* If this number is higher than 200, use 200 as your subtotal. Maintain those healthy habits that allowed you to score much higher than the average person, and try to turn any of the negatives in section A (e.g., smoking) into positives. You have the very best chance of living a long and healthy life, because these factors are totally in your control.

These self-administered tests can be both informative and enlightening, especially in highlighting the strengths and weaknesses of your lifestyle. Although no test is going to give you a firm answer as to how fast you're aging or how long you'll live, putting these scores together with the kind of information you can get from your doctor can give you a sort of early warning system, telling you where your deficits lie and giving clues to the directions you might take to correct those deficits.

Well, you may ask, will all this really help me live to the age of 110? No one can say that with certainty, of course. Still, you can surely increase your chances of living many years longer, and knowing your biological age and your rate of aging can be an important first step. As to the next steps: in the following chapters of the book I will give a number of health prescriptions, both physical and mental, that may be able to help you slow your rate of aging and lengthen your potential life expectancy. These prescriptions reflect the latest scientific findings on all aspects of life—diet, exercise, appearance, love, mental acuity, sex—that can affect how long you'll love and how much you'll enjoy living.

Take them in good health.

Eating
for
Longevity

In the 1960s, when food consciousness became a national pastime, one of the theme songs of newly enlightened dieters was "You are what you eat." Now that many of those ex–flower children are in the midst of middle age, the tune is changing slightly: the new chorus is "Eat for long life." More and more people are realizing that what we eat or don't eat may have a powerful effect on how long and how well we live, and that the traditional American diet, with its oversized portions of red meat, fats, and sugars, may actually be shortening our lives, or at least keeping us from living out our maximum life expectancy.

That's not just hippie folklore: a panel of experts working under the auspices of the National Dairy Council (they included E. A. Young, a professor in the department of medicine at the University of Texas Health Science Center in San Antonio, and Dr. R. M. Russell, former acting director of the USDA Human Nutrition Research Center at Tufts University) recently concluded that "an adequate diet is one of several factors which may help postpone chronic diseases and therefore improve life expectancy and the quality of life."

The key question is: What do the experts mean by an "adequate diet"? The hundreds of diet books that flood our bookstores and the thousands of "good eating" articles that fill the pages of our newspapers and magazines show us that there's probably no single answer to that question and that there's a great deal of controversy even among the experts. This has left the door open to an almost inconceivable number of diets, all of them billed as "healthful." Some of these are undoubtedly solid and sensible; others are a bit extreme but still based on principles that the majority of experts agree to be sound; while still others are so exaggerated that they seem to border on the loony. (My personal favorite, published a few years ago in a tabloid newspaper, was the "All Ice Cream Diet.")

Small wonder that most of us remain confused and bewildered in the face of this assault of dietary advice. But we don't have to go on being confused. First, each of us needs to establish an overriding, long-range personal goal—something more basic and more fruitful than "I've got to be able to get into this dress in time for Tina's wedding." The fact that you're reading this book in the first place means that that goal is probably already in place: you want to maximize your chances of living the longest and healthiest life possible, and you want to look good at the same time. Once you have that goal firmly in mind, the next step is to develop your own personal maximum longevity diet, incorporating your own needs and tastes with what's known—or strongly suggested—about the longevity-promoting values of certain foods. Here you'll have plenty of help. That's what this chapter is all about.

To help you develop your maximum-longevity diet, we're first going to focus individually on each of the major aspects of aging, giving clues *supported by evidence from respected scientific laboratories* as to what effect certain foods and food supplements may have on, for example, the heart, the brain, the skeleton, and the immune system. We'll talk not only about what you eat but about how and when, and at the end of the chapter we'll sum up with a comprehensive dietary plan designed to help keep your body humming youthfully along even in old age.

Eating for the Heart

If you're concerned about heart disease and have recently gone to your doctor for dietary advice, you've probably been told point-blank to lower your cholesterol. That advice is based on a huge number of studies that show a statistical link between high levels of cholesterol in the blood (these days anything over about 240 milligrams per deciliter is considered "high") and an increased risk of heart disease.

The theory is that high cholesterol levels in the blood promote the formation of sludgy plaque on the inner walls of arteries, and more particularly of the small coronary arteries which feed the heart. These plaques cause a hardening and narrowing of the arteries themselves. Known as *atherosclerosis,* this disease can eventually choke off the blood supply to the heart or the brain, resulting in a heart attack or a stroke.

The majority opinion in the medical community holds certain kinds of cholesterol responsible for these life-threatening conditions. But it may surprise you to know that the case against cholesterol is still not proved, and that some scientists, including a team from Stanford University, have expressed doubts about the value of lowering cholesterol under 200 for many adults—especially women—who have no symptoms of heart disease.

Still, as long as the scientific jury stays out, the prudent approach is to follow the guidelines set down by the National Heart, Lung, and Blood Institute's National Cholesterol Education Program and the American Heart Association, both of which recommend keeping blood cholesterol below the "safe" 200 level. There's at least some scientific evidence that a number of foods may be able to help you do just that. Perhaps the best-known and most highly publicized of these has been oat bran, now found in an increasingly bewildering variety of cereals, breads, pancakes, and even cookies. Some studies have shown that eating 100 grams of oat bran a day can lower cholesterol by as much as 20 percent. The catch, according to the Center for Science in the Public Interest in Washington, D.C., is that it can take anywhere from almost three cups a day of hot oat bran cereal to *fifteen* cups of some cold oat bran cereals to get your 100 grams of oat bran. Obviously, this gives new meaning to the phrase "eat like a horse."

It seems, though, that there are some foods that can lower cholesterol significantly even when eaten in reasonable, human-size amounts. The carrot is one. An original study by Martin A. Eastwood of the Western General Hospital in Edinburgh, Scotland, and follow-up studies by Peter Hoagland and Phillip Pfeffer of the USDA's Eastern Regional Research Center in Philadelphia suggest that eating two carrots (200 grams) a day can lower your cholesterol by as much as 10 to 20 percent. The key here is the calcium pectate in the cell walls of carrots, which speeds up the way the body burns cholesterol. The same may be true of dried beans, Great Northern whites, kidney beans, black beans, chickpeas, lentils, and split peas. Studies at the University of Toronto indicate that two or three cups of dried beans a day can bring cholesterol down by up to 14 percent. Here the theory is that the beans are metabolized so slowly that the production of insulin, which is linked to the production of cholesterol, is reduced.

Many experts now think that the overall cholesterol count is less significant than the relative amounts of "good cholesterol" (high-density lipoproteins, or HDLs) and "bad cholesterol" (low-density lipoproteins, or LDLs). Statistical profiles show that most heart disease victims have high levels of LDLs and low levels of HDLs. No one is quite sure why this is so, but a study by Jere P. Segrest of the University of Alabama at Birmingham suggests the HDLs may absorb artery-damaging toxins that are released when fats are broken down in the blood. To keep HDLs up and LDLs down, some experts suggest switching from saturated fats found in dairy products and palm and coconut oils, to monounsaturated fats, in oils made from olives, almonds, sunflowers, or rapeseed.

Many experts think that, in general, the best way to lower cholesterol is to reduce your intake of fats across the board. At least one study suggests that it's the fat, not the cholesterol, that makes the important difference. Donald McNamara, a professor of nutrition and food science at the University of Arizona, put two groups of healthy middle-aged men on diets. Both groups spent six weeks on a low-cholesterol diet (250 milligrams per day), then spent six weeks eating a high-cholesterol diet (800 milligrams per day). The only difference in the two diets was that one was high in saturated fats, while the other emphasized polyunsaturated fats. When the results were in, two-thirds of the men experienced no increase in blood cholesterol even after six weeks on the high-cholesterol diet. But when those who had been on the polyunsaturated diet switched to the saturated fats, half of them showed an increase in blood cholesterol. As far as McNamara is concerned, this shows that fat, not cholesterol, is the real villain. "People may not have to give up food items like eggs," he says, "just because they're rich in cholesterol." (Speaking of eggs, the U.S. Department of Agriculture has recently determined that egg yolks actually contain about 22 percent less cholesterol than previously believed.) My personal belief is that what matters is what the *chickens* eat. I grew up eating eggs from chickens that ran free around the farmhouse, and now that I have a country home I have free-ranging chickens that are fed on fruits, vegetables, table scraps, corn, oats, and whatever grubs and insects they can find. Both my husband and I are very fond of eggs, and both of us have low levels of cholesterol.

It's easier than you think to significantly reduce the amount of fat in your diet. You don't even have to give up entire food groups—dairy products or meats, among others—to do it. Instead, it can be a simple matter of replacing a high-fat food with something similar that's much lower in saturated fat. Replacing a cup of whole milk with a cup of skim milk will save you 4.8 grams of saturated fat; a cup of ice milk instead of an equal amount of ice cream saves you 11.2 grams; a cup of yogurt instead of sour cream saves you a whopping 27.7 grams. Replacing a tablespoon of butter with a tablespoon of margarine (made from liquid safflower, sunflower, corn, or soybean oil) saves 5.3 grams of saturated fat; eating a bagel instead of a croissant saves 3.2 grams. Among meats, there are significant savings in fat gained by switching from dark meats to light meats; from cheaper, fatter cuts like chuck to leaner ones; and from spareribs to loin chops. It can even help to make changes in the desserts you eat: substitute angel food cake for pound cake, and you'll eat 3 grams less of saturated fat.

You'll want to know, too, that there are some kind of fats that may actually be *good* for your heart. They're called *omega-3 fatty acids* (such as eicosapentanoic acid, or EPA, and docosahexanoic acid, or DHA), and they're found in a number of cold-water fish, especially salmon, tuna, lake trout, whitefish, herring, sturgeon, and anchovies. Another of the fatty acids which I take religiously is gamma linoleic acid (GLA), one of the principal components of evening primrose oil. Not only do these oils lower triglycerides, they may also reduce blood pressure, slow the thickening of the linings of blood vessels, and reduce clotting—all factors in the development of heart disease and heart attacks. In South Wales, Michael Burr of the Royal Gwent Hospital gave dietary instructions to two thousand male heart attack survivors for two years. The one thousand who ate fish high in omega-3 fatty acids twice a week or took an equivalent amount of fish oil capsules were 30 percent more likely to be alive after two years than those who didn't eat fatty fish. "If I had a propensity for heart disease," concludes William Harris, lab director of the Lipid and Arteriosclerosis Prevention Clinic at the University of Kansas Medical Center in Kansas City, "I'd eat more fish, and consider taking fish oil capsules as well."

While you're at it, you may want to season that salmon with healthy doses of garlic. Researchers at the University of Western Ontario in Canada studied typical diets in fifteen countries and found a significant correlation between high-garlic diets and low rates of mortality from heart disease. Other studies have shown that garlic lowers blood pressure and cholesterol, and reduces the risk of a heart attack's causing blood clots. It's not yet known what it is about garlic that seems to yield this protection, but Eric Block, a chemist at the State University of New York in Albany, is testing the idea that garlic may contain various sulfur compounds that help inhibit the formation of free radicals, which can cause damage to arterial walls.

While you're seasoning your pasta or fish with garlic, you may want to garnish the plate with helpings of nuts, radishes, or mushrooms. These foods are good sources of selenium, a trace mineral that has been linked to healthy hearts. When researchers at the Zuiderziekenhuis Hospital in Rotterdam, The Netherlands, compared eighty-four heart attack patients with eighty-four healthy people, they found that selenium levels in the heart attack group were significantly lower. In one district of China, where selenium levels in the soil were especially low, scores of children developed heart disease. This was in the 1930s; the problem was corrected in the next generation simply by adding selenium supplements to the regional diet. (One caution: if you're going to take selenium supplements, don't take more than 200 micrograms a day unless you know you're deficient. In any case, check with your doctor first.)

Getting an Accurate Cholesterol Count

Cholesterol counts can fluctuate from twenty to forty points a day depending on diet, exercise, illness, and other factors. Three experts tell us how to get an accurate one.

Diane Stoy, R.N., operations director, Lipid Research Clinic, George Washington University, Washington, D.C.:
Make sure to stick to your regular diet for at least two weeks before being tested. If you have been to Europe, eating richer

foods than you normally do, your reading will be higher than it probably is normally. On the other hand, if you usually eat a lot of meat but go on a temporary fish-only diet before your test, you will get a count that's unrealistically low. Any major health event, surgery, or even the flu can also affect cholesterol levels. The Laboratory Standardization Panel of the National Cholesterol Education Program advises waiting two months after illness or surgery before being tested.

Margo Denke, M.D., endocrinologist, Center for Human Nutrition, University of Texas Southwestern Medical Center, Dallas:

Since levels vary so much, have at least three measurements taken, at least one day apart, and have your doctor determine the average. Also, for several hours after exercise your blood is more concentrated, and your cholesterol count is higher. So you should not work out before having a reading taken.

Basil Rifkind, M.D., chief, Lipid Metabolism and Atherogenesis Branch, National Heart, Lung, and Blood Institute, Bethesda, Maryland:

Sit down—but for no longer than five minutes—before having your blood taken. Research shows that cholesterol counts decrease as much as 10 to 15 percent in people who have rested more than twenty minutes before having blood drawn.

Eating for Weight Loss

This is a tough one. Ever since it was first shown that being overweight increases one's risk of developing heart disease, the message—hammered home by a virtual assault from the media— has been diet, diet, diet. Millions of Americans, especially women, have heeded the call and have dedicated themselves to furious and often futile rounds of calorie cutting, often making themselves and their families miserable in the process.

The sad truth seems to be that over the long run mere calorie cutting will probably not help you keep your weight down. First of all, it's becoming more and more apparent that the tendency to be overweight is not simply a matter of overeating or lack of exercise—although these can certainly be important factors. The fact that the degree of obesity is similar among members of the same family probably indicates a hereditary component to the regulation of body fat. "Saying people get fat because they over-eat," concludes William Ira Bennett, editor of the *Harvard Health Letter*, "is like saying the sun comes up because it's morning."

To make matters worse, the calorie-cutting approach to losing weight often sets up a vicious circle in which people go on strict diets and lose a commendable amount of weight, only to gain it all back—and sometimes add a little extra—when they fall off the diet wagon. "We have become a nation of yo-yo dieters," says psychologist Kelly Brownell of Yale University, "our weight constantly cycling—down, up, down, up—perhaps inching a bit higher than before." This is in part because during the diet phase, the body probably thinks it's starving. In response, an enzyme called lipoprotein lipase signals the body's cells to store more fat as a hedge against what it mistakenly thinks are hard times. The result? The diet may produce smaller weight losses than you expect or, worse yet, you may lose no weight at all.

Not only is yo-yo dieting an ineffective and sometimes counterproductive way to lose weight, but it can actually be dangerous. If experimental data on animals hold up in human trials, the up-and-down cycle will be shown to increase blood pressure and raise cholesterol, thus increasing the risks of developing heart disease and diabetes. A study of a group of obese men who were yo-yo dieters by the West Los Angeles Veterans Administration Center showed that 80 percent of them eventually developed diabetes and 25 percent died of heart disease. Their rate of premature death was *thirteen times higher* than that of a similar group of obese men in a Scandinavian study who did not diet at all!

So what's the answer? One key for overweight people, according to psychologist and obesity researcher Janet Polivy of the University of Toronto, is to stop dieting, accept one's body style for what it is, and try to develop a positive attitude toward oneself. Polivy has developed a ten-week program designed to deemphasize diet and maximize self-esteem. When people finish this program, Polivy says, they are "happier, feel better, and have a higher opinion of themselves. And," she adds, "they don't necessarily gain weight."

Still, most experts feel that people who are more than 20 percent overweight should try to trim down—even if just by 10 percent. For those who are still determined to do battle by diet, the key is to take it very slowly. Avoid crash diets, and try to take off no more than half a pound a week until you've reached your goal. This means a more moderate diet, one that you can stick with even after you've lost the desired amount of weight. That way you will eliminate the yo-yo cycle that can be so frustrating, and will greatly increase your chances of staying permanently trim.

Remember, too, that *what* you eat may turn out to be much more important than how much. In particular, cut down on fats —they're fattening, especially the saturated fats. In a study reported in the *American Journal of Clinical Nutrition*, two groups of women ate diets that contained the same amount of calories, but one of the diets got 40 percent of its calories from fats, and the other only 20 percent. As you might expect, the women on the high-fat diet gained weight more easily than the women on the low-fat diet. As a goal, you might try following the guidelines established by the American Heart Association: get no more than 30 percent of your total calories from fats, and no more than 10 percent of these from saturated fats.

Eating for the Brain

There's nothing surprising about the notion that eating well can help preserve the body. But there's increasing evidence that what you eat can have an important effect on your brain as well. Scientists are finding that specific kinds of foods can influence mood and behavior, and can also help improve mental performance, memory, and learning.

If, for instance, you want to be alert and on your toes, eat protein.

That's the advice of Judith Wurtman, an expert in nutrition and behavior from the Massachusetts Institute of Technology and author of the book *Managing Your Mind and Mood Through Food.* Wurtman and her neurobiologist husband, Richard, have spent years studying the link between diet and brain function. In the process, they've found that protein-rich foods are high in the amino acid tyrosine, which stimulates the brain to produce the chemicals dopamine and norepinephrine—two of the neurotransmitters that carry messages from one part of the brain to another. "When the brain is producing these neurotransmitters," says Wurtman, "distinct changes take place. People think more quickly, react more rapidly, and feel more attentive. Solving problems, even difficult ones, often seems more manageable because of heightened brain power."

Wurtman estimates that a 3- to 4-ounce serving of lean protein will keep the alertness chemicals flowing in the brain. (Fat seems to have the opposite effect on the brain, making one slow and lethargic.) The best food sources of high-tyrosine lean protein, she says, are shellfish, chicken, veal, and other lean meats. She also recommends low-fat dairy products, like cottage cheese and skim milk, and legumes like soybeans and lentils.

When you want to come out of your alert state and relax, Wurtman suggests eating carbohydrates. These trigger a complicated metabolic process that ultimately delivers the protein tryptophan to the brain, and tryptophan is known to be a relaxer and an inducer of sleep. Among Wurtman's recommended foods to produce the relaxation response are low-fat cookies, popcorn, low-fat candy like jelly beans, potatoes, bread, rice, and pasta. One 30-gram serving of carbohydrates, says Wurtman, will do the trick; but she recommends that you eat that serving on an empty stomach, not after eating protein.

Eating for Immunity

The idea that you can fortify your immune system by eating certain foods is still considered highly controversial. Research on the subject began only within the past few years, and most nutritionists think that the connection between diet and immunity has yet to be proved. It didn't help matters when the physician Stuart Berger contended in his book *Dr. Berger's Immune Power Diet* that almost everyone suffers from some food allergies and that these allergies compromise the immune system in a way that can lead to frequent infections. Mainstream opinion among allergists is that only about 1 to 2 percent of the adult population suffers from food allergies. In a 1983 study that appeared in the British medical journal *Lancet*, only four out of twenty-three people who thought they had food allergies actually had them.

Obviously, then, the immune-diet connection is still tentative. There are some tantalizing hints that for some foods, at least, that connection might be real. Yogurt is one. A study by researchers in Italy indicates that eating 7 ounces of plain yogurt a day can stimulate the growth and proliferation of certain immune system cells. These cells help fight the bacteria that can cause intestinal infections and diarrhea.

Zinc is another nutrient that's recently gained some attention as a possible immunity booster. Here the focus is on the thymus gland, which, you may remember, helps regulate the functioning of the immune system, and which shrinks into virtual invisibility as we get older. In Italy, Nicola Fabris, scientific coordinator of the Gerontological Research Department of the Italian National Centers on Aging, found that when he gave daily oral zinc supplements of 15 milligrams to people over sixty, their production of thymic hormones was almost completely restored. When John Bogden of the New Jersey Medical School in Newark studied the effects of zinc on immune function in the elderly, he found that natural killer-cell activity improved at doses of 100 milligrams a day, but only transiently. However, another indicator of immune function showed the greatest improvement in the group of volunteers who received no zinc at all. If you're inclined to try zinc supplements, stick to the 15-milligram doses used in the Italian study. The nutritionist Nancy Jordan of New York University cautions that higher doses, especially those of over 1 gram a day, can cause nausea and stomach irritation.

Of all the nutrients that have been tentatively linked to the healthy functioning of the immune system, the one that at this point seems to show the most potential is vitamin E. The immunologist Adrianne Bendich of Hoffmann–La Roche in Nutley, New Jersey, fed large doses of vitamin E—up to twenty times the amount normally found in their diet—to lab rats, and discovered that the higher the amount of the vitamin in their blood, the stronger the response of their immune systems. "There wasn't much of an effect at normal doses," she says, "but we never found a dose so high that the immune system did not respond to it by becoming even stronger." She concludes, "Vitamin E is the most important immune stimulant I have ever seen."

Until recently, no one was quite sure how vitamin E works to get these dramatic results in the laboratory. But a study published in 1990 by the nutritionist Jeffrey Blumberg and his colleagues at the USDA's Human Nutrition Research Center on Aging at Tufts University has shown that vitamin E supplementation appears to suppress the production of the hormone *prostaglandin E2,* which has been linked to age-related declines in immune system vigor. The microbiologist Robert Tengerdy of Colorado State University has done research which suggests that vitamin E enhances the function of some kinds of T-cells by protecting them against damage from free radicals and possibly by improving the receptor function of their membranes.

So far, only some researchers are willing to make an out-and-out recommendation as to how much vitamin E one might take to stimulate the immune system. Blumberg, whose study concludes that the vitamin supplementation "unequivocally increases immune responsiveness in healthy older adults," says it would appear that taking the vitamin in supplements is reasonable if you aren't getting enough in your diet. Protective benefits would be obtained from 100 to 400 IUs of vitamin E per day. Especially good food sources are vegetable oils and margarines, seeds, grains, nuts, wheat germ, and green leafy vegetables such as spinach, kale, and swiss chard.

Eating Against Cancer

The role of diet in promoting or preventing cancer is still unclear, but in recent years there have been a number of strong hints that diet could be a factor in as many as a third of all cancer cases. One tantalizing bit of evidence comes from comparative studies of Japanese and Japanese-Americans. Japanese who stay home have a much higher rate of stomach cancer than do Americans. But when Japanese come to the United States their incidence of stomach cancer falls significantly within one generation, while their colon cancer rates tend to rise during the same time period. Many experts suspect the explanation may lie in dietary differences: the American diet is much higher in fats, especially saturated fats; and this may be increasing the risk of colon cancer. (High-fat diets have also been implicated in a higher risk of breast cancers in women and prostate cancers in men.) The high consumption of salted raw fish in Japan puts the Japanese at much higher risk for cancers of the stomach.

There are also interesting though still technically unproven clues that certain specific foods may help forestall the development of some kinds of cancer. Garlic, for example: the various sulfur chemicals that give garlic its distinctive taste and odor "without doubt have cancer preventive properties in most experimental studies," according to Michael J. Wargovich of the M. D. Anderson Cancer Center in Houston. Following the garlic trail, the National Cancer Institute compared cancer rates in several provinces of China where garlic was used liberally with those in provinces where garlic was used only lightly. The result? Much less stomach cancer in the garlicky provinces. The explanation? It may be that sulfur compounds found in garlic stimulate the activity of liver enzymes that detoxify carcinogens.

There's some early evidence that yogurt, a great low-fat food, as we have suggested, may also be helpful in battling cancer. Community health professor Barry R. Goldin of Tufts University School of Medicine fed *Lactobacillus acidophilus*—the bacterium found in one kind of yogurt culture—to lab animals, and found that it slowed down the development of colon tumors. Encouraged, Goldin went on to give yogurt fortified with acidophilus culture to a group of human volunteers. The yogurt seemed to suppress the production of cancer-promoting enzymes.

Yogurt mixed with citrus fruits like grapefruit may form an even stronger cancer preventive because of a natural chemical called *nomilin* that is present in grapefruit. Luke K. T. Lam, a chemist at the University of Minnesota, tried an experiment with two groups of lab mice, giving nomilin to one group and not the other. Then he exposed both groups to the cancer-causing chemical benzopyrene. All the mice in the group that did not receive nomilin developed tumors. In the group that received nomilin, almost one-third of the mice remained free of tumors. There's a standard caution here: these are mice, not people, and what works in one may not work in the other. Still, it can't hurt to add moderate amounts of citrus fruit to your diet.

Women concerned about breast cancer might want to consider the soybean connection. In Japan and China, women get much of their dietary protein from soybeans, and they have much lower rates of breast cancer than American women, or even Oriental women who emigrate to America. The pharmacologist Stephen Barnes of the University of Alabama at Birmingham tested the connection in lab rats by feeding them varying amounts of soybeans, then injecting in them a chemical that causes breast cancer. In the rats who got large amounts of soybeans, tumors appeared much less quickly. Barnes says, "The more soybean in their diet, the bigger the effect in staving off tumor development."

There's also a possible link between calcium and certain kinds of cancer of the colon. Research with lab rats suggests that high-fat diets stimulate overactive cell division in the colon, and this overactivity can be a prelude to the development of cancer. According to Warovich, "when people at high risk of colon cancer were given 2,000 milligrams of calcium daily—about twice the recommended daily allowance—almost everyone's colon-cell activity quieted down. Within a month, the rate of cell division returned to a low-risk profile."

A dietary agent that has received a great deal of attention in recent years as a possible cancer preventive is beta carotene. A chemical precursor to vitamin A, beta carotene is found in many vegetables and fruits, especially carrots, broccoli, sweet potatoes, pumpkin, and cantaloupe. When Japanese researchers studied 250,000 people, they found that those whose diets were low in beta carotene had an increased risk of a number of cancers, including cancers of the colon, lung, stomach, prostate, and cervix. In England, researchers tested beta carotene and vitamin A on people who chewed betel nut or tobacco leaves, both of which habits are known to promote cancers of the mouth. In those who got supplements of vitamin A or beta carotene, abnormal, potentially precancerous cells were reduced by as much as two-thirds. Although not all experts agree, Dr. Michael Colgan, formerly a senior member of the science faculty at the University of Auckland, New Zealand, and now the director of the Colgan Institute in Encinitas, California, declares that "there is no longer any doubt that vitamin A and beta carotene can prevent cancer."

That doesn't mean you should concentrate exclusively on carrots and broccoli to get your beta carotene. As far as vegetables are concerned, variety may be the key. At the Cancer Research Center of Hawaii, the epidemiologist Loic Le Marchand and his colleagues gave dietary questionnaires to almost one thousand men and women aged thirty to eighty-four, 332 of whom had lung cancer. While men who concentrated on carrots had half the lung cancer risk of those who ate few vegetables, men who ate a wide variety of vegetables had only one-third the risk. For women, the results were even more impressive: one-third the risk for women who concentrated on carrots, but only one-*seventh* the risk for women who ate a variety of vegetables. In general, eating many different kinds of fruits and vegetables seems to be the going advice in anti-cancer diets. Most experts also recommend cutting down on saturated fats and eating healthy amounts of fiber—the same prescription, as a matter of fact, that applies to reducing the risks of heart disease.

Eating Against Hypertension

For years, the standand advice for people with high blood pressure (hypertension) has been to cut down on salt or eliminate it altogether. Lately, that wisdom has been challenged. A huge study, known as "Intersalt," which was recently published in the prestigious *British Medical Journal*, looked at over ten thousand people in thirty-two countries and concluded that "salt has only small importance in hypertension" and that other factors—obesity, alcohol consumption, and potassium deficiencies, in particular—were more significant dangers. Still, many experts remain convinced that salt is a major villain. If you do have high blood pressure, talk to your doctor before you reach for that saltshaker.

In the meantime, you may want to pay more attention to your intake of potassium. A study by G. Gopal Krishna and his colleagues at Temple University in Philadelphia took ten men with normal blood pressure and put them on a low-potassium diet for nine days. Then they increased the dietary potassium with supplements for another nine days. Sure enough, blood pressure went up when potassium intake was low and returned to normal when potassium was increased. Although Krishna is not ready to recommend potassium supplements, he does recommend eating moderate amounts of such high-potassium foods as orange juice, bananas, bran, and unsalted nuts.

Eating Against Bone Loss

You probably know that women are prone to lose bone mass as they get older. It may surprise you to find out that this potentially crippling condition, called *osteoporosis,* also strikes a great number of men. It's just that men have more bone mass in the first place, so the losses may not be so apparent. In either case, there are some dietary prescriptions that can help reduce the losses.

Most of these prescriptions involve calcium. Although amounts will vary with the individual, most experts recommend maintaining a daily calcium intake of about 800 milligrams, the amount found in, say, three cups of milk. But many scientists think that even 800 milligrams may not be enough. "A reasonable target," says Stanford University professor of medicine Robert Marcus, "is about 1,000 milligrams a day, starting at age ten and lasting forever." For postmenopausal therapy, Marcus recommends a total intake (including diet and supplement) of as much as 1,500 milligrams a day.

Dairy foods are especially good sources of calcium—an 8-ounce serving of yogurt, for example, contains 415 milligrams of calcium, while a cup of milk has 300 milligrams. Many people as they get older have increasing trouble digesting dairy products. Food sources such as green leafy vegetables, salmon and sardines (the latter with bones in), and almonds are helpful, but massive amounts would be necessary to meet the Recommended Daily Allowance. (Note: Beth Dawson-Hughes, head of the Calcium and Bone Metabolism Laboratory at the USDA Human Nutrition Research Center on Aging, says that the calcium in spinach, while plentiful, is not used effectively in the human body.) Thus you may want to consider commercial calcium supplements. These can be good sources, although there are differences among them. Calcium gluconate and calcium lactate, for example, actually contain significantly less calcium per tablet than other forms. And many experts agree that such supplements as bonemeal and dolomite can actually be dangerous, in that they're sometimes contaminated with heavy metals like lead, mercury, or arsenic.

There's a further word of caution here. Simply increasing your calcium intake doesn't guarantee that the calcium is going to get into your bones. To properly absorb calcium the body needs other nutrients as well—magnesium, for one, and other vitamins. Exercise, particularly weight training, helps the bone retain its calcium. "Without consideration of these effects," says the nutritional biochemist Dr. Neil S. Orenstein of Lenox, Massachusetts, "no amount of calcium supplementation will prevent osteoporosis."

That's a brief discussion of dietary prescriptions that may be able to help you ward off life-shortening or debilitating diseases. But you'll probably want to integrate those prescriptions into an overall dietary plan. So, with the help of the registered dieticians Genell J. Subak-Sharpe and Anastasia Parathyras-Schepers, we've developed one for you: a sensible, scientifically supported diet that incorporates guidelines set down by the federal government, the American Heart Association, the National Cancer Institute, the American Cancer Society, and the American Diabetes Association. Not only does it have all this scientific weight behind it, but the diet's actually easy to follow, and it should give you all the nutrients you'll need to help prevent disease and boost your overall health as you get older.

Note: This diet assumes a daily intake of 1,800–2,000 calories for moderately active men and 1,500–1,800 for moderately active women. For every ten years of age past thirty, you should reduce your caloric intake by 2 percent per day. Pregnant or nursing women should consult their doctor before going on any kind of diet. For a list of calories per ounce of food see the books and computer software recommended in Appendix II.

SUNDAY
Breakfast: orange slices, wheat germ pancakes with berries, beverage.
Lunch: chick-pea salad, corn bread, pear, beverage.

Dinner: sliced tomato salad, wine-poached chicken breast, brown rice, sweet and sour brussel sprouts, orange tapioca, beverage.*

MONDAY

Breakfast: dried prunes, oatmeal with milk, beverage.

Lunch: tuna salad in pita bread, fresh fruit, low-fat milk.

Dinner: green salad with dressing, meat loaf, noodles, broccoli and sweet pepper stir-fry, raspberry ice, beverage.*

TUESDAY

Breakfast: cantaloupe, whole-wheat English muffin with cottage cheese, beverage.

Lunch: tomato soup, pasta salad, oatmeal cookie, beverage.

Dinner: turkey meatballs, baked potato, spiced red cabbage, carrot-raisin slaw, baked apple, beverage.*

WEDNESDAY

Breakfast: grapefruit half, whole-grain cereal, low-fat milk, beverage.

Lunch: vegetarian chili with rice, celery sticks, low-fat milk.

Dinner: gazpacho, baked lentils with Parmesan topping, green beans, whole-wheat rolls, spiced peaches, beverage.*

THURSDAY

Breakfast: orange juice, oatmeal with raisins and cinnamon, beverage.

Lunch: bean soup, rice cakes, yogurt with fresh berries, beverage.

* Diet soda, black tea or coffee without sugar, or water.

For more long-range diet planning, or to customize the diet according to your personal tastes and needs, look back over the prescriptions earlier in this chapter to find substitutes. Drink a lot of water—eight to ten glasses a day—and keep the alcohol down to two daily beers or glasses of wine, or two ounces of hard liquor. Finally, allow yourself one forbidden treat a day—it'll help keep you from falling off the wagon entirely.

Dinner: savory lamb stew, kasha, steamed spinach, julienne vegetable salad with lemon dressing, ginger snaps, beverage.*

FRIDAY

Breakfast: citrus juice, whole-wheat toast with cottage cheese and peach slices, beverage.

Lunch: minestrone soup, corn muffin, fresh fruit, beverage.

Dinner: spinach salad, poached salmon fillet, cracked wheat with peas and scallions, steamed baby carrots, chocolate angel food cake, beverage.*

SATURDAY

Breakfast: fresh berries, oat bran muffin, beverage.

Lunch: turkey and tomato on hard roll, almond/apricot squares, low-fat milk, beverage.

Dinner: mixed green salad, kidney bean and tomato casserole, steamed broccoli, rice-raisin pudding, beverage.*

So *salud,* and *bon appétit!*

Dietary Supplements

If you look back over the prescriptions in the last chapter, you'll notice that in most cases they describe getting the nutrients you need from the foods you eat. Anyone who's ever been to a health food store knows that the shelves are groaning with food supplements—pills, powders, and liquids that are intended to supply extra amounts of nutrients, or "proper" amounts of those nutrients when dietary sources are lacking. (We've already seen, for example, that it takes at least three cups of hot cereal a day to get enough oat bran to lower cholesterol.)

The supplement approach to healthful eating is still highly controversial. For every expert who advocates taking supplements of calcium or vitamin E, there's another who says that sufficient amounts of all nutrients are available in foods and that taking supplements is unnecessary, ineffective, and even dangerous. On the one hand, listen to Stephen Barrett, a psychiatrist and member of the board of the National Council Against Health Fraud: "Most of the products that the health food industry markets are useless, unnecessary, or irrationally formulated. Of the useful products, most are not suitable for self-medication, but should have medical supervision." A report by the National Research Council, an arm of the National Academy of Sciences, warned that supplements in excess of RDAs "not only have no known health benefits, but may be detrimental to health."

On the other hand, there's Michael Colgan of the Colgan Institute, who writes, "If anyone tells you that Americans get adequate nutrition from their good mixed diet, don't believe them." Or Oliver Alabaster, an associate professor of medicine at George Washington University in Washington, D.C., and author of *The Power of Prevention*: "Epidemiological and experimental evidence suggest that certain vitamins and minerals may prevent cancer. Some of these vitamins, especially those that are anti-oxidants, may not only reduce risks of heart disease and cancer, but may even slow aging. There may be advantages to taking selected supplements while waiting for results of many long-term scientific studies presently under way."

It's all very confusing, and the noisy claims and counterclaims make it hard to get at the truth. Personally, I believe in Colgan's approach and have taken his special packages (which are designed specifically for me) ever since *Omni* magazine did a story on his work at Rockefeller University in April 1982. After six weeks of the Colgan package, I realized that my chronic hay fever had disappeared. After having to take antihistamines almost every day since I was about nine years old, I felt this was nothing short of miraculous. I also felt more energetic, and it was his assurance that I could avoid gaining weight that encouraged me to quit smoking.

My personal daily supplement package, which I certainly don't recommend for everyone, but which works for me, contains the following:

Vitamin A   (retinol)   7,500 IU
Vitamin A   (beta carotene)   12,600 IU
Vitamin B_1 67 mg
Vitamin B_2 67 mg

Vitamin B$_3$ (niacin) 54 mg
Vitamin B$_3$ (niacinamide) 104 mg
Vitamin B$_5$ (pantothenic acid) 250 mg
Vitamin B$_6$ 79 mg
Vitamin B$_{12}$ 227 mg
Vitamin C (ascorbic acid) 2,102 mg
Vitamin C (calcium ascorbate) 650 mg
Vitamin C (ascorbate palmitate) 54 mg
Vitamin C (magnesium ascorbate) 54 mg
Vitamin D$_3$ 402 IU
Vitamin E 602 IU
Vitamin K 96 mcg
Bioflavonoids 250 mg
Biotin 554 mcg
Boron 10 mg
Calcium 796 mg
Chromium (picolinate) 308 mcg
CoEnzyme Q10 11 mg
Copper 890 mcg
Folic acid 980 mcg
Gamma linoleic acid 66 mg (I take an extra 6,000 mg a day
  for my eyesight.)
Gamma linolenic acid 99 mg
Iodine 136 mg
Inositol 122 mg
Iron (picolinate) 19 mg
L-Cysteine 190 mg
L-Glutathione 95 mg
L-Methione 75 mg
Manganese 6,800 mcg
Magnesium 650 mg
Molybdenum 80 mcg
Paba 61 mg
Phosphatidyl choline 122 mg
Phosphorus 42 mg

Potassium   152 mg
Rutin   36 mg
Selenium   (selenomethione)   210 mcg
Zinc   (picolinate)   55 mg

Colgan's theory is that everyone is different and everyone has his or her own "vitamin profile." He does an extensive series of blood tests, hair and nail analyses, and has also developed a comprehensive lifestyle questionnaire to determine exactly what, and in what amounts, his recommended supplements should be taken. If you decide to take supplements you should make your own choice, based on your needs, on your constitution, and, most critically, on your doctor or nutritionist's advice. Our job is to help give you some of the information you'll need to make that choice objectively and intelligently. So here's a list of supplements that have received attention from respected scientific laboratories, and a summary of their pros and cons. The choice, in the end, is up to you.

Vitamin A

We mentioned in Chapter 8 that vitamin A and its precursor, beta carotene, have been shown to provide some protection against cancer in animals. There's also evidence that vitamin A promotes good vision and healthy skin, hair, and mucous membranes, and that it's needed for proper bone growth and tooth development. The USRDA of vitamin A is 5,000 IUs for men, 4,000 for women. If you're getting that from the fruits and vegetables in your diet (one carrot alone can provide up to four times the RDA), you may not need supplements. If you do take supplements of Vitamin A or retinol (another precursor of the vitamin), remember that more than 85,000 IUs a day (15,000 units a day in children) can produce dizziness, severe headache, nausea, and vomiting.

Vitamin B

Vitamin B_1 (thiamine) aids in energy metabolism, appetite maintenance, nervous system function, and cell repair. The RDA for B_1 is 1.5 milligrams for men, 1.1 milligrams for women. If you eat properly it's easy to get your daily allowance from foods, especially whole-grain cereals, dried beans, pork, and other meats, so unless your doctor tells you that you're deficient in the vitamin, don't spend the money on supplements. If you're like me and travel a great deal, miss meals, and don't always get the right amount of sleep, then perhaps you should consult your doctor, or preferably a good nutritionist. (Doctors are not always the best source of nutritional information; in fact, it's only recently that nutrition has become part of their training.)

For Vitamin B_2 (riboflavin), the RDA is 1.7 milligrams for men, 1.3 for most women. Pregnant women need about 1.6 milligrams, nursing mothers about 1.8. Again, theoretically you can get all you need from food, especially dairy products, organ meats, and green leafy vegetables. The exception may be pregnant women, who may want to take supplements if their doctor advises.

Vitamin B_3 (niacin) is a bit more controversial. The RDA has been set at 18 milligrams for men, 13 for women. But it has been shown that one form of niacin (nicotinic acid) at doses of 2 to 3 grams per day can lower cholesterol and help patients suffering from schizophrenia. The problem is that even in doses as low as 250 milligrams, niacin can cause a number of unpleasant side effects: itching, burning, and flushing of the skin, and gastritis (accompanied by vomiting and nausea) if it is not taken with food. It can also harm liver function (this is usually reversible), raise uric acid and blood glucose levels, and activate peptic ulcers. Deficiencies in niacin, on the other hand, can lead to pellagra, which is characterized by skin problems, diarrhea, and even dementia. Still, because niacin is so easy to get in foods, particularly high-protein foods like meat, eggs, and enriched cereals, most doctors don't recommend supplements.

Vitamin B_6, a key agent in protein metabolism, has been shown to increase the life spans of mice and fruit flies, while deficiencies are associated with depression and increased risk of cardiovascular disease. The RDA is 2 milligrams for men and 1.6 for women, although some experts recommend about twice that amount, either from food (meat, fish, nuts, bananas, potatoes, bran, and dairy products are good sources) or a combination of food and supplements. More than 500 milligrams a day can be toxic, producing difficulty in walking and other side effects of the nervous system.

Vitamin B_{12}, which helps release energy in foods, has been touted as an energy and performance booster for athletes. But Judith Stern, a professor of nutrition at the University of California at Davis, warns, "If you're not deficient in the vitamin, being super-sufficient won't give you more energy." Deficiencies are extremely rare, partly because the RDA is extremely small: 2 micrograms for most people, 2.2 for pregnant women. You can get all that and more from a small piece of liver or a bowl of cereal. (I hate both and never eat them.)

Vitamin C

Vitamin C may be the best known—and most argued about—of all the food supplements. One thing nearly all the experts seem to agree on is that it's a potent antioxidant, meaning that it helps fight off cellular damage caused by free radicals. It's also a vitamin that the human body can't manufacture on its own. There's some evidence that vitamin C can restrain the development of cancer cells and stimulate the immune system, but assertions that it can ward off flu and colds have yet to be proven. The RDA is set at 60 milligrams, but expert estimates of optimal amounts range from 500 milligrams (Jeffrey Blumberg, assistant director of the USDA Human Nutrition Research Center at Tufts) to a huge 18 grams (Nobel Prize winner Linus Pauling of the Linus Pauling Institute in Palo Alto, California). Pauling, who for years has been the most public and vocal of the vitamin C champions, swears that it can be "the keystone of a program to extend life by twenty-five to thirty years."

Vitamin D

There's some preliminary evidence from Columbia University and the Harvard Medical School that a combination of vitamin D and parathyroid hormone (PTH) increases bone density, and thus may eventually be of help in staving off osteoporosis. Many experts warn against self-dosing supplements of vitamin D. First of all, taking the vitamin in excess of the RDA (200 IUs) can actually *cause* bone loss. Even worse, the vitamin can be highly toxic, resulting in hardening of the organs and even deafness. The safe way to get the vitamin is in food—fortified milk, salmon, and sardines—and from the sun.

Vitamin E

Once described as a vitamin in search of a disease, vitamin E is another potent antioxidant which, as we've already seen, may stimulate the immune system and help protect against cancer, heart disease, and cataracts. It may even have some anti-aging properties. Here supplements may really be of help, in that it's very difficult to get even the conservative United States RDA of 30 IUs from diet alone. A recent study at the University of Toronto showed that supplements of 1,000 IUs a day for twenty-one days significantly reduced free radical production, and some experts think that 1,000 IUs a day is a safe dose. Most, however, recommend about 400 IUs a day.

Calcium

We talked about calcium and its possible role in preventing both cancer and osteoporosis in the previous chapter. Just as a reminder, experts recommend 800 milligrams of calcium a day. Dairy products, leafy vegetables, canned salmon with bones, and almonds are good food sources. If you want to take supplements, avoid calcium gluconate and calcium lactate (not enough calcium to justify the expense); and especially avoid bonemeal and dolomite, which can be contaminated with toxic heavy metals.

Chromium

The role of this trace mineral in preserving health is just beginning to be understood, and it could turn out to be quite important. In tests at Bemidji State University in Minnesota, the biochemist Gary Evans found that daily supplements of 1.6 milligrams of chromium picolinate (containing 200 micrograms of chromium) increased levels of "good" cholesterol (HDL) and lowered levels of "bad" cholesterol (LDL). It also helped normalize blood sugar levels in diabetics with hypoglycemia (low blood sugar). Perhaps most amazing was Evans's finding that chromium picolinate supplements helped a group of weight lifters gain a significant amount of muscle mass! "There's no doubt," says Evans, "that chromium picolinate could be a nutritional alternative to risky anabolic steroids."

The only foods that have significant amounts of chromium are brewer's yeast and kidneys. There are trace amounts in whole-grain cereals. Refined sugars, on the other hand, deplete the body's stores of chromium. Evans thinks that 1.6-milligram supplements of chromium picolinate are safe.

Magnesium

Along with chromium, this is a mineral that many Americans neglect. Dr. Burton M. Altura, a physiologist at the State University of New York's Health Science Center in Brooklyn, reports that sufficient levels of magnesium can help reduce the risk of a number of age-related illnesses, including heart disease, stroke, hypertension, and atherosclerosis. But the body's stores of magnesium can be depleted by vigorous exercise and by alcohol and some pre-scription drugs.

Magnesium is found in highest concentrations in nuts, fish, whole grains, unprocessed cereals, and green vegetables, but get-ting the RDA of 350 milligrams for men and 280 for women takes an estimated 2,500 calories of food (2,000 calories for women). "Those on low-calorie diets should seriously consider magnesium supplements," says Sheldon Saul Hendler, author of *The Doctor's Vitamin and Mineral Encyclopedia.* In that case, you may want to stay away from bonemeal and dolomite supplements, which can contain impurities, and stick with forms such as magnesium glu-conate, magnesium oxide, or magnesium chloride. *Note:* If you have a kidney disorder, don't take magnesium supplements without checking with your doctor.

Potassium

This mineral has been shown to reduce blood pressure, which can help prevent heart disease and stroke. It also seems to play a role in keeping the heartbeat regular. The recommended daily dose is about 50–75 milli-equivalents (mEq) for men, about 25–50 for women. Since potassium is found in a great many foods, including dairy products, fruits, vegetables, fish, meat, beans, and nuts, most experts think supplements are unnecessary. Diabetics and people with kidney trouble should probably avoid potassium and supple-ments altogether.

Selenium

We've already seen that this mineral has been linked to healthy hearts. There's also some evidence that, as an antioxidant, it may help prevent cancer. The RDA is 70 micrograms for men and 55 for women. Since it's relatively easy to get this amount from food—nuts, seafood, mushrooms, and radishes are good sources —most experts don't recommend supplements. Intakes of up to

200 micrograms a day of selenium are safe. At very high levels it can be toxic.

Zinc

As I mentioned in the last chapter, there's some evidence that zinc can be an immune-system booster for some people. The RDA is 15 milligrams a day for men, 12 for women. If you've not been found deficient in zinc by your doctor, be careful about supplements: 100 micrograms a day can cause nausea and stomach irritation.

Ginseng

Back in the 1960s, this Oriental herb became the national supplement of an entire generation of hippies. It was thought to calm you down, pep you up, and even activate your sex life. More recently, it's been touted as a performance booster and enhancer of longevity. In fact, one Soviet study showed that daily doses of ginseng increased work endurance in lab animals by 25 percent, while another indicated that lab rats who got ginseng in their drinking water lived 10 percent longer than those who didn't. But when Walter Lewis, a professor of biology at Washington University in St. Louis, ran a similar endurance test, the rats who got ginseng didn't do any better than the others. According to Doel Soejarto, a professor of pharmacognosy (the study of the physical characteristics and botanical sources of crude drugs) at the University of Illinois at Chicago, ginseng does seem to have some value as both a tranquilizer and an energy-booster. "It produces a sort of stress-neutralizing action," he says, "that calms you."

These are some of the most common food supplements, especially those that may have an effect on longevity. Of course, there are hundreds of pills, powders, and potions that claim to have anti-aging properties; in general, we've tried to include only those items that have at least some scientific evidence on their side.

In closing this chapter, let me give you a sort of buyer's guide to supplements, a compendium of advice collected from eight experts recruited by *Longevity* magazine. They say:

Don't take doses of vitamins and other supplements far in excess of Recommended Dietary Allowances. Some of these substances are not absorbed by the body when taken in excess; others can be downright toxic. As a guideline, twice the RDA should be the upper limit.

Buy products made by major pharmaceutical manufacturers. They're more likely to be pure.

If you can, buy directly from pharmaceutical supply houses. This can amount to a savings of up to two-thirds. You should be able to get catalogues from your doctor or nutritionist.

Make sure there's an expiration date on the label. This ensures that the manufacturer is operating under U.S. Food and Drug Administration regulations.

Check the amounts of each nutrient in any formulation you buy. If there are only token amounts of some nutrients, skip it. They're listed just to make the product seem more robust than it actually is.

Don't take vitamins and supplements all at once. Spread them out throughout the day—after each meal, for example. That should keep the levels in your blood relatively constant.

Take protein with your vitamins. That helps the body absorb them. Milk, for example, is better in this respect than orange juice.

Don't pay more for products that are labeled "natural." There's really no difference between a "natural" vitamin and one that's synthetic.

Don't take iron along with vitamin C. The vitamin could make your body absorb more iron than it needs.

Here is a list of what the experts themselves do, or don't, take.

- **Joan Smith-Sonneborn, University of Wyoming.** Multivitamin, plus extra C, calcium, and magnesium. When under stress she takes extra B complex.
- **Roy L. Walford, M.D., University of California.** Multivitamin, 50.5 grams of C, 100 IUs of E, and 50 milligrams of selenium.
- **Leonard Hayflick, University of California School of Medicine.** None.
- **Denham Harmon, M.D., University of Nebraska College of Medicine.** 110 to 220 IUs of E, 100 micrograms of yeast, which contains 50 micrograms of selenium, and 1,500 milligrams of C.
- **Nathan Shock, former director, Gerontology Research Center.** None. Believes megadoses of supplements are potentially dangerous.
- **Linus Pauling, two-time Nobel laureate.** 18 to 50 grams of C, 800 IUs of E, twenty-five times RDA for B complex. Also takes zinc and selenium.
- **T. Franklin Williams, M.D., former director, National Institute on Aging of the National Institutes of Health.** Avoids supplements.
- **Ruben Andres, M.D., deputy director, Gerontology Research Center.** Is unconvinced that vitamin or mineral supplements do anything for anyone who is not vitamin deficient.

In the last two chapters, I've given some standard recipes for helping to ensure maximum longevity through foods and food supplements. Next, we want to turn our attention to a new idea, one that's receiving increasing scientific attention and, although still quite controversial, seems to be amassing an ever-growing body of evidence in its favor. That idea, put in its simplest form, is:

Eating less means living longer.

10

Dietary Restriction

Imagine yourself taking an early-morning jog along the beach in Venice, California. You hear footsteps in the sand behind you, and suddenly you're being passed by a slender man with a bushy mustache and a shaved head. As he flashes past, you catch a glimpse of his sly grin, and you wonder briefly if the man who has just left you in the dust was a guru or a gambler. Actually, you'd be partly right either way. This fellow once broke the bank at the Palace Club in Las Vegas, and he attracted quite a following in the 1960s as a radical college professor. He's also been a writer, an underground journalist, and a guerrilla theater impresario. Even if you were somehow able to guess all these things about him, the one thing you'd probably never get right is his age. Lean and muscular from a comprehensive exercise program, brimming with the energy that comes from an alert mind and a positive attitude, Roy Walford looks at least twenty years younger than his sixty-seven years.

For the most part, there's nothing really mysterious about Roy's youthful vitality. He keeps his weight down (at five-eight, he weighs about 140), exercises religiously—stationary bike every day, swimming and weight lifting twice a week—and helps keep himself feeling young by dressing in message T-shirts and neon bomber jackets. His work as a gerontologist at nearby UCLA keeps him mentally alert, so much so that he's won dozens of prestigious awards and research appointments. He challenges life with an attitude of adventure: his idea of a vacation is to hitchhike across Africa or to ride a boat Bogart-style down the Congo River. This "do-it" philosophy led Walford to sign up as a crew member for a two-year stay in Biosphere 2, the sealed-in experimental world near Oracle, Arizona.

What makes Roy Walford truly unique is his daring goal in life and his means of achieving it. Roy Walford wants—*plans* is a better word—to live to 120. The means? While even the most health-conscious among us gorge ourselves on up to 2,000 or 3,000 calories a day, Walford consumes only 1,650 calories.

At sixty-seven, Walford thinks his life is only about half over. For the rest of it, he is using his own body to answer—in personal terms, at least—what to him may be the most important of all scientific questions: Can a human being increase his chance of living out his maximum life span—that's 120 years or more—not only by living a healthful life, but simply by eating less?

From a scientific point of view, this question has yet to be answered—for human beings, at least. For the present, most of the experts in the field of dietary restriction remain reluctant to recommend Walford's approach to eating. "At this point," says Angelo Turturro, a toxicologist at the Food and Drug Administration's National Center for Toxicological Research in Jefferson, Arkansas, "I definitely would not recommend a calorie-restricted diet for people. There are still too many unknowns about its physiological effects that we have to sort out." Turturro says that experiments with dietary restriction in laboratory animals suggest a number of possible negative effects, including reduced toleration to cold, chronic elaboration of stress hormones, and significant impairment of fertility and reproduction.

These are daunting cautions, to be sure. Although I try to eat

carefully, I have no plans—not currently, anyway—to get my caloric intake down that low. A word of extreme caution: *the threat
of anorexia is very real, particularly for teenagers.* I watched a friend
die of anorexia—slowly, painfully, inexorably, apparently helpless
to stop herself from literally starving to death. She and I began to
diet together. We were both students at the Royal Ballet School
in London. She was from Australia and I was from South Africa,
and both of us had put on weight as a result of the change in our
diet from fruits and salads to the stodgy English fare. Soon we
had lost too much weight, and the headmistress became concerned.
We were sent to see a doctor, who lectured us about the terrible
damage we were doing to ourselves. I became very frightened at
the prospect of going blind—among other nasty side effects—and
stopped starving myself. She either ignored the advice or was
unable to take it, and continued to diet. She had this terrible vision
of herself as fat (a ballet dancer's nightmare) and nothing, it
seemed, could help her shake it. A few months later she was taken
to the hospital. Her name was Clover, she was fourteen years old,
and she weighed forty-six pounds when she died. I will never
forget her.

In spite of the apparent risks (only one of which is anorexia)
for humans, there's no denying that the dietary restriction story is
fascinating—there's just too much evidence from laboratory tests
on animals to hint that its benefits might just be real. Otherwise,
why would the federal government, noted for its conservative,
mainstream line on the links between diet and longevity, be spon-
soring a massive research project to find out if dietary restriction
really works?

The hullabaloo about dietary restriction, which is beginning to
reach a crescendo in the early 1990s, began as a whisper more
than fifty years ago, when Clive McKay, a researcher at Cornell
University, began a series of experiments with two groups of lab
rats. In one group, McKay allowed the animals to eat as much as
they wanted. In the other, he restricted their diets to close to 60
percent of their normal caloric intake, and supplemented the restricted diet with vitamins and minerals. McKay soon noticed that

the rats on restricted diets seemed unusually healthy in comparison with those in the eat-all-you-want group: their coats were shinier, they got fewer infections, and they were more active.

What really opened McKay's eyes was that after almost three years of experimenting, all the rats in the normal group had died. But some of the rats on the low-calorie diets were still alive and kicking—in fact, they went on living almost twice as long as normal rats. Furthermore, the rats on low-calorie diets actually stopped growing, even though they remained remarkably healthy and bright-eyed. It was as if by reducing the amount of food they ate, McKay had actually stopped development (and perhaps, by implication, the clock of aging) in its tracks. Sure enough, when he put the low-cal rats on a normal, eat-all-you-want diet, they started growing again.

Fascinated by McKay's results, other researchers soon got into the action. In the 1940s A. H. Carlson and F. Holzel tried a variation on McKay's experiments. They let groups of lab rats eat all they wanted most of the time, but put them on enforced fasts (approximately 14 percent restriction) every second, third, or fourth day. Carlson and Holzel found that while normal rats lived an average of 645 days, the rats which fasted intermittently lived longer: an average of 690 days. Ten to twenty years later, Morris Ross of the Institute for Cancer Research in Philadelphia did even better. Based on the controls he used, his group of low-calorie rats lived *60 percent longer* than rats on normal diets.

Enter Roy Walford. The UCLA gerontologist knew that all these earlier experiments had been started when the rats were young pups—just after weaning, as a matter of fact. Walford wanted to know if he could get similar life-extending results if he started dietary restriction only when the animals were fully grown adults. So in the late 1970s he began a series of experiments in which he put mice on restricted diets at the age of one year—middle age in a mouse's life, about the equivalent of thirty-five years for a human. Sure enough, even the adult mice benefited: they lived up to six months longer.

Obviously, dietary restriction was having a dramatic effect on the animals' life spans. Walford then began to wonder what was causing this remarkable life extension. Was dietary restriction somehow keeping the animals healthier, preventing them from getting killer diseases? He set out to take a comparative look and was astonished by his findings. As many as 50 percent of the mice on a normal diet eventually developed cancer, compared with only 13 percent of those on a low-calorie diet. That's not all. Walford and other researchers also found that in lab animals, restricted diets actually seemed to have a pronounced anti-aging effect. Blood cholesterol levels, for example, normally increase with age, but they didn't in diet-restricted mice. Certain liver enzymes, on the other hand, usually decline in aging mice; in diet-restricted mice the decline was substantially postponed. In perhaps the biggest payoff of all, immune system responses in mice on restricted diets were much more vigorous than in their gluttonous cousins; so much so, that Walford concluded that the immune systems of low-calorie mice had actually been "rejuvenated."

All this proved to be too much for even the staid medical research establishment to ignore. At the University of Texas Health Science Center in San Antonio, the physiologist Edward J. Masoro ran a version of Walford's experiments (in rats instead of mice) and got similar results: By the time they reached the age of 800 days, all the normally fed rats in his study had developed kidney disease, but only 25 percent of the diet-restricted rats were thus afflicted. In rats as in mice, blood cholesterol levels normally increase with age, but they didn't in diet-restricted rats. The results were similar for blood vessel disease and heart disease: 63 percent and 96 percent in eat-all-you-want rats, only 10 percent and 26 percent in diet-restricted rats. The occurrence of cancer, though not prevented, was delayed. All in all, the low-calorie rats ultimately lived about 60 percent longer than their overfed contemporaries, and sometimes died without any evidence of major disease processes. "When we look inside them," Masoro says, "they're completely clean."

In 1985, with fifty years' worth of intriguing results from laboratories like Walford's and Masoro's, the federal government finally got into the act. At a former biological warfare laboratory near Jefferson, Arkansas, scientists at the Food and Drug Administration's National Center for Toxicological Research (NCTR)— in conjunction with the National Institute on Aging—have undertaken what is undoubtedly the most massive and thoroughgoing laboratory investigation of the possible benefits of dietary restriction. Well over a hundred researchers are involved, both at the Jefferson facility and at laboratories across the country; they're working with as many as 20,000 animals—mice, rats, rabbits, even monkeys.

Basically, the scientists are already convinced that caloric restriction works—in small, short-lived animals, at least. Now, among other things, they want to know if it works as well (or at all) in more complex, longer-lived animals, such as monkeys. (There are colonies of monkeys and chimps currently under study at the National Institute on Aging, and at the University of Wisconsin's Regional Primate Center.) Perhaps even more important, these scientists are at last getting at the how and why of it: what changes take place in a body on a minimal diet, and why do those changes seem to spell a healthier and longer life?

At this writing, however, the monkey and chimp studies are not yet completed, and the only definite evidence supporting caloric restriction is that monkeys on low-calorie diets have leaner body mass and still look healthy. But the scientists are beginning to get answers to their more vital and fundamental questions. They already know that caloric restriction doesn't extend life span simply by slowing down growth rates, because it seems to work just as well in fully grown animals as it does in young ones.

What happens, then? What goes on in the small animals' bodies and brains when they eat less? First of all, their body temperature drops. When the bioengineer Peter Duffy of the NCTR measured body temperatures in animals on restricted diets, he found that some of them cooled down to what in humans would be a temperature of 82.4 degrees. When this happens, the animals tend to alternate between a slow, torpid state that looks almost like hibernation—"almost all hibernators outlive their close zoological relatives," Duffy reminds us—and a normal metabolic state that enables them to do far more work on far fewer calories. The writer Carol Kahn, who visited Duffy's laboratory in Jefferson, watched in amazement as a group of two-year-old mice, the equivalent of sixty-year-old humans, "jumped up and down in their cages like boxers in training."

"We make them smaller, more metabolically efficient," remarks Duffy.

While the animals' body temperatures decline, so do their blood sugar levels—by about 15 percent, according to Masoro's experiments. Less blood sugar (glucose) means fewer AGEs (advanced glycosylation products—we talked about them in Chapter 3), which in turn may mean less cellular damage due to cross-linking and disruption of enzyme function. In other words, less of the "normal" wear and tear that occurs in most cells as they get older.

There's also some early evidence that eating less may mean less damage from free radicals. When the body burns up its stored fats, says the NCTR's Ritchie Feuers, large bursts of free radicals may be created as a by-product. Since low-calorie rats tend to build up less fat in the first place, the production of free radicals due to oxidation of fats should be significantly reduced. Masoro's colleague Byung Pal Yu has indirect evidence that this is true: he's found far less free radical damage to cell membranes in low-calorie animals. Meanwhile, Feuers, Julian Leakey, and their colleagues at the NCTR have discovered that animals on restricted diets produce significantly more free radical scavengers like superoxide dismutase and effective levels of catalase and other liver enzymes such as lauric acid 12-hydroxylase and 4-nitrophenol hydroxylase. The more free radical scavengers, the fewer free radicals—and, as a probable consequence, the less free radical damage bodywide.

The early indications are that the bodies of animals on restricted diets do a much better job of reducing the levels of a wide variety of damaging toxins, or even of fighting them off entirely. Aflatoxin, for example, is a highly toxic and carcinogenic substance produced by a fungus that contaminates grain crops. When William Allaben and his colleagues at the NCTR fed the carcinogen aflatoxin to animals, those on low-calorie diets cleared the toxin from their bodies much more quickly and formed significantly fewer tumors than those on normal diets. Much the same seems to be true for chemical carcinogens such as benzopyrene (skin cancer), diethylnitrosamine (liver cancer), and dimethylbenzanthracene (breast cancer), as well as for cancers triggered by ultraviolet light and radiation. In all these cases, tumor formation was reduced in lab animals who were on restricted diets. At the same time, the NCTR researcher Kenji Nakamura found that in low-calorie animals, cancer-triggering oncogenes switched on at much lower rates. To put it plainly, then: in experimental tests with lab animals, *eating less meant less cancer.*

Eating less may also mean a more vigorous immune system, especially in old age. In the late 1970s, Walford and Richard Weindruch did a battery of tests in which they challenged the immune systems of both eat-all-you-want mice and mice on low-calorie diets. Their conclusion? "The immune system in the underfed mice stayed younger longer and this was associated with increased longevity." Almost ten years later, a similar study by S. Ping and his colleagues at Texas A&M University, in collaboration with Ronald S. Hart of the NCTR, reached much the same conclusion.

Rejuvenated immune systems, lowered body temperature, reduced blood sugar, protection against cancer and free radical damage—if the early evidence is any indication, dietary restriction has a tremendously broad impact on the aging body. Perhaps the greatest payoff of all this—theoretically, at least—would be if the effects of dietary restriction added up to a measurable slowdown in the overall rate of aging. Here again, there's early but intriguing evidence. One tantalizing clue involves an enzyme called *protein kinase C*, which is involved in helping muscles in the heart and blood vessels to contract, a vital function that decreases markedly with age. Eltan Friedman of the Medical College of Pennsylvania in Philadelphia notes that this decrease in cardiovascular function "has been found in early studies to be prevented by lifelong dietary restriction." (Friedman is now investigating whether or not a low-calorie diet has a similar effect in the brain, where protein kinase C helps trigger the release of important neurotransmitters.) At the same time, Harbans Lal of the Texas College of Osteopathic Medicine in Fort Worth found that animals on restricted diets showed less age-related decline in physical ability, motor coordination, and cognitive functions—all strong indications that aging rates had been slowed down. David Olton of Johns Hopkins University in Baltimore discovered that lifelong underfeeding altered sensory-motor skills in aging rats, and may even have shored up their short-term memories.

It all seems to add up to a compelling case for the low-calorie diet. But keep in mind that although the news from the labs has a lot of experts intrigued and excited, it's still very early in the story, and the jury is still out. In 1988, for instance, when the biologist David Harrison of the Jackson Laboratories in Bar Harbor, Maine, put three different strains of mice on restricted diets, many of the members of one of the strains died prematurely while most members of the other two strains lived considerably longer than normal. To date, no one knows why. Other experts caution that what works in short-lived animals like rats and mice may not work in longer-lived animals like monkeys and humans. That's why they're so eager to see the results of dietary restriction tests on rhesus monkeys. Finally, remember that few experts recommend that you copy Roy Walford and put yourself on a minimal diet as a means of extending your life.

If this leaves you undeterred, if you're determined to try caloric restriction for yourself, here's how Walford suggests you do it: First, establish your "set point" (your normal weight when you're neither overeating nor undereating. For most people, that's what you weighed when you were in your twenties, assuming you weren't overweight or underweight at the time). Then establish a level of caloric intake that allows you to lose weight gradually, over a period of three to six months. Walford's basal level is about 1,500 calories a day, but some people will need more to keep from losing weight too fast. When you plan your menu, calculate that you'll want to get 12 to 24 percent of your calories from protein (that's about 60 to 90 grams per day), no more than 20 percent of your calories from fat, and the rest from carbohydrates—preferably complex carbohydrates like fruits, vegetables, rice, potatoes, and pasta. Keep your cholesterol intake below 300 milligrams per day, and be sure to include 40 to 60 grams of fiber per day.

There are some of us, and I'm one, who lead the kind of lives that make sticking to special diets totally impractical. My personal diet is based on the idea that most if not all things should be consumed in moderation. Here's a typical day.

BREAKFAST
Fresh fruit,
one slice whole wheat toast with a little butter and marmite,
tea with low-fat or skim milk.

LUNCH
Generally a business lunch in a restaurant. Unfortunately, restaurant portions are often far too large, so I end up eating half or less. If this is difficult for you, try ordering two appetizers instead of an entrée. Luckily, I grew up with a mother who never told me to "eat everything on my plate because of the starving Chinese," as so many American children seem to have been told.

Here's what I usually order: green salad; small portion of red meat (one day a week only), fish, or chicken; green vegetable; club soda; water (I drink 8 or more large glasses of water a day).

When I don't have to go out I tend to either skip lunch or grab a tuna salad to go and eat it in the car or at my desk.

DINNER

Unless I'm traveling I nearly always eat dinner at home. Bob is a superb cook, and even though we employ three other cooks, he still enjoys doing it. We almost always have pasta made with plenty of garlic, olive oil, and combinations of tomato, clams, tuna, anchovies, and mushrooms. There's usually a salad, and a dessert made with fruit or sherbet. I like wine, and generally have a couple of glasses with my meal. On the days that we entertain I try to eat less for lunch and eliminate snacking.

When I do snack, I love fresh fruit or raw vegetables. I rarely drink distilled spirits, and I dislike nearly all fatty meats and most sweets, candy, cakes, pies, and cookies. My weaknesses are salty nuts, dates, and cheeses, and once in a very long while I spend the day at Great Adventure or Disneyland and gorge myself on junk food.

11

Working Out

On New Year's Eve, 1986, Gary Clark competed in a triathlon —a grueling three-way torture test that included a 1-mile swim, a 25-mile bike ride, and, for dessert, a run of 6.2 miles. What was unusual about Clark's participation was not the fact that he finished the race—finished it ahead of three hundred other competitors— but that he started it at all. Four months earlier, in October 1985, Gary Clark's heart was little more than a shell of white ash. A victim of an incurable heart infection known as viral cardio-myopathy, Clark was lying in an Arizona hospital, so weak that in the last forty-eight hours before his lifesaving operation, the simple act of lifting his head drove his heart rate up to 160 beats a minute. Thirty-four days after entering the hospital, his sick heart stopped beating entirely. Only a dramatic last-minute heart transplant saved his life.

Like many of us, Clark had been asking for trouble for a long time. A busy executive—he was vice president of an insurance company—he lived life at a frantic pace, leaving his health in the hands of the fates. His average day, he says, "began by eating a bologna-and-cheese sandwich and downing a couple of Tylenol to get rid of the hangover." Then came the dash to work, the three-cocktail lunch, happy hour, and a high-fat business dinner. Exercise? No thanks—no time.

It all started to catch up with him in 1983, when at the age of forty-four he felt the chest pains that signaled the development of his heart infection. Two years later came the lifesaving operation that gave him the heart of a nineteen-year-old boy. Soon after the successful transplant, Clark's rehabilitation therapists told him that if he wanted his new heart to remain healthy, he'd have to exercise. They suggested that for starters he might try a relatively gentle 5-kilometer fitness walk. "For the first time in twenty-five years," he says, "I began to listen. I had to, in order to survive."

Though certainly no major athletic feat for a normal person, for Gary Clark that 5-kilometer walk was the beginning of a new way of life. "I was overwhelmed," he says. "Not just by the fact that I could walk that distance, but that I was putting forth the effort and actually enjoying it. I know that sounds corny, but I found such an inner feeling of accomplishment."

That feeling led Clark to get serious about exercise. He now lives in Las Vegas, where he trains demonically, running 30 miles, biking 125 miles, swimming four to five hours every week, and doing five hours a week of light weight training. "I guess time will tell if all this will lengthen my life span," he says. "But I'm not really concerned about that at this point, because every day is one more day I didn't have six years ago."

Gary Clark's story is unique because of the heart transplant—he is the first heart transplant patient ever to finish a triathlon. But there are other people whose stories are almost as dramatic. There's Noel Johnson, the 90-plus-year-old hard-liver who went from the door of a nursing home to the finish line at the New York Marathon. Then there's Sam Freeman, an administrative judge from New York City who at the age of sixty-seven ran from Los Angeles to Washington, D.C.—the equivalent of a marathon every day for five months in a row! "It's really no big thing to run a marathon,"

he says. "Anyone my age in reasonably good health can do it."
Then there's Priscilla Welch, once an overweight, chain-smoking
clerk for the British Royal Navy, who started jogging for fitness at
the age of thirty-five, and at forty-two won the 1987 New York
Marathon, running the twenty-six miles in two and a half hours.
"It's a new era," she says. "Before, women forty and over felt they
couldn't do anything. Now they look at me and say, 'If she can
do it, I can.' "

All over the country, people like you and me are turning off
their televisions, getting up off their couches, and doing it—jogging, swimming, hiking, cycling, rowing, playing tennis, pumping
iron, dancing—whatever it takes to work up a good old-fashioned
sweat. More and more we're reaping the rewards that come with
exertion: getting slim and trim, strong and shapely, relaxing, feeling
great, even getting high. The biggest bonus of all may come toward
the end of life, in the form of extra wellness and even extra years.
Listen to Jane Brody, the well-known health writer for *The New
York Times*: "Even if you've been sedentary for decades, exercise
can help restore your vitality and rejuvenate your body." Or to
Dr. Roy J. Shephard, an expert in exercise and aging from the
University of Toronto: "You'd have to go a long way to find
something as good as exercise as a fountain of youth."

Of course, as with everything in life, there is a down side to
exercising. People with a family history of early death from heart
disease have to be extremely careful in determining how and how
much to exercise. Otherwise, they risk the fate of Jim Fixx, the
man who started the whole jogging craze in the late 1970s and
who died of a heart attack at fifty-two—while running. There's
also some evidence that exercise produces bursts of free radicals
in the body—the very free radicals that have been implicated in
so many aspects of aging.

For most of us, perhaps the biggest concern is the beating the
body can take during exercise. When you play tennis or basketball,
do aerobics, or even when you jog, your body is absorbing far
more impact than it does in everyday activity. This jarring impact

can mean serious chronic injuries to the joints and other parts of the body. I'm sure we all know tennis nuts who have to give up the sport for months or even years at a time because they develop the painful form of tendinitis known as tennis elbow. Obsessive swimmers often develop small tears in their shoulder muscles, and serious runners are famous for wearing out the cartilage between the kneecap and leg bone, one of the conditions grouped under the heading "runner's knee." The National Institute of Health estimates that as many as 17 million Americans suffer at least one injury a year "as they break down their body parts in an effort to build them up."

There are ways to reduce the risk of exercise-related injury, and I'll go into them a bit later in this chapter. For now, let's examine Dr. Shephard's statement that exercise can be a fountain of youth. Actually, the idea that exercise can promote longevity and effectively add years to your life has been highly controversial. In the mid-1980s, Ralph S. Paffenbarger, Jr., of the Stanford University School of Medicine conducted a huge study of 16,936 men who had entered Harvard between 1916 and 1950. Although Paffenbarger found that death rates were a fourth to a third lower among vigorous exercisers, in the end that translated to a longevity gain of only a little more than two years. At first, says Paffenbarger—himself a regular exerciser—the result was "a bit disappointing. I would have guessed that it would have been longer. On further consideration, I realized it was a significant extension of life."

Paffenbarger's study is not the last word on the possibility of this important connection between exercise and longevity. At the Institute for Aerobics Research in Dallas, Dr. Steven Blair spent fifteen years accumulating data from some 13,000 men and women of all ages and in various degrees of physical condition. The result? The death rate among unfit people was twice as high as that of people who were even slightly fit—people who did little more than, say, take a brish half-hour walk every day. Blair's study, declared the editors of *Sports Illustrated,* provided "conclusive evidence that being physically fit can prolong your life."

If these studies haven't convinced you that exercise can indeed lengthen your life, try thinking about it this way: What happens to you—your body, your mind, and your spirit—when you *don't* exercise? First of all, you open yourself up to dangerous weight gain. Listen to University of California at Davis researcher Carol Meredith: "It's not age that causes people to get fat, but rather inactivity." Meredith and her colleagues did an elaborate study in which they compared a group of physically active men aged forty-eight to fifty-eight with a group of similarly active men in their twenties. For the same amount of time spent training per week, the middle-aged men had about the same body composition and stayed as physically fit as the young men. The bottom line, as far as Meredith is concerned, is that "if people stop exercising, the body ages faster."

Not only that, but when enough people don't exercise, it costs the rest of us a good deal of money. Emmett B. Keeler, an economist with the Rand Corporation in Santa Monica, California, measured the economic impact of people with unhealthy lifestyles, and the results were staggering. Couch potatoes—that's the one American man in eight and the one woman in five who never exercise—miss 18 percent more workdays than people who exercise moderately. They also need 12 percent more outpatient treatment and 30 percent more hospital stays than more active people. Translate this into dollars, as Keeler did, and you get $1,650 for every couch potato, bringing the total cost to the rest of us to $1 billion a year.

That's fine, you may be saying, but what will exercise do for me personally? If it gets me only an extra two years of life, is it really worth it? The answer is an unqualified yes. In addition to the extra years—whether it's two or many more—there's a long list of other rewards for breaking a sweat, rewards that can be just as powerful as extra years of life.

First, it makes your heart a more efficient pump—it can pump more oxygen-rich blood with less effort, thereby increasing your ability to work or play without getting tired. It also enables your muscles to burn more fuel more efficiently, to remove oxygen and waste chemicals from the blood, thus delaying muscular fatigue. It lowers blood pressure and normalizes blood sugar. It increases the mass and strength of your bones and the flexibility of your joints.

The most obvious benefit of exercise is that it can help you shed weight and stay trim. According to Scott Weigle, associate professor of medicine at the University of Washington in Seattle, "Dieting alone isn't really a satisfactory treatment for obesity. A better idea is to exercise as you diet, or exercise instead of dieting—for some people, exercise actually helps them to eat less." Although many experts recommend slow easy workouts for weight loss—the body burns a greater percentage of fat when the pace is slower—Dixie Stanforth of the University of Texas at Austin, using data from previous research, has recently discovered that turning it up a notch, say, from a walk to a jog, can burn up to 40 percent more calories, including even greater numbers of calories from fat.

So there's the first payoff of an exercise program, and a vitally important one. It may be even more important to know that exercise seems to help fight off diseases. There's impressive scientific evidence to show that moderate exercise actually boosts the immune system, giving you extra protection against common illnesses like sore throats, runny noses, and coughs, and perhaps against more serious infections like influenza and pneumonia. At Arizona State University, researchers performed a study on thirty-seven men in which they measured levels of immunoglobin-A (IgA), an antibody that provides the body's main line of defense against upper-respiratory infections. After the first measurement, the volunteers were put on a moderate exercise program, in which they rode stationary bicycles for 20 to 40 minutes three times a week for twelve weeks. The researchers then assessed the level of fitness of each volunteer, and measured the level of IgA in his saliva. Sure enough, the fitter the volunteer, the higher his level of disease-fighting IgA.

I can attest to these benefits myself. I exercise regularly, and in spite of my grueling schedule I have very few colds, sore throats, or ailments of any kind. Of course, no one can guarantee that you'll be as lucky as I've been, but there's evidence to suggest that even if you do get a cold, the sniffles may be shorter-lived and less severe if you're in reasonably good shape. At Loma Linda University in California, researchers took a group of forty obese, sedentary women and put half of them on a mild exercise program—a 45-minute walk five days a week—and left the other half on their couches. Over the winter, some of the women in each group caught cold. Among the inactive women, the colds lasted on average three times longer than they did in the women who were doing moderate exercise.

Colds are one thing, but the word today from scientific laboratories is that exercise may help reduce the risk of getting serious diseases. Heart disease, for one. Lars-Goran Ekelund, an associate research professor of medicine at the University of North Carolina at Chapel Hill, led a study in which researchers followed 3,106 healthy men aged thirty to sixty-nine for eight and a half years, keeping careful records of their physical activities and their level of fitness. Ekelund found that the least fit men were 3.2 times more likely to die of heart disease than the men who were in the best physical shape—irrespective of other risk factors, such as cholesterol, smoking, and blood pressure. The same holds true for women. You don't have to be young for your heart to reap the rewards of exercise. Dr. Steven Van Camp, medical director of the Adult Fitness Program at San Diego State University, reports that exercise can significantly improve the heart's functional capacity and ability to use oxygen—even in people in their eighties.

There are also cautious indications that exercise may help protect against cancer. In the study by Ralph Paffenbarger mentioned earlier in the chapter, the death rate from cancer was significantly lower among men who burned 2,000 calories a week exercising than in those who burned less than 500 calories. A 1984 study of 3,000 men showed that active men have two-thirds less risk of colon cancer, while a 1987 report indicated that nonathletic women have twice the risk of breast cancer and two and a half times the risk of cancers of the reproductive system that athletic women have. No one is yet sure how exercise works to combat cancer, but there's some early evidence that exercise may boost the immune system's production of natural killer cells, which then act as sentries, shooting down cancer cells as they appear. Although the case for exercise as a tool in the fight against cancer is not yet closed —much of the evidence is still considered preliminary—it's strong enough so that in 1985 the American Cancer Society recommended exercising moderately and decreasing food intake to maintain ideal body weight.

If the cancer-exercise connection surprises you, you may be even more surprised by some of the other rewards of working out—I know I found them quite unexpected. Most of us understand that exercise makes us feel good—it relaxes us, brightens our mood, and even gives us a mild high, probably because it promotes the release of the "feel-good" brain chemicals called *endorphins*. A recent study at Arizona State University showed that the endorphin high kicks in after only about twenty minutes of aerobic exercise and can last for as long as five hours afterward.

Exercise can also make you more mentally alert. Robert Dustman of the Salt Lake City, Utah, Veterans Administration Medical Center tested this notion on a group of men and women aged fifty-five to seventy who were woefully out of shape. After putting them on a moderate exercise program—one hour of fast walking, push-ups, weight-lifting, and stretching three times a week—Dustman found that they were much better at remembering sequences of numbers and using abstract thinking in matching numbers and symbols. They were also faster at mathematical calculation and at understanding new ideas.

If the brain and body benefit from exercise, so, it seems, do the eyes. Dynamic vision—the ability to focus on moving objects and to see while moving—can be sharpened. At the Pacific University College of Optometry in Forrest Grove, Oregon, researchers found that the visual skills of athletes with 20/20 vision far exceeded the visual skills of nonathletes who also had perfect eyesight. Regular eye exercises improved the athletes' visual fitness even more.

If you're interested in trying some Olympic-level eye exercises, here are a few developed by Jeanne R. Derber, director of the Vision Performance Laboratory at the United States Olympic Training Center in Colorado Springs, Colorado:

1. **Bull's-eye:** Hold the eraser end of a pencil about a foot away from your nose. Fix your vision on the eraser, then bring it slowly toward you until it blurs. Stop there and bring it back into focus. Next, look directly from the eraser to something in the distance—say, a lamppost outside the window. Focus on it, then look back at the eraser, and focus. Repeat twenty times.

2. **Muscle Flex:** Look straight ahead, then up as far as you can, then right, down, and left. Feel your eye muscles stretch. Repeat five times in each direction.

3. **Record Spin:** Put a disc on a turntable and set the speed to 33 RPM. As it rotates, try reading the label in the center. Repeat for as long as you can without getting dizzy. When you can do 33 RPM with ease, try 45 RPM.

Exercise can also help with another potential eye problem. As we age, many of us become more likely to get glaucoma, a disease that causes pressure to build up inside the eyeball. The usual treatments are drugs or surgery, without which the disease can lead to blindness. (Glaucoma is one of the leading causes of blindness in elderly Americans.) But Michael Passo of the Oregon Health Sciences University in Portland put sixteen middle-aged people on an exercise program in which they worked out for forty-five minutes three times a week. After sixteen weeks on the program, Passo measured the volunteers' eye pressure. The result? An average drop in pressure from 12 to 15 percent. "This doesn't suggest that exercise is a cure for glaucoma," Passo says. "But it does indicate that conditioning exercise may be used as a long-term treatment, and, for those at high risk, as a means of prevention."

Finally, there's evidence to suggest that exercise can help relieve some kinds of chronic pain—back pain, for one. A team of researchers at the University of Miami took a number of people whose chronic back pain was so troublesome that they were considered candidates for surgery and put them on a program of stretching and calisthenics. By the end of only two weeks, most of the patients were off the surgery list. "Chronic pain sufferers," explains H. Martin Blacker, director of the Pain Control and Functional Restoration Clinic at Baylor College of Medicine in Houston, "impose a mental cast on the aching part of the body. They immobilize it to the point that scar tissue forms around the joints, limiting mobility and making even simple actions painful. The best way to repair these muscles," Blacker concludes, "is to exercise them." Of course, this doesn't necessarily mean you take a seriously aching or recently injured back out onto the jogging track—consult your doctor or a bona fide physical therapist first. However, a little gentle stretching won't hurt and could help a great deal.

Certainly, if you want the benefits of exercise, you'll have to do some real work of your own. So the next questions are: What sort of exercise should you do, and how much how often? The range of choices is vast—just take a walk through any sporting goods store and you'll see what I mean. As we become more exercise-conscious as a society, we keep coming up with new sports: walley ball, battle ball, step training, even ultimate Frisbee; as well as videos on everything from ballroom dancing to Mousercise, Firm Fannies, and the ubiquitous Jane Fonda. So choose the activity that best suits your temperament, your lifestyle, and the level of your physical conditioning.

One of the first things to consider is how much exercise you feel suits your needs. It's becoming increasingly apparent that you can probably get just as much benefit from moderate exercise like fast walking or even gardening as you can from more vigorous activities like running or handball. (Although walking and gardening will never give you a body like Madonna's, there is much less risk of injury than with heavier exercise.) In either case, whether the form of exercise you choose is moderate or strenuous, the key to reaping the rewards is to burn about 2,000 calories a week more than you would if you were inactive—that's the number that researchers at the Stanford University School of Medicine and the Harvard University School of Public Health have suggested will reduce the death rate in active people compared with sedentary people.

You'll find that you don't have to run triathlons to burn those extra 2,000 calories. You can do a lot of it just in your daily activities. Climbing two flights of stairs a day, for example, will burn 300 calories a week. If you walk one to two miles a day on the job (sounds like a lot, I know, but anyone whose job keeps him on his feet to any extent will walk that much and more) burns another 750. Add about five miles a week of fast leisure walking (that's about 20 minutes a day), and two hours a week of moderate sports like golf or tennis, and you're over the mark—2,150 calories, to be exact.

The chart on page 156 will give you an idea as to how many calories you might be burning in the course of your daily activities, and how many more you can burn with moderate exercise. Use it to calculate what you need to do to get up to that 2,000-calorie-per-week mark.

If these gentler activities don't suit you, or if you're determined to challenge yourself, to "feel the burn," then you're going to want to go in for more vigorous exertions. The chart on page 157 will provide an indication of how many calories you'll burn in various forms of heavier exercise.

Another factor in making your choice is to try to strike a balance between anaerobic forms of exercise—resistance strength conditioning at high intensity for brief periods of time (sprinting and weight lifting, for example)—and aerobic exercise, which conditions the most important of all muscles, the heart. Almost any form of exercise that makes you move your legs or arms can be aerobic—it just depends on how much you accelerate your heart

Everyday Activity	*Calories per Half Hour*
Sitting and talking	40
Lawn mowing (power)	125
Lawn mowing (hand)	135
Cleaning windows	130
Mopping floors	130
Scrubbing floors	170
Vacuuming	130

Moderate Exercise	
Bicycling (5 MPH)	105
(6 MPH)	135
(8 MPH)	165
Walking (1 MPH)	68
(2 MPH)	105
(3 MPH)	135
Gardening	110
Canoeing (2 to 3 MPH)	115
Golf (using power cart)	100
(pulling cart)	135
Bowling	135
Rowboating (2 to 3 MPH)	150
Swimming (¼ MPH)	150
Badminton	175
Horseback riding (trotting)	175
Square dancing	175
Volleyball	175
Roller-skating	175
Low-impact aerobics	120

rate and for how long. The general rule is that your exercise routine should raise your heart rate to about 80 percent of its maximum and keep it beating at that level for a minimum of about 2 hours a week. Here's the formula for determining what you should go for: subtract your age from 220, and multiply the result by 75 percent (.75). The answer will be your target heart rate, the rate that will give you the most aerobic benefits without putting undue strain on your heart.

In picking an aerobic exercise, one thing to consider is how

Vigorous Exercise	*Calories per Half Hour*
Table tennis	180
Bicycling (10 MPH)	195
(11 MPH)	225
(13 MPH)	330
Walking (4 MPH)	195
(5 MPH)	220
Ice-skating (10 MPH)	200
Tennis	210
Waterskiing	240
Hill climbing (100 ft./hr.)	245
Jogging (5 MPH)	265
Skiing (10 MPH)	300
Squash or handball	300
Scull rowing (race)	420
Running (5 MPH)	310
(8 MPH)	360
(10 MPH)	450

much impact your body will have to absorb. Running and health club high-impact aerobic routines, two of the most popular forms of aerobic exercise, are famous for pounding the body to the point of injury, especially in the knees and ankles. The same is true of sports like tennis, basketball, and soccer, all of which require a lot of running and twisting. If you're addicted to these activities, as so many people are, there are some things you can do to soften the impact: wear good shoes; run on soft surfaces (cinder or rubberized tracks, for example); play tennis on clay or on rubberized surfaces instead of hard courts, and basketball indoors on wood instead of outdoors on cement.

You might also want to consider picking an aerobic form of exercise that doesn't pound your body. Obviously, cycling and rowing are much kinder in this regard, as are swimming, golf (if you don't use a cart), and just plain walking, especially up stairs. In addition, many health clubs now offer low-impact aerobic routines, which try to raise the heartbeat without jarring the body. The major problem with low-impact aerobics, though, is that they

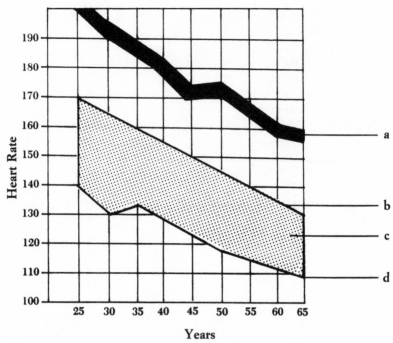

TARGET PULSE
Maximum heart rate declines with age (a). The target heart rate for aerobic exercise (c) should be 70 percent (d) to 85 percent (b) of your maximum heart rate.

may not be demanding enough to increase fitness. For example, when researchers at Ball State University in Indiana put a group of sedentary men and women through fourteen weeks of hour-long low-impact aerobic workouts, the group showed no improvement in physical fitness and no change in the ratio of fat to muscle. In the same study, when a group of high-impact aerobic dancers switched to a low-impact routine, they suffered an average fitness loss of 5 percent and an average weight gain of four pounds.

To address this problem, fitness experts Peter and Lorna Francis of San Diego State University developed a compromise routine, known, sensibly enough, as moderate-impact aerobics. The key is to substitute a springing movement for the jumping that characterizes most high-impact routines. That way, says Lorna Francis, "you get the energy of high-impact, but with more control, which allows you to avoid fast, uncontrolled landings. It feels energetic, but without the aches and pains." Many health clubs now offer moderate-impact aerobic routines. If yours doesn't, you might want to drop a hint.

Once you've settled on an aerobic exercise that suits you, you may want to have a look at the strength side of the picture. For some time, anaerobic exercise has been a sort of poor stepchild, seen as good if one wants to look like Arnold Schwarzenegger or those female body builders who take steroids, but not much in the health department. Now that picture is changing. Not only does anaerobic exercise make you look and feel better, but there are some real health and longevity benefits to be gained from simply being strong. First of all, increased muscle mass means a decreased risk of obesity, because you have to burn more calories to maintain muscle tissue than you do to maintain fat. At the same time, anaerobic exercise improves glucose tolerance, and thus helps to provide protection against diabetes.

There's little doubt that a strong body resists physical stress— even the stress of sitting at a desk—meaning less tension and less fatigue. Also, it confers a greater degree of self-reliance and independence as you get older (it's hard to negotiate life if you can't lift a bag of groceries). There's even some evidence that increasing muscle mass can increase bone mass. When researchers at McMaster University in Ontario put a group of postmenopausal women on a year-long program of anaerobic strength training, not only did their muscle size increase by 20 percent, but their spinal bone mass rose by 9 percent. It's possible, then, that strength training might help ward off osteoporosis.

A knowledgeable coach or fitness trainer can help you design a weight and exercise program that suits your individual needs. I emphasize the word *knowledgeable*: far too many so-called fitness trainers are not trained at all, and can actually cause you to injure yourself. This is something I have learned through personal experience. I work out with three different trainers four to five times a week, and I have auditioned dozens. Some were simply inept; others were downright dangerous. If you decide to lay out the money for a personal trainer, be sure you are getting your money's worth. Ask exactly what training she or he has had. On the whole, I have found that trainers who have had dance training, especially ballet, are best. If anyone starts out by saying, "What would you like to do?" forget it! Remember, you are paying *them* to tell *you* what to do.

Whatever you decide on, your routine should target all the major muscle groups: the calves, the quadricep and hamstring muscles of the thighs, the back, hip, and abdominal muscles, shoulders, deltoid and trapezius muscles, and the biceps and triceps muscles of the arms. An effective program usually calls for three sets of eight to twelve repetitions of each exercise, two to three times a week, but only every other day, so that your muscles have a chance to recover. Remember that to increase muscle mass you need to reach muscle fatigue—the point in each exercise when you feel the "burn" and can't do any more repetitions.

You should try to vary your exercise routines so that you're doing some aerobics and some anaerobics every week. That way you won't get bored. I believe that boredom is the biggest reason why people give up on exercise programs. In any event, doing the same old thing every time you work out won't benefit you nearly as much as constantly changing your routine and thereby challenging a different set of muscles each time. You can do that (as I do) by alternating trainers, videotapes, or sports activities between aerobics, swimming, calisthenics, weight training, and machines like the StairMaster. Or you can try forms of exercise that provide both aerobic and anaerobic benefits: rowing is a good example, and so is cross-country skiing (as long as they include sprinting).

Perhaps the most efficient way of combining the two is to do weight training *while* you walk, jog, or do aerobic dance—not just by holding weights while exercising, as many people do, but by actually *pumping* them. A study at the University of Pittsburgh's

Human Energy Research Lab showed that people who pumped even 2-pound weights while running burned 120 more calories per half hour than people who merely held the weights while they ran. But you don't even have to run: you can walk and pump hand weights and do at least as much work as a highly fit runner. If you can do this, says the University of Pittsburgh exercise physiologist Tom Auble, "your workout will shift from a primarily lower-body activity to full-body exercise. Since with age and disuse upper-body strength tends to decline, adding weights to a running or walking workout can help keep *all* the muscles in your body younger, longer."

Once you've decided to exercise—or even if you're already exercising, but want to shift gears from a low-key to a more vigorous workout—it's important, even crucial, to know what kind of shape you're in before you start. This is especially true if your lifestyle has been basically sedentary—you don't want to risk injury or even a heart attack by trying to do too much too soon. A visit to your doctor and a few simple tests can help let you know where your body stands and give you a prescription for breaking your body in prudently.

If you want a really exhaustive rundown, you might try to find a doctor or hospital that administers a sports fitness evaluation known as "The Profile." Developed by Lenox Hill Hospital's Nicholas Institute of Sports Medicine and Athletic Trauma in New York, this series of tests looks at what the Institute's director, James Nicholas, calls "linkage": the way your muscles, joints, and bones work together to furnish movement, speed, and strength. The Profile assesses the ability of the body's bones to meet the demands of performance. Based on the findings, the staff can recommend an exercise program that circumvents the potential trouble spots. "For example," says the Institute's executive director, Phil Rosenthal, "if we find patellar or knee problems we discourage a patient from running and direct him or her into swimming instead. If a patient is set on golf we might tell them to improve back, shoulder, and trunk flexibility and increase lower leg strength. In general," Rosenthal concludes, "we can tell people how to proceed so they gain an excellent level of fitness without getting hurt."

One more thing before you start out: if you want the maximum benefit from your exercise, it must be regular. In a study at the University of North Texas in Denton, kinesiologist David Hill looked at seventeen people who exercised intensely, cycling five days a week. Ten of them exercised only in the morning, seven only in the afternoon. After six weeks, Hill tested each group's ability to sustain vigorous cycling in the morning and in the afternoon. Sure enough, those who were used to exercising in the morning could cycle much longer during the morning test, while the afternoon exercisers could go about 10 percent harder in the afternoon. The moral of the study: pick a time of day to do your exercise, and stick with that time. Some of us are morning people, and some are not. For me, the very idea of jumping around at 7:00 a.m. is horrifying, and I love exercising! I much prefer to do it in the evening, around 6:30 or 7:00, when I get home from work. I find it relieves the stress of the day, and leaves me feeling relaxed and in good spirits.

In case you're having trouble deciding what sort of exercise to do, here are some alternatives. As I have said, my favorite way of exercising is to constantly change what I do. This means I'm always challenging myself, so I don't get bored. I make sure, though, that whatever I do gives me a good, whole-body workout, and I keep it versatile. Because I was a dancer, many kinds of exercise come quite easily to me. I rotate ballet, aerobics, yoga, weight lifting, gardening, jazzercise, calisthenics, swimming, water aerobics, and stretching. I don't feel good unless I have worked out, at the very least, three or four times a week for an hour or more. I always work out with one of my exercise coaches or a friend—I find that I work harder and have more fun that way.

If you dislike working out to videos and can't afford a personal trainer, here is a program called the "Stay Young Workout," designed by Marianne Battistone, owner and director of Sports/ Dance/Fitness Educational Projects in New Jersey and New York.

This routine emphasizes the use of the whole body in motion. It contains the five standard components of fitness—stamina, flexibility, coordination, agility, and balance. (Flexibility is very important in countering the stiffness that often accompanies getting older.) It consists of seven basic exercises:

1. **Hip mobilizer**
   A. Lie on your back with your arms and legs outstretched in an X position, with palms up.
   B. Turn the right leg inward and lift it across the left leg, sliding it along the floor as your right hip, waist, and shoulder come off the floor. Your chest, head, and right arm stay open to the ceiling. Slide and circle your right leg back across the left, and roll your body back into the starting position. Repeat on the other side.

2. **Shoulder Loosener**
   Start in an X position. Slide your right arm up along the floor and circle it overhead, letting your right shoulder and your head turn left until your right hand touches your left hand. Circle and roll your shoulder back to the starting position and repeat on the other side.

3. **Back-Saving Curl**
   Start in an X position. As you press your navel toward your spine, bend your arms and legs toward each other, bringing your buttocks and shoulders off the floor, elbows past knees. Roll back to the X position. Repeat.

4. **Posture Strengthener**
   A. Start on all fours with your back flat, your head aligned with your spine. Lift your right arm and left leg slightly outward from your body until they reach shoulder/hip level. Hold for four counts. Lower.
   B. Arch your back like a cat, tucking your pelvis under and pressing down with your arms. Return to the starting position. Repeat A and B with your left arm and right leg.

5. Torso Firmer
   A. Lie on your right side with both arms overhead.
   B. Lift your left leg, left arm, upper body, and head slightly off the floor, with your right arm outstretched for support. Lower. Logroll to the other side, repeat.

6. Full-Body Flexor and Stretcher
   A. Kneel with your knees slightly apart, your chest low toward the floor, arms outstretched.
   B. As you inhale, shift your body forward, transferring your weight onto both hands with your arms straight and your shoulders down; keep your legs relaxed but your abdomen lifted so your back doesn't collapse. Pause.
   C. As you exhale, tuck your toes under, straighten your legs, and "pike" your pelvis up so your body makes an upside-down V. Keep your arms and back straight, your heels pressed into the floor so the backs of your legs feel a stretch. Pause. Bend your knees back toward your head and lower your body to the starting position. Repeat. Try to move steadily and smoothly, without rushing or jerking.

7. Mind-Body Relaxer
   Put your favorite music on and rest on your back with knees bent and arms folded across your chest. Concentrate on breathing, letting go of tension.

If you're looking for an exercise routine that truly combines just about everything—including *reading*, believe it or not—you might want to try *cardiocybernetics*. Developed by the cardiovascular surgeon Irving Dardik (he was the founding chairman of the U.S. Olympics Sports Medicine Council), the 50-minute routine alternates between running, fast walking, bounding, slow walking, and skipping, punctuated by as many as a dozen periods of absolute rest (that's where the reading comes in). The idea, Dardik explains, is to exercise until you raise your heart to the high edge of your training range (remember the formula we used earlier in this chapter of calculating your ideal training range), then rest—read, meditate, or just muse—until it drops down into a lower cycle. Not only does this provide what Dardik calls "true physiological relaxation"—and thus relief from accumulated stress—but Dardik claims that in the resting state you'll actually become more mentally alert and better able to concentrate. The ultimate payoff? Dardik thinks that cardiocybernetics may actually prolong life—partly by reducing stress and partly by toughening up the heart, the arteries, and even the immune system.

If everything you have read in this chapter still isn't enough to get you off your couch and into the gym, here is a summary of ten compelling reasons why you should start a regular exercise program:

1. Makes your heart a more efficient pump. Your heart can pump more oxygen-rich blood with less effort, thereby increasing your ability to work or play without getting tired.
2. Enables your muscles to remove more oxygen from circulating blood. Your muscles can burn fuel more effectively; they can clear away waste chemicals faster, thus delaying muscular fatigue.
3. Keeps fatty deposits to a minimum. It reduces serum triglycerides and sometimes total cholesterol levels, and increases blood levels of high-density lipoprotein (HDL). HDL cholesterol is believed to transport artery-clogging fats out of the body.
4. Lowers blood pressure and normalizes blood sugar. (With exercise, less fat-storing insulin is needed to control blood sugar levels.)
5. Increases the calcium content of your bones. Exercising against gravity is the safest and most effective way to maintain strong bones, and even rebuild bone tissue late in life.
6. Increases the flexibility of your joints. However, carrying exercise to an unwarranted extreme can inflict joint injuries. Moderation is the key.

7. Fosters emotional stability, probably because it releases a natural tranquilizer, beta endorphin, in your brain.
8. Enhances mental sharpness.
9. Increases the speed at which nerves convey messages to muscles.
10. May help prevent or fight cancer. Women who exercise regularly have lower rates of cancer of the breast and reproductive system.

I will add an eleventh reason of my own—it keeps you looking good.

So much for keeping your body healthy. But working the body—even with years of dedicated and dutiful exercise—isn't going to turn the longevity trick all by itself. You're going to have to exercise your mind as well.

12

Mental Muscle

Have you ever noticed that some people just don't seem to know how old they are? Like my grandmother, who never revealed her age to anyone—probably not even to herself. Or the grandfather of a friend of mine, who was still writing stinging letters to the local newspaper about anything that crossed his mind—Harry Truman, college football, even the lost cause of the Confederacy —until he died at the age of ninety-four. Or an eighty-three-year-old writer friend who takes time off between books to go mountain climbing.

What these people have in common can be summed up in the phrase *continuing to grow.* Like the Roman statesman Cato, who learned Greek at the age of eighty; or Goethe, who was over eighty when he wrote *Faust*; or even old George Burns, who says he'll be tap-dancing on stage on his hundredth birthday—these people have never lost their *joie de vivre,* their ongoing willingness to learn new things and tackle new tasks, and, perhaps most important, their relentless conviction that they're only as old as they feel.

We all know such people, but it may come as a surprise to you (as it did to me) to discover that they're not especially rare. A growing number of experts have come to believe that for many people middle age is a time when they feel at the peak of their powers. "Midlife is not a period of crisis but of development," says the psychologist Gilbert Brim, director of a MacArthur Foundation–sponsored massive cross-disciplinary research program that is currently investigating every conceivable aspect of middle age—from attitudes and aspirations to brain function and hormone levels. "Study after study of the middle-aged has been done," says Brim, "without discovering that any significant part of the population has a midlife crisis." Far from it: when the American Board of Family Practice polled 1,200 adults, as many as 89 percent of them said that middle age is a time of warmth, of increasing closeness to their mates, their children, and their friends.

So, perhaps to a larger degree than we ever realized, getting old is all in the mind—or, to be accurate, in that most vital of all organs, the brain. As I've said, the brain does change with age, although the details are still a matter of controversy. It used to be commonly accepted among scientists that as we get older our brains lose cells—anywhere from 10,000 to 50,000 a day. This would mean an overall reduction in size of about 10 percent between youth and old age. The part of the brain that seems to be among the hardest hit is the *substantia nigra,* which controls some aspects of movement and thus is implicated in the development of Parkinson's disease. The cell count in the substantia nigra is thought to drop from about 600,000 in youth to around 100,000 by the time we reach eighty.

The conventional wisdom had it that this irreversible decline in the brain's cell population would make us more forgetful and less mentally acute as we aged. But these days fewer and fewer scientists are willing to accept such a pessimistic picture. At the University of California at San Diego, Dr. Robert Terry, a professor of neurosciences and pathology, has used a special imaging technique to look at the aging brain in a new light. He's discovered that many of our larger brain cells, or *neurons,* don't actually die. Instead, they simply shrink; but in so doing they lose some of their connections and thus perform less well.

Still, it seems to be true that in an important sense our brains can keep right on growing, and even repairing themselves to some extent when they get out of kilter. In the 1960s and 1970s researchers at Cambridge University in England and the University of Rochester in the United States found that as they get older or become damaged, some brain cells actually send out new "branches"—long, spidery projections called *dendrites.* These dendrites continue to grow longer and sprout more branches even as we pass our ninetieth birthdays, leading some experts to speculate that these dendritic branches are the physical embodiments of what we call the "wisdom of age."

Recently, scientists have discovered clues that dendritic branching is stimulated by powerful brain chemicals known as nerve growth factors. These chemicals—there may be dozens or even hundreds of them—are generating tremendous excitement in laboratories here and abroad.

At the University of Lund in Sweden, Anders Bjorklund immerses elderly rats in a Morris maze—a tank filled with murky water that hides a submerged platform. Once the rat can find the platform and scramble onto it, it's raised out of the water to safety. As far as the rat is concerned, the trick is to find the platform during the first immersion, then remember where it is on subsequent dunkings. The bottom line on this experiment is that rats who got injections of nerve growth factor after their first immersion remembered where the platform was and swam right for it, while rats who got no nerve growth factor floundered around the tank until they stumbled on the platform by accident. Obviously, nerve growth factor had a positive, and possibly lifesaving, impact on the rats' memories.

Some scientists think that, down the road, nerve growth factors may become the basis for treatment of human diseases like Parkinson's and Alzheimer's. In the meantime, many researchers are beginning to conclude that the much ballyhooed deterioration of the brain with age has been greatly exaggerated. "Senility or impaired cognitive function doesn't seem to appear independent of physical health problems," says Marion Perlmutter, a psychologist and gerontologist at the University of Michigan. "Older people may not be as quick in timed tests," says Robert Terry, "but they don't lose judgment, orientation, or vocabulary. There is no way that people like Picasso, the cellist Pablo Casals, or Martha Graham could have continued to be so successful on half a brain."

So, from the standpoint of sheer mental muscle, it's evident that our brains can remain vigorous, capable, and creative no matter how old we are. The key, apparently, is to keep our brain in shape the same way we keep our body in shape—by using it. The brain researcher Marian Diamond, a professor of integrative biology at the University of California at Berkeley, put groups of aging lab rats into what amounted to a rat Disneyland: an environment full of toys, swings, ladders, treadmills, and wheels that kept them active and stimulated. It turned out that the rats who lived in Disneyland had bigger and better-functioning brains than their impoverished cousins, up to the ripe old age of three—the equivalent in humans of ninety.

In many ways, then, putting the brakes on mental aging may depend on a positive and aroused response to the challenges presented by the world around us. The same is true, apparently, of our attitudes toward ourselves and others. It is said, for example, that people who are shy and timid may actually be compromising their longevity. Research by the psychologist Jerome Kagan of Harvard University has shown that children as young as two who were very quiet and cautious in the presence of strangers had accelerated heart rates, more muscle tension, and higher levels of the stress hormone cortisol in their saliva. If that shyness persists into adulthood, Kagan thinks, it makes those people more prone to panic attacks.

So how do you deal with shyness and reticence? One way may lie in changing your style of conversation. The psychologist Phillip

Zimbardo of Stanford University has found that instead of listening attentively to what other people are saying, shy people concentrate on what they themselves are going to say next. A related study has shown that blood pressure actually goes up while we're talking and goes down while we're listening. So paying close attention to what your conversational partner is saying may prove to have unexpected rewards, not only for your social relationships but also for your health.

What you talk about may turn out to be just as important as how much you talk—especially if you're the kind of person who likes to talk about yourself. Larry Scherwitz, a social psychologist at the University of California at San Francisco, taped conversations of 193 men who later developed heart trouble, and compared them with the conversations of 384 others who had no heart problems. He then counted the number of times each person used the words "I," "me," and "my." Those people who used the first-person pronouns more frequently were more likely to develop heart disease. And the more they talked about themselves, the more likely they were to die of heart attacks. "Listen with regard when others talk," says Scherwitz. "Give your time and energy to others; let others have their way; do things for reasons other than furthering your own needs. Develop an attitude of love, because love erases the imaginary boundaries between self, others, and the world."

If shyness can increase your risk of developing heart problems, pessimism can evidently be worse. For more than forty years a team of psychologists led by Dartmouth Medical School's George E. Vaillant has been tracking the connection between mental attitudes and physical health in a group of Harvard graduates. Their findings? The men who had the bleakest outlook on life at the age of twenty-five suffered from the most serious illnesses when they were in their sixties. Vaillant's colleagues Christopher Peterson of the University of Michigan and Martin E. P. Seligman of the University of Pennsylvania found a similar pattern when they studied major league baseball stars. Players with a dark view of themselves and the world—those who tended to blame losses or slumps on internal factors ("I just don't seem to give a damn") and to see bad times as predominant in the natural order ("That's the way the world is")—lived shorter lives than more optimistic players.

Seligman thinks that a pessimistic and passive outlook has a direct and deep effect on the immune system and its ability to fight off diseases. "In animals," he says, "if you manipulate helplessness, you can produce natural killer cells that don't kill, T-cells that don't proliferate, and animals that grow tumors at a faster rate and reject them at a lower rate." He thinks the same may be true of humans: a bleak outlook means a weakened immune system.

The message, obviously, is to try not to let things get you down, or, at least, try not to let them keep you down for long. The evidence is that ongoing depression can be just as dangerous and potentially life-shortening as passivity and pessimism. Dr. Robert Carney and his colleagues at Washington University in St. Louis studied a group of 52 people who had coronary artery disease. Some of these people also suffered from major depression. Among the severely depressed patients, 78 percent had a serious heart problem within twelve months—a heart attack or coronary bypass surgery—compared with only 35 percent of the nondepressed patients. Carney concluded that depression was a stronger predictor of imminent heart trouble than any other factor, including age, smoking, and even the severity of the arterial disease.

How do you avoid the dangers of serious depression? There's a hint in the work of Dr. Rick Ingram and his colleagues at San Diego State University. Ingram wanted to know why approximately twice as many women as men suffered from severe depression. When he and his team members delved into the question in a series of psychological experiments, they found that women were significantly more introspective, more focused on themselves and their feelings than men, who tended to concentrate on the external world and its workings. Now, obviously, we don't want to ignore our feelings entirely (I think Socrates was right when he said that the unexamined life is not worth living). But we also don't want introspection to lead to moodiness, bad health, and a potentially shortened life expectancy. So one prescription against depression might be to try to strike a healthy balance between looking out and looking in. My mother always lectured me about not allowing myself to be "flattened," as she put it. "Be one of those who always bounce back," she would say when I was depressed or upset. "If you do that, nothing can keep you down."

If depression is the mild-mannered way of reacting to life's raw deals, then the flip side of depression is anger. It's well known that so-called hot reactors—people with hair-trigger personalities who confront the world with an attitude that's hostile and cynical— are more susceptible to high blood pressure and heart disease than people who react with aplomb and roll with life's punches. But scientists have been looking more deeply at hot reactors, and they're finding that the real key, as far as health and longevity are concerned, is not so much the angry reaction itself, but what the reactor *does* with the reaction. The worst thing is to stifle the anger or try to deny it.

This was borne out by a pair of revealing studies. One of them was conducted by Dr. Stewart Wolf of the Totts Gap Medical Branch Research Laboratory in Bangor, Pennsylvania. Among patients who repressed anger and felt overwhelmed by circumstances, he found electrocardiographic changes that made them vulnerable to dangerous, and even fatal, heart arrhythmias. In another, Paul L. Falger and his colleagues at the University of Limburg School of Medicine in The Netherlands delved into the family lives of a group of men who had suffered heart attacks. The more they probed, the more the researchers found histories of prolonged, ongoing conflicts—problems between husband and wife or among in-laws, or school problems with children. The important thing, according to the scientists, was not so much that conflicts existed, but that they were allowed to go unresolved.

The same conflicts can and do occur outside the home. A study by the sociologist Ronald C. Kessler of the University of Michigan revealed that office battles can be even worse than domestic upsets.

That is because few people are willing to come right out and create a stir when they think their job may be on the line. Since we live most of our lives either at home or at work, the psychological strain produced by these unresolved conflicts can put a severe and some-times life-threatening tax on our hearts.

Repressed anger, depression, pessimism, egocentricity, shyness —all negative attitudes, all potential life shorteners. Add them all up and they spell stress, which may be the most dangerous of all the mind killers. In our contemporary society, a typical day is loaded with stress; this may be the most stressful epoch in human history. So as stress increases, it becomes hazardous to your health. Stress helps produce high blood pressure (hypertension), which currently afflicts sixty million Americans. It's been implicated as a factor in the development of atherosclerosis, heart disease, and some kinds of cancer.

How to eliminate stress? There's no way to do it entirely. Even if we could do it, it might be unhealthful. Studies have shown that a certain amount of stress is actually good for us, in that it keeps our minds and bodies alert and awake. The important thing is to learn how to deal with stress. There's a clue to this in some recent research carried out by James A. McCubbin, a psychophysiologist at the University of Kentucky College of Medicine. McCubbin found that young men who were in the early stages of hypertensive disease showed diminished levels of opioids—calming chemicals that our brains produce in response to stress. The key word here is *calm*. McCubbin's work suggests that there's a natural mecha-nism in the brain that helps us stay cool when we're challenged by stressful events. It's when that mechanism breaks down that stress becomes truly dangerous.

The question is: How do we gain control of our innate anti-stress mechanisms? How do we train our brains to stay cool under fire? There are enough suggestions around to generate libraries full of self-help books. Scores of ashrams and health spas are dedicated to one anti-stress approach or another. My preference (learned from working on *Longevity* and *Omni* magazines, which put me in touch with the very latest scientific findings) is a sort of mixed strategy, involving a combination of diet, diet supplements, and exercise classes. Every year or so I make a point of learning how to do something new and enjoyable, whether it's video games, scuba diving, needlepoint, or tennis. I eat healthy portions of complex carbohydrates, especially pasta, because these are thought to have a calming effect, and may actually help the brain produce opioids. I take a combination of vitamins designed specifically for me by Dr. Michael Colgan. This custom regimen takes into account the very stressful life I lead. I do an hour's worth of high-energy aerobic exercise at least three times a week. Vigorous exercise, as I have noted, has been shown to stimulate the release of endorphins. The same may be true of meditation. I like to combine meditation with music and repetitive exercise, so I'll meditate to music—usually classical or New Age—while lifting weights or stretching. I also love working in my garden on weekends in the spring and summer.

I find that this combined approach helps me keep stress at arm's length. You may want to develop your own anti-stress program, using the tactics that best suit your personality, your needs, and your individual style. Here are a few tips—what I call "Thirty-Second Stress Busters":

Step 1: Close your eyes and breathe smoothly, deeply, and evenly.

Step 2: Relax your face and smile. This increases blood flow to the brain and helps "reset" the nervous system.

Step 3: Shift your posture and stretch. This can do a lot to release pent-up emotions.

Step 4: Take a quick mental scan of all your muscles and relax, from clenched jaws to curled-up toes.

Step 5: Take a momentary pause. It will help you regain your powers of concentration and get back in control.

At the same time that you're attempting to eliminate, or at least soften, the negative, you should be accentuating the positive. Because it turns out that an affirmative attitude—a sunny, positive philosophy that invites and embraces life—can also help prolong life.

One of the most important of the positive attitudes is openness. It's been known for many years that people with secretive, closed-in personalities are more prone to hypertension, ulcers, and even cancer. In his book *Opening Up*, the psychologist James Penne-baker of Southern Methodist University, who's made a career of studying the effects of secretiveness and self-revelation, likes to tell a true story that illustrates the difference between the two styles. During a period of economic hard times, a worker embezzled a large sum of money from his company. For years afterward the worker experienced all the physical fallout of psychological stress, including high blood pressure and accelerated heart rate. Finally, as his company began to investigate the possibility of embezzle-ment, the worker came forward and confessed. Even though he faced jail and financial disaster, his heart rate and blood pressure almost immediately dropped to normal—a powerful and tangible testimony to the unexpected rewards of confession.

In a scientific study, Pennebaker and his colleagues, the psy-chologist Janice Kiecolt-Glaser and the immunologist Ronald Glaser of Ohio State University, asked twenty-five college students to spend twenty minutes a day for four days in a row writing about past traumatic experiences. When the four days of self-revelation were over, the researchers found that the ability of the students' immune systems to respond to challenges was significantly im-proved, and the number of visits they made to the student health center in the ensuing months declined markedly. The conclusion? "It's time," says Pennebaker, "to update the old Scottish proverb that confession is good for the soul. The fact is, it's even better for the body."

If confession is good for the body, so, apparently, is a healthy regard for one's self. The researchers Jonathan D. Brown of the University of Washington and Kevin L. McGill of Southern Meth-odist University found that among a group of 370 teenagers and college students, people with low self-esteem had a high rate of stress-related illnesses and were likely to get sick even when life was going well. People who liked themselves, on the other hand, had a much lower incidence of stress-linked diseases and seemed to thrive both physically and psychologically when good things came their way. The message is clear: If you want to feel better and live longer, learn to like yourself. Forgive yourself your faults and failings, and identify your virtues.

Self-forgiveness can also help us to cultivate some healthy self-delusions. Most of us tend to think that we are the center of the universe. It is, of course, a ludicrous illusion in view of the absolute immensity of the real universe, but wait. It's also a healthy illusion, and crucial to our sense of purpose, our well-being, and our very survival. According to the psychologist Daniel Goleman, who writes on human behavior for *The New York Times*, there are three more healthy illusions: "an overly positive sense of yourself, an unfounded optimism, and an exaggerated feeling of control over your life." Cultivate those vital illusions, concludes Goleman, and you may daydream your way to better health and a longer life.

Another incredibly powerful folk medicine is laughter—"one of the best strategies for maintaining good health," according to Dr. William F. Fry, Jr., a psychiatrist at the Stanford University Medical School. If you want living proof, just take a look at the life spans of stand-up comedians. Charlie Chaplin lived to be eighty-eight, Groucho Marx eighty-seven. Even Jackie Gleason, who smoked, ate, drank, and partied his way through a riotously unhealthy life, made it to seventy. Milton Berle, Bob Hope, Red Skelton, and Henny Youngman are still laughing—and kicking— in their eighties. And of course, there's the grand old man himself, George Burns.

There is a growing body of research to support the notion that laughter can be the best medicine. Lab studies have shown that laughter can be the equivalent of aerobic exercise (it accelerates the heart rate, improves blood circulation, and helps clear the breathing passages), can stimulate the production of enzymes that aid digestion, and can fight stress by lowering the level of arousal chemicals in the brain (catecholamines) while at the same time raising the levels of endorphins. There's even evidence that laughter can help stimulate the immune system. The editor and author Norman Cousins used laughter instead of drugs to fight off a spinal disease that his doctors had considered a death sentence. (Cousins wrote about his stirring battle in his groundbreaking book *Anatomy of an Illness.*)

It takes a healthy sense of the absurd to find life consistently funny, and this same appreciation for the offbeat and the off-center can in itself help one live longer. That's the conclusion of David Weeks, a psychologist at the Royal Edinburgh Hospital in Scotland. Weeks studied two hundred people whom he classified as eccentric or unconventional. Beneath their oddities, Weeks says, "these people have a very strong sense of self and purpose in life. They're curious, they have a robust sense of humor, and they love ideas." Their eccentricities, Weeks concludes, are signposts of an unflagging zest for life and an unending appreciation of its rewards. "To an eccentric," Weeks says, "anything is possible."

The kind of zaniness that characterizes the true eccentric can be put to work for all of us. The key—and it can't be repeated enough—is to stay busy and involved. If you're like me, you may have found that the busier you are, the happier you are—and the more you take on, the more you get done. It seems to me that during the periods when I'm at my most active, I never get sick —it just doesn't occur to me, and even if it did, I couldn't afford the time.

There's something very powerful going on in the too-busy-to-get-sick syndrome. Staying busy, involved, and purposeful can not only help keep you in good health, it can actually add years to your life—especially if you're a woman. In the late 1980s, the sociologists Phyllis Moen, Donna Dempster McCalin, and Robin N. Williams, Jr., of Cornell University studied 427 women from upstate New York who had originally been interviewed in 1956. In the ensuing thirty-plus years, 80 of the women had died, but the researchers managed to find most of the rest of the women and interviewed them again. Their conclusion: women who from a young age had juggled motherhood, a career, and other activities—church, club memberships, community service, and the like—typically lived much longer than women who simply stayed home and took care of the kids.

The idea is to tap the potential life-extending power of taking charge of your own life. If you feel that you've lost that sense of control and purpose, do whatever you have to do to regain it. Being in charge, says the Yale University psychologist Judith Rodin, is "of central importance in influencing psychological and physical health, and perhaps even longevity." In the mid-1970s, Rodin and her colleagues tested this notion on the elderly residents of a nursing home in New Haven, Connecticut. The residents, aged sixty-five to ninety, were divided into two groups. The first group was told that the staff wanted to make the home a happy place in which to live. "We want to know anything that you want," they said to that group, and "we'll do it for you." The second group was told to take charge of things. "We're having a movie next week," the staff said to this group, "but *you* tell *us* when you want to see it."

Eighteen months later, the psychologists checked in on the two groups. Sure enough, the people in the take-charge group were much more alert, more active, and significantly happier than their passive peers. Their feisty attitude had tangible rewards in terms of physical health: they had lower levels of the stress hormone cortisol and a greatly reduced need for medication in general. The ultimate payoff, in addition to better health and greater happiness, was longer life: at the end of a year and a half, twice as many of the take-chargers were still alive and kicking.

So identify the things in life that are important to you—it may be a career, creativity, finances, politics, or the feeling of satisfaction that comes from serving your community—and put yourself in command. Assert yourself, express yourself, take control. You'll be more satisfied with yourself and your life, and you might actually live longer, too.

This concept is so important that one expert has invented a

name for it. Charles Garfield, a psychologist and associate clinical professor at the University of California in San Francisco, and the author of *Peak Performers: The New Heroes of American Business*, calls it *vertical longevity*. He defines it as "the art of living as fully as possible during each moment of chronological life.

"The source of vertical longevity," Garfield explains, "is having a high sense of mission, having some goal or end to which you're willing to devote your life." He cites as an example a former colleague, a technical manager at Grumman Aerospace Corporation in New York, who had spent most of his career working on obscure, seemingly purposeless projects and then was suddenly assigned to the team that was helping to put the first man on the moon. "Do you know what it's like," he asked Garfield, "working forty to sixty hours a week, not knowing if your effort makes a damn bit of difference to anybody? For years I was a piece of furniture—until this thing came along." With his new assignment, Garfield says, the once moribund manager suddenly came alive: he looked younger, more animated, and more in charge of himself and his life. "When you have this kind of personal, powerful mission," Garfield observes, "something extraordinary happens. Just by transcending the tick of the clock and reaching for something higher, you seize a little piece of immortality."

Over the past ten years, there's been an explosion of evidence linking the power of the mind to the health of the body, and experts in the new field of *psychoneuroimmunology*, or PNI, are gaining a greater understanding of how the brain and the body can cooperate to fight off illness. It's been discovered, for one thing, that there are nerve fibers in the thymus, the immune system's master gland, as well as in the spleen, the lymph nodes, and the bone marrow—all vital parts of the immune system. Some immune system cells have receptors for neuropeptides, chemicals that are produced within the brain itself. In other words, there's a growing body of evidence to suggest that the brain talks directly to the immune system via this electrochemical version of AT&T.

Sometimes this electrochemical link between brain and body

can be mobilized to produce astonishing, seemingly miraculous results. A middle-aged woman is diagnosed with terminal lung cancer and given only a few months to live. "I can't die," she says, "I have four children to raise." Ten years later, her cancer in remission, she watches her youngest child graduate from college. A man with a terrible secret—he knows that his father has committed murder—suddenly develops throat cancer. The night before surgery to remove the tumor, he breaks down and tearfully reveals his father's crime. Within four hours he's able to eat for the first time in a week, and the surgery is canceled. Four days later, the tumor has entirely disappeared.

These and thousands of other cases may show the potential power that the mind can bring to bear on even the most devastating diseases. People who experience spontaneous remissions seem to have extraordinary capacities for self-repair. The key question is: How can we learn to turn on those self-repair mechanisms?

One method that has already had a long history of remarkable success is "guided imagery." In this technique, first developed in the 1960s by psychiatrists O. Carl Simonton and Stephanie Simonton, patients are encouraged to develop a sharply focused mental picture of the "enemy"—a cluster of cancer cells, for example. They're then trained to imagine their own defenses—the immune system's T-lymphocytes, or natural killer cells—attacking the invading disease cells and fighting them off. Sometimes the imagery can be realistic—one woman fought off lung cancer after her daughter, a nurse, put an X ray of a healthy lung beside her bed. At other times they may be slightly surreal: one eight-year-old girl mobilized her immune system against cancer by imagining that the cancer cells were dragons and her attacking immune cells were knights bearing lances.

Although it doesn't always work, the use of guided imagery can help even the most desperate of patients nurture a fighting spirit and a will to live. As Stephanie Simonton puts it, "There's no such thing as a false hope. In the absence of certainty, hope is simply a stance you take toward an unknown outcome." For anyone with a life-threatening disease, this is an essential and potentially life-saving truth.

For the rest of us, the tantalizing question is: Can we learn to use guided imagery or related techniques not just as an end-stage strategy in the face of existing disease, but as a prophylactic, a way to keep disease at arm's length and thus extend our lives? As far as the psychologist Lawrence R. Casler is concerned, the answer is an emphatic yes. In the 1960s Casler, professor emeritus at the State University of New York at Geneseo, selected thirty relatively healthy elderly people—their average age was eighty—who were living in a New York nursing home. He left fifteen of the volunteers alone. The other fifteen he saw once a week for four weeks, giving them hypnotic-like suggestions that they "had many, many years of life ahead, years that would be vigorous years, and during which they would retain their mental and physical capacities." For the next twenty years, Casler received monthly reports on the health and mortality of each group. In the end, people in the group that had been given the "long-life suggestion" not only had fewer days in the hospital, but actually lived an average of 6.3 years longer than the group which got no suggestion!

This was enough to persuade Casler that he was on the right track. In 1970, he began hypnotizing subjects and giving them the ultimate, most audacious of all post-hypnotic suggestions: *You're going to live to be 120.* In the ensuing twenty years, Casler has kept a close watch on the original one hundred subjects, half of whom got the suggestion and half of whom didn't. The outcome has been startling. In the group that was hypnotized, there have been 22 percent fewer hospitalizations than occurred in the other group. Three-fourths of the smokers in the hypnotized group have quit, compared with only one-fourth in the control group. "The data are very incomplete," Casler says, "but the experimental group is healthier than the control group." As far as Casler is concerned, these two studies are "partial confirmation of my belief that to a great extent the human life span is under mental control."

Can hypnotism really help extend life? Not all hypnotists think so. "It would be hard to prove that hypnosis helps longevity," says the San Francisco obstetrician and hypnotist David B. Cheek. "But certainly hypnosis can be a tremendous help in decreasing stress." Casler stands by his treatment, telling himself every night that he's going to live to be 120. "In essence," he says, "we are hypnotized by society into believing that when we reach a certain age—three score and ten, or whatever—we just don't have a chance. So what I'm really doing is *de*-hypnotizing—getting rid of the psychological garbage that leads to early death."

You don't have to resort to hypnotism to begin to use your brain as a weapon in the battle against aging. Programmed relaxation techniques like meditation, which are actually similar in many ways to self-hypnotism, may do the trick in and of themselves. When the psychologists Charles Alexander of the Maharishi International University in Fairfield, Iowa, and Ellen Langer of Harvard University taught transcendental meditation to a group of octogenarians in eight Boston-area nursing homes, 100 percent of those who practiced TM for twenty minutes a day were still alive three years later, while 38 percent of their peers who did not meditate had passed on. This is reminiscent of legends of Himalayan yogis using similar techniques to live more than a hundred years. "Of course, these stories have to be taken with a grain of salt," Alexander says, "but meditation does seem to extend life."

Alexander is one of a growing body of scientists who believe that we can muster the power of our brains to stay healthy, to heal ourselves when we're sick, and, quite possibly, even to extend our life expectancy. I'm definitely in their camp; in fact, I think that the guided imaging techniques of the Simontons and the hypnotic approach of Casler are just the beginning. I'm convinced that within the next ten to twenty years we'll gain such a thorough understanding of the mind-body link—and develop such powerful techniques for strengthening and exploiting that link—that spontaneous "miracle cures" will become more and more frequent, and many of us will actually be able to use our minds to effect what amounts to the ultimate cure: to lengthen our lives.

13

What's Love Got to Do with It?

Imagine two babies crying in a crib. Let's say they're identical twins, so that with the exception of their names (we'll call them Diana and Donna) nearly everything about them is virtually the same—their genetic endowment, their life history, their environment, even their birthday. There's one crucial difference: every time Diana cries, she's ignored; whereas every time Donna cries, her mother picks her up, cuddles and soothes her, and asks her what's wrong.

What happens to Diana and Donna as adults? Diana grows up feeling helpless, worthless, and unloved. By middle age she's a confirmed alcoholic, several times married and several times divorced, a failure at each of the many jobs she's held. By fifty she's dead. Donna, on the other hand, grows up with a solid sense of self-confidence, a feeling of mastery over herself and her life. She lives a rich and healthy life, full of achievement and rewarding relationships, until she dies at ninety.

The only difference between Diana and Donna is love: Donna got lots of it early in life, and Diana didn't. Love, and only love, made the difference between the two. Of course, this is an imaginary story. But to Leonard Sagan, a California physician and epidemiologist, it's a powerful illustration of what has become his central belief: all other things being equal, the more love you have in your life—especially love at an early age—the longer you're going to live.

Sagan first outlined this belief in his 1988 book, *The Health of Nations*, which grew out of twelve years of exhaustive epidemiological research, during which he studied disease and death rates in cultures all over the world, in some cases going back as many as five hundred years. Sagan came out of that study convinced not only that love has a powerful influence on the longevity of the individual, but that early love, in the form of a warm, nurturing childhood, is the single most important factor in the great leap in human life expectancy that has taken place over the past century.

That leap—from an average life expectancy of about forty in the nineteenth century to today's industrial world average of seventy-plus—has usually been explained in terms of advances in medicine and sanitation. The advent of antibiotics, vaccines, and modern plumbing, most experts contend, combined to act as a barrier against the infectious diseases—tuberculosis, typhoid, and pneumonia, among others—that had been massive killers throughout history. But Sagan found that these theories "were not borne out by the historical record." First of all, he discovered, killer diseases like tuberculosis and typhoid were on the decline *before* the appearance of their medical remedies. Death rates from diseases for which no vaccine had been developed declined at about the same rate as those for which there were vaccines.

As far as Sagan is concerned, there's only one possible explanation. He attributes the great leap in longevity to the increased strength of the family, and especially to changes in the rearing of children. "Until the late nineteenth century," he says, "children were seen as miniature adults. Child rearing was mostly a matter of harsh discipline and authoritarian attitudes." To the rich and ennobled, children were either potential heirs—and often rivals

—or marriageable daughters, used to fashion alliances with other powerful families. To the poor, children were extra hands to help around the farm, the mine, or the home.

But Sagan thinks that in the twentieth century, with the spread of democracy and economic bounty, came the rise of smaller, gentler families, families in which the welfare of children was at least as important as the needs of the adults. In general, children came to be treated with the kind of loving care and concentrated attention that meant the development of "disease-resistant personalities"—people who were healthy, strong, and resilient enough to foster vigorous immune systems, which, in turn, help them live longer lives.

Sagan's contention is considered interesting but controversial, in that most scientists find it hard to give up the idea that medical breakthroughs and improved sanitation have had a huge impact on human life expectancy. But Sagan is certainly not the only expert to preach the vital connection between love and longevity. Over the past several years, a large body of evidence has accumulated to suggest that positive childhoods, strong emotional bonds, and a healthy network of social ties ultimately pay off in better health and longer life.

For the past twenty-five years, as I indicated earlier, psychiatrist George E. Vaillant of the Dartmouth Medical School has been keeping track of a group of Harvard men who were sophomores between 1940 and 1942. By the time they reached their mid-sixties, Vaillant found, the single most important factor in determining good health—more important than not smoking, exercising, and even having long-lived parents and grandparents—was a "warm childhood environment."

Of course, what you do as an adult can be just as important as what was done to you—or not done to you—as a child. High on the list of social ties that promote long life is that strongest of all possible bonds between adults, marriage. It's long been suspected that married people outlive their peers who stay single, and that suspicion was confirmed by a huge study, results of which appeared in 1990. Yuanreng Hu and Noreen Goldman of Princeton University looked at almost thirty years' worth of statistics for sixteen industrial countries, including, among others, England, Portugal, Finland, Taiwan, Japan, and the United States. In those countries, the researchers found, the average death rate for unmarried men was over twice that of married men, while the average death rate for unmarried women was about one and a half that of married women. The young divorced and the young widowed fared particularly badly: they had death rates up to ten times higher than their married peers.

Goldman thinks there are two possible explanations. It may be, she says, that healthier people tend to find mates more easily, leaving their unhealthier counterparts in the unmarried category. Or it may be that sharing lives is an effective way of coping with stress—not only the stress that accompanies pure loneliness, but the hassles and nicks of simply being alive in this most stressful of centuries.

Although marriage does seem to be an important plus in the longevity equation, this doesn't necessarily mean that people who stay single are doomed to live shortened lives. It may be loneliness, not singlehood, that seems to spell the difference. (Indeed, the psychologist Janice Kiecolt-Glaser and the immunologist Ronald Glaser of Ohio State University have found that people who scored high on a "loneliness index" had relatively sluggish natural killer cells, the immune system cells that help fight off tumors and infectious diseases.) The key, apparently, is to develop social and emotional ties that replace the bonds of family life—ties with friends, ties with lovers, ties that can nurture in all sorts of ways.

The epidemiologist Lisa Berkman of Yale University conducted a six-year study of 4,775 residents of Alameda County, California, in which she asked people to list four kinds of social ties that might potentially be important features in their lives: marriage, contacts with family and friends, religious institution membership, and other sorts of group affiliations. Berkman found that those who scored low on her "social network index" were more than twice as likely to die during the next nine years as those whose lives were enriched by emotional bonds. A similar study of 2,000 Tecumseh, Michigan, adults by the University of Michigan sociologist James S. House came to a similar conclusion—a death rate twice as high in unsociable women, and up to three times as high in unsociable men.

Significantly, marriage in and of itself was not an important factor. According to Berkman, "unmarried people who maintained many contacts with close friends and relatives had the same mortality rate as married people with fewer contacts. There isn't any one relationship that's critical," she concludes. "What *is* critical is having—or not having—close connections with people."

Also critical, if the experts are right, is the *style* of those connections. Relationships that are characterized by selfishness, manipulation, and exploitation are probably going to create more stress than they alleviate, and thus are not likely to help tip the scales of longevity in one's favor. The majority opinion has it that the kind of relationship that's most likely to have a positive impact on health and long life is the one that is cemented by altruism— a willingness to extend a helping hand and, at least in times of crisis, to put the other person's needs before your own.

The link between altruism and longevity is of great interest to Allan Luks, former executive director of the Institute for the Advancement of Health, and now director of Big Brothers/Big Sisters in New York. During the late 1980s, Luks undertook a study of helping behavior in which he distributed questionnaires to 3,000 volunteer participants. Not only was it clear that, in Luks's words, "people who help others frequently report better health than people who don't," but more than 90 percent of those people actually experienced positive physical sensations linked to their helping— feelings of exhilaration, increased strength, and a deep sense of tranquillity. Luks thinks these sensations may be caused by a release of endorphins (the same brain chemicals that are released during exercise to produce the "runner's high"), or that helping others generates a mental and spiritual state similar to that induced by yoga and meditation. In either case, it's becoming increasingly clear that a helpful, caring attitude toward others may be a ticket not only to a happier and more productive life, but to a longer one as well.

The watchword is to reach out and touch someone—not just in the metaphoric sense, as in extending a helping hand, but also in a physical sense. It turns out that physical contact, especially at an early age, has an amazingly powerful impact on health and longevity—in rats, at least. In 1988, the Stanford University neuroscientist Robert Sapolsky and his colleague Michael Meaney of the Douglas Hospital Research Center at McGill University in Montreal spent fifteen minutes a day for three weeks handling a group of newborn lab rats. When those rats reached the age of twenty-eight months—doddering old age in rat terms—Sapolsky and Meaney found that they could swim mazes considerably better than their relatively untouched peers: they could swim them, in fact, just as well as young rats.

Fascinated by this finding, Sapolsky and Meaney dug deeper, looking for a biomechanical explanation for the intellectual rejuvenation of the handled rats. They found that the hippocampal regions of the brains of the handled rats had developed extra receptors for glucocorticoids, powerful hormones secreted by the adrenal glands during episodes of stress. These extra receptors apparently made the hippocampus more effective in regulating the secretion of glucocorticoids, keeping the stress hormones at levels that ultimately did less damage to the hippocampus. A healthier hippocampus seemed to spell better performance on the maze tests. Although Sapolsky cautions that what's true in rats may not be true in humans, he points out that there are similarities in the nervous systems of the two species. In the end, he remains impressed. "Something incredibly subtle that occurs way back in infancy," he says, "may protect the brain forever."

The point of all this is that touching can pay long-term dividends in helping to ensure better health and longer life. This seems equally true of almost everyone's favorite form of touching: sex.

First of all, the sex act—whether intercourse or masturbation —has a number of important rewards in terms of overall health: it helps lower blood pressure, relieve arthritis pain, alleviate insomnia, and reduce stress. Does regular sex also prolong life? The jury is still out on that question—for humans, at least—but many researchers think that once the facts become known, the answer will be a resounding yes. "The evidence is out there," says Ann Beatty, a psychologist at Southern Illinois University at Edwardsville. "There is no doubt in my mind that continued sexual expression is a factor in prolonging life."

Of course, sex does change with aging. Some of the changes are purely physical: in men, semen production declines; it takes longer to achieve an erection ("You can't expect a seventy-year-old man to have an erection at the drop of a bra," says the famous sexologist William Masters) and longer to get to orgasm. Impotence, whether the causes are physical or emotional, becomes somewhat more frequent. In women, the production of estrogen slows down, especially after menopause, while the walls of the vagina become thinner, drier, and somewhat less elastic. These physical changes can be reflected on the emotional side of sex: a feeling that sex is inappropriate, or that desire itself is on the wane.

On page 191 there is a decade-by-decade rundown of the changes you can expect. Remember that these stages represent an average for the whole population. Individuals age at different rates and in different ways.

Fortunately, science is hard at work on developing new ways to cure, or at least alleviate, the physical problems that can compromise our sexuality as we get older. Perhaps the most common—and the most feared—is impotence in men. In the past, it's often been difficult to sort out whether impotence is a purely biological problem (that's true, the experts say, in over half of all cases) or whether it's caused by some sort of ongoing emotional difficulty. A new test developed by the Boston University School of Medicine urologist Irwin Goldstein and the registered nurse

Age *Women*

20 Estrogen levels are eight to ten times higher than those of childhood. Inner vaginal lips are now fully grown.

30 Estrogen production peaks. Vaginal lubrication is at its height. Sexual desire and orgasm are at their greatest intensity.

40 Arousal takes longer. With menopause approaching, the length and amount of menstrual flow begins to decrease.

50 Mons is less cushioned. Vaginal walls grow thinner, stiffer, and drier. Estrogen levels decrease. Clitoris becomes uncomfortably sensitive. The average age of final period is fifty.

60 Estrogen production is low. Breasts become less full and firm.

70 Slight shrinkage of the clitoris. Labia are thinner.

Age *Men*

20 Semen production is 3 to 5 milliliters every 24 hours.

30 Testosterone production levels out.

40 Arousal takes longer. Semen production waning.

50 Erotic thoughts no longer sufficient for arousal. Semen production declines. Impotence, about half of it physically caused, increases.

60 Less sensation leading up to climax. Ejaculation only once in every two to three sexual episodes.

70 Testes shrinking. Several days needed between ejaculations. Erection fades rapidly after ejaculation.

Terry Payton can help determine whether impotence is biological or psychological.

In that test, a series of "cocktails" of the drugs papaverine, phentolamine, and prostaglandin E-1 (PE-1) are injected into the penis until a "bedroom quality" erection is produced. In normal men, these drugs, which stimulate blood flow to the penis, will produce an erection in about fifteen minutes. If there's no erection, then the doctors know that something physical is impeding the blood flow to the genitals.

Poor blood flow is often due to blood pressure problems, which can be caused by clogging or hardening of the arteries. "If men have high blood pressure and a poor diet," says Dr. Helen Kaplan, director of the Human Sexuality Program at the New York Hospital–Cornell Medical Center, "the penile arteries will clog up, too." Luckily, there are remedies, essentially the same remedies for anyone whose arteries are constricted: diet low in saturated fats, exercise, and reduction of stress. "All these," Kaplan concludes, "can slow down the progression of vascular impotence and maintain penile functioning."

In some cases, impotence can be an unwelcome psychological by-product of problems with the prostate, the gland near the bladder end of the urethra that manufactures some of the ingredients of semen. In youth, the prostate is about the size of a walnut, but as men age, about 75 percent of them will experience swelling of the prostate. If it swells enough, the gland can choke off the urethra, causing urinary problems that can be severe. In the most troubling cases, part or all of the prostate has to be surgically removed to restore proper urinary flow.

That's where the psychological sexual problems can come in. The common belief is that prostate surgery almost invariably causes some degree of impotence, or at least a decline in sexual functioning. According to Laura Creti of the Behavior and Sex Therapy Service of Sir Mortimer B. Davis–Jewish General Hospital in Montreal, this can become a self-fulfilling—and sexually self-defeating—prophecy. "Men may fear surgery itself. Not just prostate surgery, but any surgery may interfere with penile and erectile functioning," says Creti, who studied thirty-two men who had had prostate and herniography operations. "And it appears that there is a relationship between what men believe will happen and then subsequently what does happen." On the other hand, Creti found, men who've had a healthy sex life before the operation and expect to continue enjoying sex afterward often do. "These well-functioning men," Creti concludes, "don't have much to worry about."

For the men among you who continue to fear that prostatectomy will mean the end of your sex life, there's further good news. All over the country, scientists are busily at work developing knife-free alternatives to prostate surgery. One of these involves inserting a small, deflated balloon through the tip of the penis and up the urethra. When it reaches the prostate, the balloon is inflated, thus compressing the swollen prostatic tissue and relieving the pressure on the urethra. (The results of this procedure are not permanent in all cases, and it sometimes has to be repeated within a few years.)

In an even more recent experimental procedure, doctors at Pennsylvania Hospital in Philadelphia used ultrasonic aspiration on fifty-nine men with BPH (benign prostatic hypertrophy, or noncancerous swelling of the prostate). Eighteen months later, none required further surgery. For those who want nothing to do with hospitals, an experimental drug called Proscar has been effective in reducing prostate swelling in about 30 percent of the cases, and seems to have no effect on sex drive or potency. Proscar could be available by the mid-1990s. There's even good news for the one man in ten whose prostatic swelling is caused by cancer. (Prostate cancer is one of the three leading causes of cancer-related death in men over fifty.) The traditonal treatments for prostate cancer—either surgery or conventional radiation therapy—have often left these unfortunate patients impotent or incontinent. But now there's an alternative on the horizon, at least for prostate cancers that are detected early. Called TheraSeed Palladium 103, this treatment involves implanting a radioactive "seed" or pellet directly into the tumor. The seed then releases timed bursts of radiation, which kill the tumor while causing only minimal damage to surrounding tissue. At a price of $7,000–$8,000, it's about half the cost of surgery, and it takes only about forty-five minutes with a local anesthetic.

For women, many worries about sexual decline have to do with hysterectomy. The statistics are startling indeed. More than 500,000 American women undergo this operation every year in the United States—so many that by age sixty-five half of all American women will have had their uterus removed. In the aftermath of this surgery, many women feel depressed, chronically tired, and sexually unresponsive. Even worse, if the ovaries are removed along with the uterus, there's an increased risk of heart disease, osteoporosis, and other nasty side effects.

The shameful fact is that many hysterectomies are performed unnecessarily. Frequently, women are not fully informed of the possible consequences. My advice—no, my urgent plea—to any woman who has been told she needs a hysterectomy is to get an independent second and even third opinion.

A new use for the resectoscope, an instrument often used in prostate surgery, may help cut down the number of hysterectomies. In this country and others, a growing number of doctors are inserting a resectoscope through the cervix. A mild electric current is passed through a roller-ball electrode to vaporize the abnormal endometrium. This procedure, which can be done under local anesthesia in less than thirty minutes in most cases, will render a woman sterile, but it has a much lower risk of complications than a hysterectomy.

In a variation of this technique, the resectoscope is attached to a cutting loop electrode, and that loop is used to cut away the fibroid uterine growths that can cause heavy bleeding or infertility. This version of the procedure may allow a woman to keep her fertility if she suffers from bleeding caused by fibroid tumors. Many insurance companies have now approved resectoscopic surgery, and obstetrics and gynecology professor Phillip G. Brooks of the University of Southern California School of Medicine reports that 92 percent of the more than one thousand American women who have had resectoscopic surgery have significantly reduced uterine bleeding, while 60 percent have no bleeding whatsoever. According to Bruce McLucas, an assistant clinical professor of obstetrics and gynecology at UCLA, "Many of my patients get off the operating room table and tell me 'I can't believe you've done anything.' "

Even for those of us who are lucky enough not to have to face hysterectomy—or whose uterine problems can be solved by resectoscopic surgery—there still may be fears of the one change that will inevitably happen to all of us: the onset of menopause. The common mythology is that once the body starts to change the most significant change is a decline in the production of the female hormone estrogen. With that decline, so the myth goes, sexual desire, and sex itself, go out the window.

It doesn't have to be that way. For the past ten years Dr. Barbara Sherwin, an associate professor of psychology, obstetrics, and gynecology at McGill University in Montreal has tested three different hormone treatments on female patients recovering from operations that result in a reduced production of sex hormones. One group received only testosterone, another only estrogen, and a third received a mixture of both hormones. The women who received testosterone, either alone or with estrogen, have more sexual desires, more sexual fantasies, and higher levels of sexual arousal than the women who received estrogen only. The women on testosterone also had higher rates of intercourse and orgasm. "Testosterone in women seems to have its greatest effect on the libido," Sherwin says. "It also gives women higher energy levels and increases their sense of well-being."

In the United States, both oral and injectable hormone replacement medications with low levels of testosterone are available. Even though they have minimal side effects, the drugs are infrequently prescribed. The reason, says Sherwin, is that many physicians, and many women, do not realize the importance of testosterone in female sexuality, primarily because until recently there has been no good research on the subject. "Estrogen can help with vaginal atrophy and hot flashes, but it does nothing for sexual desire," says Sherwin.

Catherine Olevnik, a research assistant in the department of psychology at the State University of New York at Albany, has found that women who have an uninhibited and open attitude toward sex can continue to enjoy physical intimacy as long as they wish. The key, Olevnik has found, is to replace conventional feminine attitudes, especially passivity, with an active, eager, and assertive approach. "Feel free to start the ball rolling," she urges. "Express your needs and let your mate know that you understand his."

The message here is that the physical and emotional changes

that accompany getting older do not necssarily mean that your sexuality is on the wane. It's just changing, and in some ways it's changing for the better. The unbridled passion of youth may fade along with the sound of trumpets and violins, but it often is replaced by a richer sound—the sweet, slow hum of the cello. Dr. Robert N. Butler, former director of the National Institute on Aging, calls this deeper form of intimate expression "the second language of sex." "When you're seventeen," Butler says, "the first language of sex is excited, urgent, often passionate, but also amateurish and primitive. With time, you can broaden your definition of sex and acquire new skills and experience." Some of those skills can be purely physical—more touching, more fondling, more mutual stimulation. Others are emotional: tenderness, thoughtfulness, sharing; in general, putting the love back in lovemaking.

Basically, as Butler and other experts suggest, much of preserving a healthy sex life is a matter of maintaining a healthy attitude. "As we get older," says Nancee S. Blum, co-author of *Sexual Health in Later Life*, "it's easy to view the body as a repository of pain. It's good to know that the body can give and receive pleasure as well." If you believe that sex can be an ongoing feature of your life as you get older, that it can be even deeper and more pleasurable than it was when you were young—and if you're willing to adopt an attitude of enthusiasm, adventure, and continuing experiment—then the chances are that you'll be able to enjoy sex your whole life through.

Besides maintaining a healthy, adventuresome attitude, there are some other things you can do to help keep your sex life active and fulfilling. One of the most important of these is exercise— exercise outside the bedroom, that is. The behavorial scientists Phillip Whitten and Elizabeth J. Whiteside did a survey in which they compared two groups of 160 active swimmers, one group in their forties and one in their sixties, with a normal population in the same age groups. The swimmers were found to be significantly more sexually active than the sample from the normal population. The swimmers in their forties reported having intercourse at a frequency usually reported by people in their twenties and thirties. Even the over-sixty swimmers enjoyed intercourse an average of 6.7 times a month. The conclusion? "Older people in excellent physical condition have sex lives more like those of people in their late twenties or early thirties," Whitten says. "These swimmers were proud of their bodies, and they felt younger."

If regular exercise can help keep your sex life bubbling even in your sixties, so, too, can careful attention to your diet. The San Francisco physician and psychiatrist Richard Kunin thinks that there's a special sexual payoff in keeping your diet low in fats. "Anything that improves circulation," he says, "tends to enhance one's love life." Simple carbohydrates like sugar should also be avoided; these can induce hypoglycemia, drowsiness, and sluggishness, all of which can act to apply the brakes in the bedroom.

On the other hand, there are certain nutrients that act as sexual stimulants. Vitamin A, for example, found in egg yolks, liver, and most fruits and vegetables, helps maintain the production of virtually all the sex hormones. Vitamin B_6, found in whole grains, liver, fish, yeast, and avocados, decreases the production of prolactin, which is implicated in depressing sexual desire in women. In men, vitamin B_6 increases the production of the hormone that regulates testosterone. Vitamin E, found in green vegetables, whole grains, seeds, and nuts, improves circulation in general, and in women also helps boost levels of prostaglandins, fatty acids that help the uterus contract during intercourse.

Among the nutrient minerals, two in particular can help keep the fires burning. Manganese, found in nuts, whole grains, dried beans or peas, and tea, helps stimulate the brain's production of two neurotransmitters—acetylcholine and dopamine—that help fuel sexual arousal. Zinc (look for it in oysters, wheat germ, cashews, green beans, lima beans, and meats like beef and lamb) assists in the formulation of testosterone, which, interestingly enough, has been found to be a sexual turn-on not only in men but in women as well. "All these nutrients," says Kunin, "are necessary to a rich and energetic sex life."

If attitude, exercise, and diet fail, there are several drugs now being tested as potential promoters of sagging sexual desire. One of these is quinelorane hydrochloride, a substance that mimics the activity of the neurotransmitter dopamine. At this writing, tests are under way in lab animals at the State University of New York at Buffalo, and in humans at Mount Sinai Medical Center in New York, where it's being given to men and women who have low sex drives, to women who have trouble getting aroused or achieving orgasm, and to men who suffer from impotence or inability to ejaculate. Although quinelorane hydrochloride is still in the early stages of development, "it could," according to Raul C. Schiavi, director of the Human Sexuality Program at Mount Sinai Hospital, "help with sexual problems associated with aging."

A second drug that may turn out to have an impact on sexuality is buproprion hydrochloride, which goes under the trade name Wellbutrin. Originally developed as an antidepressant by Burroughs Wellcome (it was introduced in 1985), Wellbutrin has recently been tested as a sexual stimulant at the Crenshaw Clinic in San Diego. Like quinelorane hydrochloride, Wellbutrin acts on the brain's dopamine system. Although its manufacturer says the drug has only a modest effect on sexuality, Crenshaw Clinic director of research James Goldberg finds early results more promising. Along with colleagues Theresa L. Crenshaw and Warren Stern, Goldberg gave 225 to 450 milligrams of Wellbutrin per day for twelve weeks to a group of sixty-eight men and women who were suffering from inhibited sexual desire, inhibited sexual excitement, or inhibited orgasm. By the end of the study period, 66 percent of the treated patients reported themselves much improved or very much improved. Wellbutrin, says Goldberg, "perks the sexual system back up. It's like putting a higher-octane gas in the system."

While some people may feel their sexuality to be declining as they get older, for others—especially some men—the problem can be quite the opposite: overexcitement, and its anticlimactic consequence, premature ejaculation. For these men there may be some good news on the horizon in the form of the blood pressure control drug Dibenzyline. According to a report in the *Journal of Sex and Marital Therapy*, when the Argentine psychiatrist Mario Luis Gospodinoff gave Dibenzyline to thirty-nine overstimulated patients for twenty-eight days, 60 percent of them calmed down to satisfactory—and satisfying—levels.

All this leads us to one happy conclusion: our pursuit of sexual pleasure need not be interrupted by anything as trivial as aging. Surprisingly enough, the same may soon turn out to be true of nature's underlying sexual goal—the making of babies. Most of us think that childbearing stops sometime in middle age; late middle age for men, somewhat earlier for most women. Many people, of course, wouldn't have it any other way. Once children are out the door it's the beginning of long-awaited freedom. For some there is simply no substitute for the joys of childbearing—I think of a male friend of mine who, in his mid-fifties and married for the third time, is now starting what amounts to his fourth generation of children.

For those diehard parents among you, there may soon be no need to sing the empty-house blues after the last kid heads for college. First of all, the last several years have seen the emergence of a truly amazing variety of treatments for the declining fertility rate that often accompanies getting older. Probably the best known of these is in-vitro fertilization, or IVF, in which a follicle—an egg and its surrounding cells—is taken from a woman's ovaries and fertilized in a laboratory, using her husband's sperm. The embryo is then implanted in the woman's uterus, and if all goes well, which it does about 14 percent of the time, a normal pregnancy and delivery are the happy result.

A newer alternative, for women with functioning fallopian tubes, is the GIFT procedure, which is similar to IVF except that once the eggs and sperm are mixed, they're immediately implanted in the woman's fallopian tubes for fertilization. Success rates now average 21 percent, although some doctors have reported success rates of 42 percent.

An older, simpler, and cheaper method is intrauterine insemination, in which the ovaries are stimulated with hormones and the husband's sperm is inseminated directly into the uterus. At the scientific frontier is cryopreservation: freezing fertilized eggs, or even early-stage embryos, for later implantation into the mother. At this writing, over four hundred fetuses have resulted from cryopreservation. There are some as yet unanswered ethical and legal questions (what happens, for example, if a mother decides later that she doesn't want her frozen embryo?). However, these medical advances continue.

Beyond such treatments for infertility, there are some tantalizing clues that our natural fertility span can be greatly increased. One clue came from experiments with the steroid DHEA, which, as we mentioned earlier, has aroused a great deal of scientific curiosity as a potential life extender. As a by-product of DHEA testing, some researchers have found that the steroid actually seems to extend the fertility span of lab mice. Richard Weindruch of the University of Wisconsin speculates that linking DHEA supplements to a low-calorie diet may ultimately do the same for women.

Yet if DHEA doesn't fulfill its promise as a fertility extender (human tests have not yet begun), there may be other ways to trick nature into letting us have babies later in life. At Hadassah University Hospital in Jerusalem, two women *without ovaries* gave birth to healthy babies after receiving donor embryos. The women had been given estrogen and progesterone supplements to replace those their ovaries would otherwise have produced. Although the women in the test group were all under forty, Hadassah project leader Daniel Navot thinks the procedure could work at any age. "Theoretically," he says, "with this type of treatment a ninety-year-old woman could have a baby." Richard Marrs, who founded the in-vitro fertilization clinic at the University of Southern California and is now director of the Institute for Reproductive Research in Los Angeles, agrees. "We believe that a woman who's sixty years old could be prepared hormonally to receive an embryo," he says. "Her chances of implantation of that embryo would probably be as good as in a twenty-five-year-old woman with normal ovarian function."

Whether or not an older woman could withstand the strains of pregnancy—to say nothing of the strains of raising a child—raises other questions, both practical and ethical. These complex questions will have to be sorted out by the medical community, by lawmakers, and, of course, by the women involved. But the fact remains: from the standpoint of pure science, it now seems at least theoretically possible to extend a woman's childbearing years well into what used to be considered old age.

There's another breakthrough looming ahead: male pregnancy. Yes, you heard right. This age-old dream of women (and maybe a few enlightened men, although I haven't come across any) is actually on the scientific drawing board. At the George Washington University Medical School in Washington, D.C., Cecil Jacobson has implanted chimpanzee embryos into the abdomens of male chimps. Startlingly enough, as many as 50 percent of the male chimps actually gave birth—by cesarean section, of course. Jacobson's work has inspired Robert Francoeur, a professor of biological sciences at Fairleigh Dickinson University in Madison, New Jersey, to predict that male pregnancy could actually be a reality before the turn of the twentieth century. As in the chimp experiments, Francoeur says, "the embryo could be implanted in the abdominal cavity, and the delivery accomplished by cesarean."

Male pregnancy aside, the message of all this is obvious: age is no barrier to the joys of love. You can enjoy the peaceful companionship of marriage, and you can keep sexual passion simmering. You may even be able to start family life all over again. And the happiest news of all is this: chances are that the more love in your life, the longer you'll live to enjoy love still more.

14

Looking
Good

Let's say you've been lost in the jungle for thirty years, deprived of all the staples of the information age—no television or radio, no popular magazines, no newspapers, no contact of any kind with civilization. One day, out of the blue, an emissary from the outside world—say, a game show host—alights from a helicopter into your clearing, cameras whirling. He shows you photographs of four contemporary show business stars—say, Raquel Welch, Joan Collins, Tina Turner, and Goldie Hawn. If you can guess their ages, the host says you'll win a free trip back to civilization. Well, I wouldn't start packing my bag if I were you, because the chances are you wouldn't even get close to the right answers. In every case, in fact, you'd probably guess that these stars were at least fifteen years younger than they actually are.

The point is that when longevity and aging are the issues, looks can be surprisingly and deeply important. First of all, as our guessing game suggests, appearance can be a powerful indicator of the difference between chronological age (the number of years we've actually lived) and biological age (the number of years we've *effectively* lived). In that respect, if we take proper care of ourselves, as the stars mentioned here have, many of us can look younger than we are. Looking younger can make us feel younger, and with feeling younger comes the bounce, the optimism, and the enthusiastic appreciation of life that can in itself slow down the clock of aging. In other words, looking young, feeling young, and staying young can all be part of a happy, self-preserving cycle—and it can start with a simple look in the mirror.

It turns out that if you're on the young side of forty, the mirror can actually be a crystal ball, giving you a sort of general forecast of how well your face might age. So take an inventory: if you have certain kinds of features, you may have a head start in the aging game. If not, you'll have some early indications as to areas that might need attention:

Skin color: Fair skin produces less pigment to ward off damaging ultraviolet radiation from the sun—perhaps the chief factor in producing skin that looks older than it should. Dark skin produces more pigment and thus more protection. Nevetheless, even black skin can burn.

Hair color: The darker and the oiler the better. But your hair needs protection too; sun and sea and chlorine can wreak havoc. Blondes and redheads tend to have drier, more delicate hair that is even more vulnerable to damage from the elements.

Eye color: Here again, dark is good. Lighter eye shades—blue, gray, hazel—often go with lighter, less sun-resistant skin.

Bone structure: Strong features—heavy brows, prominent cheek- and jawbones—provide more support for the skin, helping to keep it from sagging.

Lubrication: Dry skin with small pores creases faster and wrinkles more easily, especially around the eyes, than oily, large-pored skin.

If you're under forty or therabouts, this little inventory can help point out areas of future concern, and give clues to help you take preventive measures now. If you're over forty (and unflinchingly honest), your look in the mirror may reveal one or more of the common signs of age: a nose that's starting to droop, sagging breasts, drying lips, spidery veins, crow's-feet, thinning or graying hair, and wrinkles around the mouth (especially if you smoke).

In either case, there's no need to throw up your hands in dismay. You're no longer helpless against these surface signs of age. Every year sees the introduction of a host of new and better way to keep your face and body looking young, fresh, and vital. From the old-fashioned facial—which, you'll find, has undergone some very sophisticated improvements—to laser-assisted plastic surgery and even replacement skin, the last decade has produced what amounts to an arsenal of new weapons in the battle against the outward signs of aging. There are liposomes and liposuction, dermabrasion, tummy tucks, chemical peels, and suntan pills. There's even a whole new industry, which, under the name of *cosmeceuticals*, has merged paint-job cosmetics with new and vigorous age-fighting drugs. And, thanks in large part to the laser beam, the art of the cosmetic surgeon has been thoroughly revolutionized.

In the next chapter we'll go into the operating room and look over the shoulder of the plastic surgeon. For now, let's start off by taking a look at some of the ways that you can help preserve your good looks without calling on the cosmetic surgeon.

Before you start your anti-aging campaign, you'll want to know exactly what's going on with your skin. Let's go back, then, to the trusty mirror, which will tell you in an instant, and sometimes quite rudely, about skin that's starting to dry or sag, and about the appearance of crow's-feet and other nasty wrinkles. But even if the mirror's tale is still soft and sweet, you may want to know in advance about problems you might face down the road—especially if your skin is fair and delicate.

To get a better, more accurate forecast, you might want to try the "Krazy Glue skin scan," a new diagnostic and therapeutic technique invented by Dr. Albert Kligman, the dermatologist who gave us Retin-A. Kligman paints a glass slide with cyanoacrylate —the same substance that gives Krazy Glue its potent stickiness.

The glue-coated slide is pressed against the skin for about thirty seconds, then removed, taking with it (relatively painlessly) a fresh sample of the skin's outermost and most vulnerable layers, as well as contents of the follicles. When analyzed under a microscope, this skin sample can detect such potential problems as minute dry spots and tiny moles, providing an early warning and suggesting ways to head off potential problems before they're real. Recently, this follicular extraction technique has become available in various salons, using another, milder cyanoacrylate, which is painted on the skin and removed on a tape. (The trade name is Exolift.)

Once you've got a good idea as to the nature of the beast, you can take the proper precautions. Most experts agree that the chief enemy is the sun, whose ultraviolet rays dry and sear the skin, bringing on the wrinkles, blotches, and even cancers that are the signposts of accelerated aging. For today's active, sports-oriented lifestyle, though, staying indoors is an unappetizing alternative— I know I'm certainly unwilling to give up my vacations on the farm in South Africa, or my gardening, country walks, and scuba-diving expeditions.

Undoubtedly the best compromise between an outdoor lifestyle and a youthful, undamaged skin is the liberal use of a sunscreen. In the United States sunscreens are the only cosmetic products that can legally bill themselves as "anti-aging." Essentially, all sunscreens act to block the sun's ultraviolet rays, and the greater the blocking action, the higher the product's Sun Protection Factor, or SPF. Although the amount of SPF you need is controversial, most experts recommend a product with a rating of at least fifteen.

Actually, there is more than one type of ultraviolet radiation. It's recently been shown that one kind, known as UVB, causes burning, drying, and wrinkling; and another variety, UVA, penetrates more deeply, damaging the elastin and collagen that make up the skin's support system and ultimately causing it to sag. The same is true of infrared rays, which go even deeper. Yet most sunscreens—even those with SPFs in the forties and above—protect primarily against UVB rays. At this writing there's not even an SPF-type rating scale for UVAs, although one is in the works.

In the meantine, there are a few products that provide significant protection from UVAs. One excellent example is Photoplex, the only FDA-approved sunscreen to use the UVA-blocking ingredient butyl methoxydibenzoylmethane, better known as Parsol1789. But you won't find Photoplex shelved with the other sunscreens. You may have to ask for it at the prescription counter, where it's sold (no prescription necessary) for $10 to $13 per four-ounce bottle. To get protection from infrared rays, you'll need a sunscreen that contains either zinc oxide, titanium dioxide, or silicone dioxide. Still in the experimental stage is a powder containing tin oxide. Developed by Robert Rubin of the University of Miami, it has the added advantage of actually cooling the skin by as much as five degrees.

(I use Pre-Sun 29 on my face and neck. It has both UVA and UVB protection and is waterproof. Most important, it doesn't irritate the sensitive skin around my eyes. Neutrogena's SPF 15 sunblock is another one I use, because it also provides a respectable amount of protection from UVAs.)

One word of caution: Recent research at the Boston University School of Medicine indicates that constant use of sunscreen while outdoors may rob the body of vitamin D. You can avoid this potential problem by drinking milk—the other good source of the vitamin—or by taking a multivitamin preparation that contains 400 IUs of vitamin D, or by allowing yourself a little time in the sun with a low-SPF block, say a six, before you put your stronger block on. According to Boston University's Michael Holick, fifteen minutes a day of ultraviolet exposure on the cheeks is all you need to produce the body's vitamin D needs. (That, by the way, is for a Caucasian in Boston in the summertime. Adjust the time upward for darker skin, downward for more tropical latitudes.)

If you'd rather not take any chances at all with the sun but still want that tanned look, you might want to try one of the many creams, gels, or powders that will color your skin while you remain safely indoors. Most of these products use dihydroxyacetone, a substance that gives a hue that ranges from an almost natural bronze to a slightly suspicious orange, and in some cases (I'm one) a decidedly jaundiced yellow. Don't mistake these tanners for sunscreens, though—if you do go out in the sun, the tanning products provide protection against UVs or infrared rays for only the first few hours. That's because they don't stimulate the skin to produce melanins, the natural skin pigments which are the root of all suntans.

Melanins may be the key to the sunless suntan of the future. Researchers at the USDA Human Nutrition Research Center on Aging at Tufts have done laboratory experiments in which they increased the amount of melanin in certain kinds of skin cells, either by bathing the cells in a special solution or by adding a synthetic version of a messenger chemical called DAG. Preliminary safety tests of melanotan have been encouraging, so stick around —in the next few years, you may see a melanin stimulant, the most elegantly natural of all suntan products, on your drugstore shelves.

Sunscreens and tanning creams are not the only way to protect your skin from the aging effects of the sun. Your mother might have reached for the face cream, which in her day would have been little more than a simple moisturizer made by a cosmetics manufacturer. Today all that has changed. There seems to be no such thing as simple cosmetics anymore; increasingly the cream and lotion business is being taken over by products that claim to have all kinds of anti-aging properties. At the same time, drug companies are jostling for a share of the cosmetics counter, either by supplying chemicals to giants like Revlon and Mary Kay, or by creating products of their own, which they market under the eye-catching and hope-raising name of *cosmeceuticals.*

It's all very confusing, especially when the manufacturers couch their claims in scientific language that can range from the suspiciously vague to the downright unintelligible. What, for example, are "complex liposomes," and what do they really do? Are they better than simple liposomes, or just more complicated? What about the "procollagen molecule"? Is it really a miracle anti-ager, or is it just the flip side of the anti-collagen molecule? Like me, you may feel that you need a chemical dictionary just to go to the cosmetics counter.

Let's try to sort out some of these products, examining them class by class and attempting to take a hard look at the science behind the claims. First come the huge number of creams, lotions, and gels that collectively call themselves *moisturizers*. These range from your mother's cold cream to latter-day products that sound like they were dreamed up by rocket scientists: "procollagen," for example; and "mucopolysaccharides." Underneath all the polysyllables, however, is a fundamentally simple idea: since dry skin tends to age and wrinkle at a faster rate, anything that helps keep the skin moist may also help keep it looking young.

There's undoubtedly a lot of truth to this, and it may well explain why the English, Welsh, Scots, and Irish, who live in a climate that's damp and rainy, have such glorious complexions. The question is, short of moving to London, what's the most effective way to keep your skin moist? There are a number of relatively new products which claim that by coming up with sophisticated new combinations, they do a better job than less complicated creams or lotions. In some of these, the not-so-secret ingredient is collagen, a protein molecule that binds to water and holds it in place. This sounds helpful, even impressive. But the problem, most experts agree, is that the collagen molecule is much too large to penetrate the skin.

Then there's glycosphingolipid, the main ingredient in a product called Glycel, which, according to its manufacturers, "oversees the retention of moisture and improvement in elasticity of the skin." Glycel was actually promoted for a time by famed heart transplant surgeon Christiaan Barnard, who billed it as an anti-aging product—until the FDA stepped in, since there has been little scientific evidence that glycosphingolipid does much of anything. The FDA eventually sent letters to twenty-three manufacturers, warning them to limit their claims so that the product sounded less like a drug and more like a cosmetic.

There is also a prescription moisturizer available called Lac Hydrin 12 percent, which contains lactic acid and supposedly penetrates the skin. I first heard about it four years ago, through a doctor I go to occasionally. I had just started using Retin-A, and my skin had become very red and sore. Almost immediately after I began using Lac Hydrin, the redness and soreness lessened markedly. I have continued using it ever since (all over my body, in fact), and have found that apart from helping soothe and heal the initial effects of Retin-A, it also works very well for sunburn.

The truth seems to be that until science comes up with something legitimately better, the best moisturizers may be among those that have been around the longest. One of these is the clear gel extracted from the leaves of the aloe vera plant, a relative of the lily. The gel is mostly water (about 96 percent), held together by the leaves' natural mucilage, or fiber. It is one of the plants I remember my grandmother using. Another moisturizer is lanolin, which has been used for years in face creams and lotions. But the grand champ, believe it or not, may still be petrolatum, as in good old Vaseline. Most moisturizers have to be used daily to have an effect, according to the dermatologist Arthur Balin of Philadelphia. But Vaseline, which coats the skin and slows down the process of evaporation that can leave it dry and vulnerable, helps keep the skin moist for as long as two weeks after each application. "Vaseline is the best therapeutic moisturizer around," Balin says. "No one has to spend as much money as they do now on cosmetics." Maybe he is right. A friend of mine, the dress designer Mary McFadden, who has wonderful translucent white skin, is a firm believer in Vaseline.

Whether you opt for plain old Vaseline or for an up-to-the-minute moisturizer, keeping the skin wet is certainly a tried and true strategy for maintaining a youthful look. Another is to keep the skin firm. There are a number of products in a number of forms—masks, creams, ampoules—that claim to firm and tone the skin, implying that this will help reduce wrinkling and give the skin a youthful look. While there's no proof that the active ingredients in any of these products (yeasts, or plant or animal protein) can strengthen skin collagen so as to provide long-lasting firming, they can cause a temporary effect by mildly irritating the skin or slightly dilating the underlying blood vessels. Their greatest benefit, according to the dermatologist Diane Baker of Portland, Oregon, may lie in the fact that "they tend to be excellent moisturizers."

Another, more recent entrant you might want to consider trying is *exfoliating*. This technique is designed to stimulate the natural process by which old, dry skin on the surface is replaced by fresh cells migrating up from deeper in the skin. You can encourage some degree of exfoliation simply by scrubbing your skin briskly with a washcloth.

If you want something a little more high-tech, you might try a cell renewal enhancer. These range from Buf-Pufs, slightly abrasive sponges with or without an added deep cleanser, to Chanel's Skin Regeneration Treatment, an elaborate kit that sells for about $110. Basically, the principle is the same: get rid of the dry surface skin and speed up the development of the fresh young skin underneath. A caution: if used too vigorously, mechanical cell renewal enhancers like Buf-Pufs can rough up the skin too much, making it more vulnerable to the enviroment; while the chemical versions (other examples besides Chanel's are Elizabeth Arden's Millenium and Lancôme's Force Vital de Nuit Tissue Firming Cream) can irritate the skin. Still, when used according to directions, these cell renewal enhancers can help produce a smoother, more youthful-looking skin.

More controversial are a pair of relatively new entrants on the cosmeceutical scene: liposomes and thymus extracts. Liposomes are synthetic fats, the molecular structure of which is virtually identical to that of skin cell membranes. This is supposed to give them, so the cosmetics manufacturers claim, extra penetrating power, making them ideal delivery vehicles for other skin-renewing chemicals. Expert opinion is divided as to whether or not liposomes really do penetrate the skin. Thymus extracts, taken from the thymus glands of animals, are said to stimulate cell renewal. In lab tests at Tufts University the extracts made cells more proliferative in culture dishes. But the researchers, led by Barbara Gilchrest, are quick to point out that the skin is not a culture dish, and what happens in the laboratory may not happen in the skin of a human face.

Liposomes and thymus extracts are still being evaluated, both in the laboratory and in the crucible of the marketplace. But the product that has everyone buzzing these days (and certainly my favorite) is Retin-A. Its active ingredient is retinoic acid, a potent derivative of vitamin A. Retin-A was approved in 1971 as a prescription drug against acne. As it came into widespread use, though, it started to become apparent that Retin-A produced some unexpected and delightful rewards. Over the next several years Retin-A's developer, Albert Kligman, began receiving enthusiastic reports from patients about the product's unanticipated but highly desirable side effects: fading spots, vanishing wrinkles, and rosy, youthful-looking skin. For the next ten years, Kligman and a host of other researchers did exhaustive clinical trials, and came to a virtually unanimous conclusion: Retin-A did appear to retard or even reverse the effects of sun-inducing aging.

Retin-A is not yet approved by the FDA as an anti-aging ingredient, and you probably won't see it popping up in over-the-counter cosmetics even if approval is obtained. The only way to get it is as a prescription drug against acne. If the early signs are any indication, though, many doctors are willing to prescribe it as a skin-smoother and a wrinkle-eraser. In fact, during the twelve months following publication of results of clinical trials in 1988, sales of Retin-A almost quadrupled.

Although I have found it every bit as good as it's supposed to be, a few notes of caution are in order. First of all, Retin-A is an extremely potent drug, and when first used it can cause peeling and reddening of the skin that can last many weeks, depending on the amount of sun damage you have. Its long-term effects, especially in older users, are not yet fully known. I would strongly recommend that you use it under the supervision of a dermatologist. I have found, after five years of careful experimentation on my own skin, that I get the best results by using a high-strength form of Retin-A (0.1 percent) on the center, relatively oily part of my face—chin, nose, and forehead—and a relatively weak form (0.005 percent) around my eyes and on my cheeks and neck.

"You don't just hand somebody a tube of it," says Kligman. "The average person will press out the same amount they use for brushing their teeth, which is about eight times too much." (The recommended amount is a dab about the size of a small pea to be spread evenly about the entire face.) You also need to use it on totally dry skin. A friend of mine claimed it was doing nothing for her. After questioning her about exactly how she used it, I found out she was washing her face, putting on her normal night cream, and *then* applying Retin-A. I have found that the best way to ensure that my skin is completely dry is to wash my face, then wait a half hour or so before applying it.

Another note of caution: if you use Retin-A too close to the corners of your mouth, it can cause a sore or ulcer. This goes away quickly with the application of Synalar or similar creams available over the counter. A good way to prevent its happening is to put a minuscule dot of Synalar on the corners of your mouth before applying Retin-A. The drug also interferes with the skin's natural protection against UVAs (I can vouch for this), so experts are recommending either using a sunscreen or staying out of the sun entirely.

There is another serious potential danger in using Retin-A, and that is overuse or abuse. Another friend of mine who uses Retin-A had suffered severe acne as a teenager and was very sensitive about her skin. Although she had used Retin-A safely (under the supervision of her doctor) for a while and was benefiting from it, one day a pimple appeared on her cheek. She was so upset about the pimple that she used her Retin-A several times that day and the next. The result was a nasty sore on her cheek, which took months to heal.

If you stop using Retin-A, wrinkles and blotches may return.

When I first started using it, I applied it every night, but now, to maintain its effects, I use it three times a week, alternating it with a cream containing Nayad, another promising newcomer. I don't use Retin-A if I'm going to be in the sun, and I always use a sunscreen, winter and summer. If I know I will be in the sun for any length of time, I take a hat along too.

In the rush to cash in on all the publicity surrounding Retin-A, a number of cosmetics manufacturers have been calling attention to products that already contain other derivatives of vitamin A— retinyl acetate, for example, and retinyl palmitate. But there's no real evidence that these distant relatives have the same effect as Retin-A. "It's like comparing diamonds to coal," says the New York City dermatologist Ronald Sherman.

In the end, once the cautions are duly noted, most dermatologists remain enthusiastic about Retin-A. "There isn't anything being studied in dermatology that's more exciting," says Ortho Pharmaceutical director of research George Thorne, M.D. "Provided the drug is used under the supervision of a dermatologist," says Tulane University Medical School professor Nia Terazakis, "there's no question that better skin can result."

Even newer than Retin-A—and, in the minds of some experts, perhaps equally promising—is Nayad. Technically beta glucan, Nayad is an active chemical taken from the cell walls of certain kinds of yeast. Its manufacturer, the small West Coast biochemical firm ImmuDyne, says it stimulates Langerhans cells, immune system cells embedded in the skin, which are vulnerable to damage from the sun and from aging in general. The Langerhans cells help activate other immune cells, macrophages, which give orders to produce collagen and elastin—the connective tissues that keep skin from sagging and wrinkling. Although at this writing the beneficial effects of Nayad have yet to be confirmed by an independent study, the dermatologist Peter Pugliese, who has tested the substance for ImmuDyne, found it at least 50 percent as effective as Retin-A in reducing wrinkles in mice. If you can't wait for the results of further tests, Nayad is available by mail from

Louise Bianco Skin Care in Van Nuys, California. Newer versions of Nayad are Immunage UV Defense Hand and Body Lotion (Elizabeth Arden) and DeJoria (John Paul Mitchell), sold in department stores and beauty salons throughout the world. More Nayad products from other manufacturers are sure to follow. (Remember to check the amount of Nayad in whatever product you settle on—that's what counts.)

Most of these anti-aging tactics, from simple sunscreens and moisturizers to space-age products like Nayad, are in the do-it-yourself category—things you can do at home in the privacy of your bedroom or bathroom. If you're willing to take an occasional trip to the beauty salon or even to the doctor's office, a brave new world of ultra-tech treatments opens up for you.

Let's start with the facial, which used to be little more than a deep cleaning of the pores (still, according to the experts, the most important benefit of this procedure), followed by a stimulating massage. No more. Thanks to the explosion of new products and techniques, and in particular to the advent of chain department store facial salons sponsored by the likes of Lancôme, Adrien Arpel, Clarins, and Estée Lauder, during the course of a facial you can now get exfoliated, rebalanced, hydrated, recharged, and even "effleuraged"—a state-of-the-art massage technique that borrows heavily from Japanese shiatsu. All this can be had for prices that can range from as little as $20 to as much as $175.

If you're interested in a more thorough makeover, or in undoing a summer's worth of sun damage, you might want to consider a chemical peel. This basically means applying a chemical, such as phenol, that strips away the top layer of skin, exposing the fresh and presumably rosy skin underneath. (I have tried this, and it really works, but be prepared to take three or four weeks to recover entirely.) Lightweight versions of the chemical peel, which often use resorcinol, are available at beauty salons. Heavier-duty peels, using substances like trichloroacetic acid (TCA), can be done only by dermatologists. A reminder: peels can leave the new skin feeling raw and sensitive for months. They can also produce temporary discoloration and in some cases, even permament scarring if the skin fails to heal properly. Some dermatologists are now trying to head off these problems by taking the skin off in gradual stages over a period of several months. In any case, chemical peels are obviously not to be taken casually.

An equally radical treatment, available only from dermatologists, is dermabrasion. In this case the doctor sprays a freezing solution on the skin, then holds it taut as he scrapes off the outer layer with a diamond-coated instrument. As with heavy chemical peels, the new skin is extremely tender and easily irritated, and should not be exposed to the sun during the healing period, which can take several months. If you're willing to put up with this inconvenience, dermabrasion can remove acne scars, brown spots, and even some shallow wrinkles.

A more recent and somewhat gentler tool in the dermatologist's closet is a technique called *microlipoinjection.* Here the doctor uses a hypodermic needle to draw small amounts of fat from elsewhere in the body—the hips, say, or the abdomen—and then injects the fat into the facial skin, where it can fill out wrinkles or hollow cheekbones. As an alternative to fat, some dermatologists use collagen. However, the effects of collagen last only a few months and many people are allergic to it. Silicone and fibrel, a collagen-stimulating compound composed of the patient's blood, gelatin, and a clotting agent, are in the experimental stages, although some dermatologists are now using silicone.

But microlipoinjection is iffy; in some people, the injections fail to take, and the fat shrivels into scar tissue. In others, all goes well and the improvement in appearance can last up to three years. If you're interested, you should know that the procedure has been performed in this country for only a few years, so make sure your dermatologist or cosmetic surgeon has some experience with it. By the way, almost all the strategies we've talked about, including Retin-A, peels, dermabrasion, and injections of collagen, silicone, or fat, can work just as well on your lips as on your facial skin.

You may be wondering if, instead of working from the outside in with creams, facials, peels, and the like, it might be possible to keep your skin looking young by working from the inside out. Well, there are a host of pills and potions reputed to do just that, some of which have been around for a while, others that are brand new, and still others that are still in the experimental stage.

The best known of these are vitamins A and E. In the case of vitamin A, the story is a bit disappointing, which seems especially unfortunate in that A has long been held to be the "skin vitamin." Sorry, says clinical dermatology professor Paul Lazar of Northwestern University Medical School in Chicago, but "no supplements are especially helpful to the skin"—including vitamin A. In fact, Lazar warns, in excessive amounts—more than three times the RDA of 5,000 IUs—vitamin A can be poisonous. "In addition to causing dry skin and cracked lips, brittle nails and loss of hair," he cautions, "vitamin A poisoning can result in bone pain, arthritic changes, disturbed menstrual cycles, tooth and eye problems, and depressed thyroid functions." The only vitamin A relative that's been shown to help the skin is Retin-A, and you certainly wouldn't want to eat that.

Vitamin E and other antioxidants may eventually be a better bet. Because there's so much evidence that vitamin E is beneficial in so many ways—some of which we've discussed in earlier chapters—many health-conscious people think of E as not only an immune-booster, but a skin-preserver. There is one theory that holds that aging in skin, and wrinkles in particular, are caused by damage from free radicals, and since vitamin E is an antioxidant, it may prevent some of that damage. Although there's no real evidence that vitamin E taken orally will have any effect on overall skin structure, hope remains, even among cautious experts. "Antioxidants," says Warwick Morison, associate professor of clinical dermatology at Johns Hopkins University in Baltimore, "offer the greatest possibility for development of an oral sunscreen"—and thus an anti-aging pill for the skin. (One way in which Vitamin E really works is for minor burns. I always keep a bottle of 1,000 IU capsules handy in the kitchen. I have saved myself blistering from stove burns on many occasions. Simply prick a capsule, squeeze out a liberal amount on the burn, and you will find that it alleviates the pain almost immediately.)

To prevent sun damage before it occurs, researchers at the University of Arizona in Tucson are busy developing what might be the dream of all unredeemed indoorsmen: a suntan pill. The chemistry professor Victor Hruby and the biology professor Mac Hadley were using an analogue derived from the hormone MSH, which stimulates the pituitary gland to produce skin pigment cells, as a test for skin cancer. When they found that the MSH analogue was nontoxic, even when taken internally, they realized that the substance was a strong candidate for a tanning pill. So far they've tested it on animals and on human skin cells in culture, and have found that MSH can, under lab conditions, produce a tan that lasts for weeks or even months. At this writing, tests on humans are under way, and the initial studies show that long-term skin darkening does, indeed, occur.

If you can get a suntan from a pill, can you also wipe out wrinkles and make the skin look youthful just by swallowing a tablet or capsule? Not yet, but that doesn't mean that no one's trying. A number of researchers are experimenting with oral retinoids—in other words, Retin-A in a pill. Among those who seem to be furthest along is Harry Miller of Daltex Medical Science in West Orange, New Jersey. Miller has tested his oral retinoid for two years on one hundred men and women in the United States and Germany, and has found that the drug helped shrink enlarged pores, improve skin elasticity, and clear up pimples, scaly redness, and even the "liver spots" that sometimes appear with age. Retin-A inventor Albert Kligman is impressed. "Daily dosages," he says, "can moderate or reverse a number of these problems with no side effects."

If testing continues to go well, you can look for retinoid pills to hit the market with an enormous splash by about 1995. On the slightly more distant horizon, watch for pills or potions based on human growth hormone (hGH). Since hGH seems to hold great promise as a general anti-aging substance, we'll have much more to say about it later in the book. For now, let's just note one of its many results from human testing: taken over a period of six months, hGH made skin thicker, rosier, and in general more youthful-looking. It may well be that products based on human growth hormone will become the anti-aging skin treatments of the future.

Let's say you've just been introduced to someone, and you're trying to guess that person's age. After you scan his or her face for crow's-feet or frown lines, what do you check next? Probably the hair. Along with the face, the hair is the feature that's among the most vulnerable to aging—as in *gray*. The vast majority of us (me included) don't like to see gray pop up in our hair. We'll go to almost any lengths to hide those streaks of gray, and so the hair-dye industry continues to be a multibillion-dollar business.

These dyes come in a truly bewildering variety of stains, rinses, semipermanent and permanent colors. Unfortunately, there are some disturbing suggestions that some of these products could possibly be dangerous for some people. Many permanent hair dyes contain a class of chemicals called aromatic amines, a small amount of which can be absorbed by the scalp. Most people's systems are capable of breaking down these chemicals and rendering them harmless. But in some people—perhaps as many as 40 percent—that breakdown process occurs more slowly. These people may be at higher risk of developing systemic lupus erythematosus, an autoimmune disorder that can bring on aches, fever, skin lesions, and in some cases death.

The hair dye–lupus link is very controversial. Representatives of the dye industry point out that aromatic amines are a huge chemical family, one of the members of which is aspirin. A great deal more research is needed, they say, before any kind of scientific indictment can be brought against the amines in hair dye. For the most part, scientists agree. Brian Strom, a professor of medicine and pharmacology at the University of Pennsylvania, is now conducting a five-year study of six hundred people—two hundred lupus patients and four hundred controls—to see if the hair-dye connection stands. In the meantime, the epidemiologist Lambertina Freni, formerly of the U.S. Centers for Disease Control in Atlanta, suggests that anyone with a family history of connective tissue disease "hold off on using hair dyes until more is known."

For most of us, though, dyes continue to be relatively safe. A few, especially permanent and semipermanent colors, can cause allergic reactions. It's important that you follow the manufacturer's instructions and test a small amount behind the ear or in the crook of the elbow before using dyes on your scalp. Others can be messy, expensive, or hard on the hair itself. Still, if your main concern is hiding the gray, most of them will do the job. I recommend that if you're contemplating anything major, you go to a good hairdresser. If you are blond, try streaking instead of a full bleach. You have to have it retouched only every two months instead of every two weeks, and it's much kinder to your hair.

If you're already a blonde or want to disguise the gray by going blond, you may soon have a new ally: the laser beam. Researchers at Clairol have been working on a finely modulated laser that breaks down pigments in the hair fibers, bleaching the hair blond in a matter of seconds. Because the laser light is competely absorbed by the pigment, there's no damage to the hair. The ultimate goal? Connecting the laser to a comb with fiber-optic teeth so that a woman can go blond simply by combing her hair. "It sounds pretty far out," says the product's co-inventor John Menkart, "but it could happen in a few years."

While almost all of us are going to have to deal with graying hair, very few women have to worry about going bald. Although some men like and even cultivate the Yul Brynner look, for most of them hair loss is one of the most obvious and unpleasant aspects of aging. Until recently, hair growth formulas occupied the same unsavory pharmacological niche as snake oil and youth potions—although they all made exuberant claims, none of them really worked. Over the past ten years, though, that picture has changed to some degree, so that now there's even a prescription hair-growing formula that's approved by the FDA.

That product is Rogaine, the key ingredient of which is minoxidil, a drug used for treating high blood pressure. It's been documented by lab testing that minoxidil really can grown hair—at least on the crown of the head. But critics note that it worked for only about a quarter of the test subjects, and even then the concentrations of minoxidil in the laboratory version were about twice as high (3 to 5 percent) as in Rogaine. Still, nearly everyone agrees that it's better than nothing.

These days, the search for something better is beginning to amount to a race, with laboratories across the United States and in Europe scrambling to be first with the next generation of effective hair growers. The Upjohn Company, the makers of Rogaine, are testing what they hope will be an improved version of their product, in which minoxidil is mixed with retinoic acid, in the hope of giving it more penetrating power and more oomph. Another candidate is diazoxide, which, like minoxidil, is a blood pressure drug. Tests have so far shown that it can grow hair in 10 to 60 percent of bald men, and that it can help many others retain their hair they have. Then there's omexin, which promotes blood vessel growth and which has just been tested at New York University. There's also cyoctol, an anti-androgen being developed by Chantal and tested at UCLA.

All these substances are essentially drugs intended for some other purpose that incidentally seem to help some men grow hair. But the real breakthrough will come when science deciphers the mechanics of the balding process itself. At this point, no one fully knows what happens to make some men go bald while others remain bushy-headed throughout life. At the University of Miami School of Medicine, the dermatology research scientist Marty Sawaya and her colleagues have identified several small proteins that may be implicated in the balding process and are now trying to formulate a drug that could correct imbalances among the proteins. Meanwhile, Arthur Bertolino of New York University is looking at the genetics of balding, trying to learn how to switch off the genes that cause hair loss while switching on those that keep hair growing.

These newer approaches could ultimately lead to the dream product: a pill or lotion that reverses balding entirely. This sort of tonic would then take a special place in the growing armory of anti-aging products and techniques that are helping us win the battle of the mirror.

Then there are the fingernails. While most men take their nails for granted, for women they are important, especially since the first telltale signs of aging, split, brittle nails, can show up as early as the thirties in women but don't normally appear until the fifties in men.

Sometimes changes in nail color, shape, or texture can be a sign of a serious medical condition. Clubbing, when nails become very rounded and bluish, can be a sign of chronic lung and heart disease, and pale nails can be a sign of anemia. Ridges indicate a propensity for the skin condition psoriasis, according to David Orentreich, M.D., an assistant clinical professor of dermatology at Mount Sinai Medical School in New York. Texture changes such as ridging and thinning are due to changes in the nail protein keratin, which becomes weaker and thinner with age. Orentreich recommends applying a sunscreen to the whole nail area to slow the damage. He also debunks the notion that eating gelatin will do anything to strengthen nails. Clinical data, he says, suggest that methionine, an amino acid, might strengthen nails as well as vitamin D. However, more research is needed before either can be prescribed.

My friend Josephine, who does the manicures for many of the beautiful hands and nails you see in high-fashion magazines, suggests the following:

1. Always file your nails in one direction to avoid splitting.
2. Apply hand cream often. Keep a bottle in the office, by your bedside, and in your purse. Get into the habit of using it four to five times a day.
3. Between manicures, take your polish off for at least twelve hours. This allows your nails to breathe.
4. After you shower or bathe, push the cuticle back gently. It's softest at this time.
5. Always use a base coat. It protects your nails and helps prevent staining.
6. Carry the paper from a tea bag and some Krazy Glue in your purse; that way you can repair a broken or split nail in seconds. Apply the tea-bag paper to the damaged nail using a few drops of Krazy Glue. Let dry. Now buff the nail until the suface is smooth. Add another coat of glue. Allow to dry, buff again, and polish.

While nails are important mostly to women, teeth are a concern to almost everyone. Those with really serious discolorations or misshapen teeth may have to go the cosmetic-dentistry route. There are plenty of products and dental services to check out before you reach that point. Which procedure you select depends on how stained your teeth are and how much you are willing to spend. Lightening and brightening can cost as much as $2,000 to $3,000 or as little as $2.00.

Here are some of the options:

1. **Fluoride toothpaste.** Mild abrasive, good for superficial stains. To preserve enamel use a pea-size amount twice a day.
2. **Tartar-control toothpaste.** Mild abrasive, good for superficial stains that cling to plaque and tartar. Used twice a day, it can help control tartar buildup.
3. **Tooth polishes.** Abrasives which remove mild food and tobacco stains. Should be used twice daily. Caution: some

experts think they are too strong and could damage the enamel.

4. **Epismile.** A mild abrasive with fluoride and a whitener which removes mild food and tobacco stains. Use twice a day. Contains nonabrasive baking soda.

5. **Hydrogen peroxide and baking soda.** Baking soda polishes without abrading enamel; diluted peroxide is an antiplaque agent and tooth whitener. Use once a day. Keep in separate covered jars, dip toothbrush into a fifty-fifty solution of 3 percent peroxide and water. Mix in baking soda, and brush as usual. Does not taste great.

6. **Professional cleaning.** By far the best. The dental hygienist removes tartar manually or with ultrasound, then polishes teeth with a paste to remove hard stains or calcification. Removes stubborn food and tobacco stains. Should be done two or three times a year. Much more thorough than everyday brushing. Can erase discoloration caused by coffee, tea, or red wine.

7. **Bleaching.** The patient is fitted by the dentist with a retainer-like arch containing a mild bleaching solution. The bleach-filled arch is worn ten to twelve hours a day and the solution is changed about every one and a half hours. Removes moderate yellow to brown stains linked to aging and diet. Tetracycline and fluoride stains are more difficult, and bonded teeth or teeth that have had a root canal operation may be a problem. Normal staining fades in three to five days; deeper stains take up to two weeks. Must maintain with regular office checkups and proper dental hygiene.

8. **In-office bleaching.** Bleach is applied to teeth, then activated by a special light. Three to five sessions are needed to lighten teeth significantly. Produces the same results as doing it at home, only it's less messy. Maintenance similar to that of #7. Back teeth are not usually done because of the difficulty in isolating them.

Many of the most exciting of these new techniques are not available at cosmetic counters, in drugstores, or even in dermatologists' offices. They are in the hands of the people who, late in this century, have become the high priests and priestesses of the anti-aging movement: the cosmetic surgeons.

15

The New Plastic Surgery

If you had gone to a cosmetic surgeon during the Dark Ages—
say, fifteen or twenty years ago—you would have found that what
he did was a lot like tailoring. The key words were *trim* and *tighten:*
the surgeon lifted the skin from your face, or your belly, or your
thighs, cut away the excess, then stretched the remaining skin
tightly and sewed it back in place—much as a tailor would take
in the waist on a pair of pants. Today all that has changed. There's
more than one way to lift a face, trim a nose, or tuck a tummy,
and the contemporary cosmetic surgeons have become not only
physicians and craftsmen, but space-age scientists, with a bevy of
avant-garde, high-tech tools and techniques at their disposal.

The nose job is the perfect example. It used to be that having
your nose redone meant a less-than-delicate procedure from which
you emerged looking as if you'd just had an argument with Mike
Tyson: eyes black and blue, face swollen almost beyond recogni-
tion. It usually took weeks in hiding before you could venture out
to show off your new nose—which, by the way, inevitably looked
as if it had been cloned from Doris Day's. "The operation that

was done through the 1960s removed a considerable amount of structural tissue," says Dr. Norman Pastorek, a New York facial surgeon. "The result, though it looked good, could easily be identified as an operated-on nose."

Today surgeons have learned to take away much less tissue. "We try to reshape rather than remove," says Pastorek. "The goal today is to make the patient look normal, so that when someone looks at his or her face, they don't see just a nose." The modern nose job takes forty-five minutes in a doctor's office under a local anesthetic. Large doses of vitamins C and K help prevent bleeding and bruising, so you can go back to work in just a week, and without looking like a raccoon. Best of all, there's no mallet—the surgeon uses a tiny, razor-like instrument to make minute incisions in the bone.

While some of us are eager to have our noses remodeled, others are more concerned about their breasts. Since the procedures were introduced in the 1960s, some two million women have gone to the plastic surgeon (and to a lot of just plain surgeons with their eyes on saving money) for breast implants. Cosmetically, this surgery can be an absolute disaster, especially when it is performed by a surgeon without the proper training and experience. I know because I've seen thousands of bad breast jobs among the pictures of hopeful centerfolds submitted to *Penthouse*. I have seen nipples that point in opposite directions, one breast noticeably larger than the other, and breasts that looked like coconut halves hastily inserted under the skin. On the other hand, I have also seen breasts that look terrific and totally natural. Invariably, these were done by qualified cosmetic surgeons.

Be aware, though, that breast implants carry with them some important health concerns, important enough to generate a movement to ban them entirely. One is capsular contracture, an often painful condition caused by internal scar tissue forming around the implant. Over time, the scar tissue contracts, hardening and sometimes deforming the implant. The scar tissue can be removed by surgical and nonsurgical means, but it can't be prevented from recurring. A new kind of silicone implant with a textured surface is reported to reduce the risk of capsular contracture.

There is another potential problem. Although evidence is by no means conclusive, there are some indications that in certain sensitive people, the silicone in breast implants may bring on an autoimmune disorder called scleroderma, a connective tissue disease that can cause the skin to tighten and harden, and can even affect the vital organs. Researchers at the University of Texas Medical Branch at Galveston are now hard at work developing a test to help determine in advance which women might be susceptible. "We view this as an allergic reaction," says the UT-Galveston surgery professor John Heggers. "Not everyone will respond adversely to silicone."

It may turn out that scleroderma and other allergic reactions to silicone are extremely rare. But the remaining health problem is something that could potentially concern the one out of every nine women who is in danger of developing breast cancer. There's some evidence, although it's not yet conclusive, that leakage of silicone or polyurethane may be linked to increased risk of breast cancer. At the same time, implants may make existing cancers harder to find. The trouble is that X rays can't penetrate silicone implants, so that developing cancers may not be detected by X-ray mammography until they are already in an advanced and far more dangerous stage. If you're considering breast implants, you may want to have a mammogram beforehand—this will at least help reveal any existing cancer before it's covered up by the implant.

The problem won't really be solved, though, until there's either a reliable implant that's also transparent to X rays or a mammography technique that can get around or through the implant to the tissue underneath. It's heartening to know that considerable progress is being made on both fronts. Some experts are now doubling the number of X-ray views they take during a mammography, enabling them to see around the implant. Others are using the Eklund, or displacement, method, in which the X-ray technician pulls the breast tissue away from the implant, then flattens the implant against the chest with a device that looks like a paddle. In as many as 50 percent of patients, this technique significantly improves the view—and thus increases the chances of catching a developing cancer.

Even the Eklund method isn't foolproof, though. Many experts think the best solution will be implants that act like windows for X rays instead of walls. One possibility is an implant in which a thin layer of silicone envelops a center made from a combination of peanut and sunflower oils. This implant, currently being tested at Washington University in St. Louis, is more transparent to X rays than are implants with higher silicone contents. So far there have been no adverse or allergic reactions to these implants, and researchers estimate that if tests in humans go well, these vegetable oil implants could be available to the public as early as 1992.

In the meantime, the FDA is paying increasing attention to breast implants. In 1991, the agency passed a regulation requiring all implant manufacturers to inform doctors of three possible health risks: infection, hardening of breast tissue, and the shielding of possible tumors. At this writing, makers of silicone gel and saline implants must submit data on the safety and efficacy of their products to the FDA or remove those products from the market. Bristol Myers Squibb Company has already withdrawn Surgitek, its polyurethane implant, and in July 1991 the FDA seized eight hundred unapproved implants made by Bioplasty, Inc.

No one has yet suggested pumping up drooping facial skin with vegetable oil, but over the last few years the old-fashioned face-lift has undergone what amounts to a revolution. In the old days, if you wanted to have the bags under your eyes removed, the surgeon had to cut into the skin to do it, leaving you with bruises. Now the knife has given way to the heater, so that the fatty bags can actually be melted away. Surgeons simply peel the skin of the lower eyelid down, then heat the fatty skin underneath with an electrically heated probe. In two to three seconds, the fat is evaporated. No scarring, no postoperative droop, and no hollow, ghostly look.

There's also a new procedure that helps avoid one of the most common causes of face-lift failure: postoperative sagging. The culprit here is often the buccal fat pad, the subcutaneous fat that makes kids look apple-cheeked but can droop as we get older, giving us a jowly look. The buccal pad is usually left in after a face-lift, and even though the skin above it is now tight, the pad underneath can still slip and sag. But a number of physicians now make a tiny incision inside the cheek and then use tweezers to gently lift the buccal pad out. This takes about five minutes, then the rest of the lift is performed.

The key tool in this procedure, as in most cosmetic surgery, has traditionally been the scalpel. But the knife is giving way to a much more elegant device: the laser. Argon lasers generate an intense blue-green light that selectively heats up the red pigment in the blood, so it can be used to treat blood-related blotches like port wine stains and spider and varicose veins. Tunable dye lasers emit a yellow light that can remove birthmarks even from children or people with very fair skin. And carbon dioxide lasers can do deep peels and dermabrasion without chemicals. (For more information on laser-assisted cosmetic surgery, and for recommendations of surgeons in your area who practice it, send a stamped, self-addressed envelope to the American Society for Laser Medicine and Surgery, 2404 Stewart Square, Wausau, Wisconsin 54401. Recommended surgeons are all members of the society.)

While many surgeons have learned to work with lasers at the level of the skin, others are taking facial surgery much deeper—right down to the bone. These "facial architects" want to attack skin aging where it often begins, in the skeleton. "The bones in the face appear to shrink a bit with age," explains Edward Terino, director of the Plastic Surgery Institute of Southern California. "We know the jawbone diminishes to a considerable degree, and we believe the soft tissues over the cheekbones may shrink in volume. Just pulling the skin tight—as we do in a face-lift—doesn't solve the underlying problem."

Terino and other plastic surgeons are actually shoring up the structure of the face, using custom-sculpted implants made of plastic. The implants themselves have been around since the sixties, but the early models often gave people's faces a thin, angular Abraham Lincoln look that made them appear older. Today, Terino and his colleagues have so refined the plastic implant that they've become works of art in their own right. Terino used banjo-shaped Silastic silicone implants, which he inserts smack against the cheekbones, where they fit so snugly that they don't even need temporary stitching to hold them in place. The operation takes less than an hour and, at about $2,000 to $3,000, is about one-third the cost of the average face-lift. Recovery time is two to three weeks before swelling and bruising are gone, and about six months for total recovery. This is about the same as, or even a bit shorter than, conventional face-lifts. Although some surgeons have had trouble getting both cheeks to look identical, Terino says his newest implants are so carefully molded that this problem should be greatly reduced.

While Terino works to shore up the cheekbones from above, the Los Angeles plastic surgeon William J. Binder goes even deeper. Binder, a clinical faculty member of surgery at UCLA, has developed an implant that goes not on the cheekbone, but *under* it. This *submalar* implant—like Terino's, it's made of silicone Silastic—actually lifts up the entire middle third of the face, filling in hollow cheeks and reducing folds and lines around the mouth. "Think of it as scaffolding," says Binder, "which can help prop up sagging skin." The operation, which at this writing is being performed by as many as 1,500 surgeons across the country, takes about forty minutes at the doctor's office, and costs $2,500 to $4,000. Postoperative swelling lasts for a few weeks. Binder, who has been performing the operation for more than nine years, reports no major complications. He has also developed a computer program that he uses to "take the guesswork out of facial reconstruction" after injury to the face. The patient's injuries are scanned and fed into a computer, which generates a three-dimensional image that allows Binder to custom-tailor each implant in increments of one-eighth of a millimeter. "These Silastic parts will be perfect replacements for people who've had traumatic facial injuries," says Binder. He's now adapting the system to create custom parts for cosmetic surgery.

If Terino and Binder have made the cheekbones their special province, Harry Mittelman's territory is the jaw. Mittelman, an associate clinical professor of facial plastic surgery at Stanford University, has found that as we get older, most of us develop an indentation above the sides of the chin. It's that groove which can give us double chins, sagging skin, and a generally jowly look. Mittelman has developed a chin implant that, he maintains, will benefit 80 percent of all face-lift patients. Made of Silastic, the implant wraps around the chin and jaw, giving strength and structural support to the lower part of the face. The implant adds about $1,200 to the cost of a face-lift, but it can also be performed alone, with a price tag of $1,600 to $1,800. There's a bit more bruising and swelling with this procedure, but the initial recovery time is still about ten to fourteen days.

If you've always had good strong bones, you may not need a restructuring of your facial architecture. But if you're troubled by a certain fleshiness, you may want to consider *liposuction,* in which the surgeon goes after that extra fat with a vacuum cleaner. He makes a half-inch incision in the area to be treated, inserts a tiny cannula—the latest models are so small that twenty of them take up no more than an inch—and simply sucks out the fat. When it was first introduced in the early 1980s, liposuction was performed almost exclusively on the thighs. Now, thanks to the development of miniature cannulae, it's being done all over the body: the face, the neck, the stomach, even the ankles. As with other forms of cosmetic surgery, expect a couple of weeks' worth of bruising and swelling. And don't expect it to take the place of dieting in reducing a paunch—liposuction is only for small but stubborn concentrations of fat that dieting alone cannot get rid of. "Liposuction is not a cure for obesity," warns plastic surgeon Gary Brody. "If you take more than four pounds, you begin to challenge the body's fluid balance, and that can be dangerous."

If you've already been through the dieting process and have lost a significant amount of weight—or if you've recently been pregnant—you may be disappointed to find that no matter how hard you exercise, there's still some loose, even sagging skin that droops down from your tummy. If that's a problem, you may want to consider a stomach tuck. Like some kinds of face-lifts, this procedure is essentially an exercise in tailoring: the surgeon cuts out a band of skin and fat in the abdomen, then sews the skin that's left tightly together. The incision is made below what would be the top edge of a bikini so that the slight scar remains hidden. Recovery time is ten days to two weeks.

Most of these procedures involve modifying or manipulating existing skin, along with the fat layers underneath. In the not so distant future, though, you may be able to simply replace your tired skin, with its folds and droops and wrinkles, with a fresh batch. In the laboratories of Organogenesis, Inc., in Cambridge, Massachusetts, a company founded by former MIT biologist Eugene Bell actually manufactures replacement human skin, which the company calls "living skin equivalent" (LSE). To make LSE, Organogenesis scientists take skin fibroblast cells from infant foreskins removed during circumcision, and cultivate them in a lab dish to increase their number. These cells are mixed with nutrients and structural molecules, mainly collagen, which forms a gelatin-like polymer. The sheet of material thus formed is called a "dermal equivalent." The Organogenesis scientists then add a suspension of cells, an "epidermal seed," that over a few weeks will develop into the epidermis—the top layer of skin.

Because LSE lacks a specific kind of cell that would normally trigger an alarm in the immune system, grafts of the new skin are not rejected by the recipient. So far LSE has been used in clinical tests, primarily to provide new skin for burn victims. But its application in cosmetic surgery may not be far off.

If you've been tempted to try cosmetic surgery but have always held back, what I've described may have piqued your interest sufficiently so that you're ready to cross the threshold. In that case, you'll want to devote a good deal of time and energy to choosing the right surgeon. I've had some experience with all this, and I know how important it is to make that choice, yet how difficult it can sometimes be to choose wisely.

Basically, I've found that there are three kinds of doctors who can perform these procedures. First, there is the nonspecialist, a doctor or surgeon who may be competent but doesn't have specific training or certification in cosmetic techniques. (Any doctor can open an office and perform a nose job or a breast augmentation.) The second variety is the specialist, the bona fide cosmetic surgeon. He or she has extensive training and in most cases is quite competent. But if I were you, I'd look for the third type, which I call the "rejuvenation surgeon." Much more than a surgeon, this doctor is an artist and a sculptor—his or her medium is tissue and bone, and they work with the painstaking care of a fine craftsman. While other doctors or clinics do as many as twenty operations a day, with patients running through as if on a conveyor belt, the rejuvenation surgeon may take two hours just to do your eyes.

My personal rejuvenation surgeon has been Dr. Bruce Connell of Santa Ana, California. He's done my nose, my eyes, my forehead, and my chin, and I've been thrilled with the results—the man is an artist. I have asked several board-certified plastic surgeons to provide me with suggestions on how you might find your personal version of Dr. Connell. Here are some important guidelines from Dr. John Sherman, Dr. Norman Cole, Dr. Gary Brody, and other authorities:

Choosing a good plastic surgeon is not easy. The patient-to-be can expect to hear claims that may be misleading, and the lack of government and peer control is worrisome. Ask physicians about their precise credentials, training, and field of expertise. If advertisements say "board-certified," find out which board and whether it is accredited by the American Board of Medical Specialties. Be aggressive in your questioning. Dr. Cole says, "I am amazed at how few questions people usually ask me about my training and credentials."

Ask physicians about the hospitals where they have operating privileges. Contact those hospitals and ask if the physician has privileges to perform the specific operation you are considering (even if it's being done in a private office).

If a physician "guarantees" results from cosmetic surgery, avoid him. In the uniform opinion of top plastic surgeons, there are no guarantees.

Obtain recommendations from former patients. Your family doctor may be able to provide background on a plastic surgeon you are considering. Get a second and even third opinion on the procedure, asking about risks and benefits, and whether or not it will benefit you in particular.

To that advice I would add the following: Don't worry about how near or far away the surgeon might be—just add the airfare to the cost of surgery. Don't haggle about the price or try to make deals; your face and body are too important to ask for discounts.

Ask these questions: What are the surgeon's credentials? What procedures does he use? How long is the recovery period? Will you need nursing care, and if so, who arranges it? What can you expect physically during recuperation? Mentally? How long will the results last? Will you need surgery again in a few years?

Even when you've found a surgeon who seems to be absolutely right for the job, and even if he or she has answered all your preliminary questions to your satisfaction, you're still probably going to be a little nervous going in. You've never done this before, after all, and no matter how soothing and thorough the surgeon's pre-op lectures, you still don't know quite what to expect. To give you a better idea, here are some tips from a friend of mine who's been through it, and who even kept a diary of her experience:

Once you've made the decision, plan well in advance, at least a few months ahead. You don't know how quickly you'll heal or how long it will be before you're comfortable being seen. If you have a special event coming up, use that as a possible target date for your emergence.

In the meantime, whom do you tell, and when? If you're

married and have grown children, perhaps you should tell them in advance. In many cases, their reactions will be negative. Expect this, and don't let it upset you. Their fears stem from the fact that they love you as you are, and they're afraid that you won't come back. Assure them that this isn't what happens, and tell them not to worry.

You might also want to tell your very best friend, simply to have someone to discuss your plans and share your doubts with —someone who agrees with you and will encourage you. If you're a working person, you might want to tell one or two people whom you work closely with so you can keep in contact with your office through them while you recuperate. But swear them to secrecy! That way you won't have to answer a lot of distracting or upsetting questions.

Unless it's impossible to arrange, it's better to have someone with you immediately before and after surgery. Remember, this is a major operation. You may be very emotional when it's finished, and in need of support. Just knowing that someone is there caring for you can make you feel a lot better. Remember that even though the operation itself may take only a few hours, it takes time for the anesthesia to wear off, and a good deal more time to heal.

My friend was entirely happy with her cosmetic surgery experience. She got satisfying, even stirring results with very little pain and absolutely no psychological trauma. She might have been even happier, however, had she spent part of her recovery period in one of the many dedicated post-op "retreats" that have sprung up in recent years. At prices ranging from $95 to over $300 a night, these specialized facilities combine the privacy of an exclusive resort with medical and nursing care custom-tailored for the recuperating plastic surgery patient.

At the Facial and Plastic Surgery Center in Abilene, Texas, for example, the famed cosmetic surgeon Howard A. Tobin is on hand from six in the morning until eight at night, and on call—he lives only five minutes away—twenty-four hours a day. There is no charge for staying in the guest suites, and patients can be picked up by the center's private plane. The Armway Grand Plaza Hotel in Grand Rapids, Michigan, has five plastic surgeons available, and also has an in-house beauty salon, shops, and even its own art gallery. If you want the ultimate in pampered luxury, Le Petit Ermitage, a small, private facility for postoperative recovery in Beverly Hills, California, will pick you up in a limo and feed you room service haute cuisine from the famed L'Ermitage Hotel next door.

Being catered to in one of these posh post-op retreats can make you feel like a kid again—sort of like the ice cream we all got as a reward when we had our tonsils taken out. Of course, feeling like a kid again, and especially *looking* like a kid (or at least like the youngest possible version of the present you), is what cosmetic surgery is all about. And there's no doubt that a face-lift or a tummy tuck can make you look and feel years younger. But what we're after is even more audacious—we want to slow down the entire aging process so much that we will in effect *be* younger.

Here we come to the wave of the future. Today scientists in laboratories all over the world are determinedly searching for tomorrow's breakthroughs. They're developing not only replacement organs but replacement bones and blood. They're deciphering the role that hormones play in aging, and even beginning to home in on the genes themselves. There's a growing confidence among many of these scientists that this concentrated effort will soon pay off in three-digit life expectancies for many, if not all, of us. The scientists freely admit that in some respects they're only beginning, but judging by the research reports that are streaming in on an almost daily basis, they're off to a roaring start.

For more details on finding the right doctor see Appendix I, page 287.

16

Spare Parts

In a stainless-steel cylinder at a Cambridge, Massachusetts, laboratory, an incubator houses sheets of replacement human skin. In another room artificial human blood vessels are taking shape. This is not a scene from a twenty-second-century techno thriller by Michael Crichton. It is an eyewitness description of the laboratories at Organogenesis, a Cambridge biotech company that specializes in fabricating what will become an inventory of spare parts for human bodies. In effect, Organogenesis is what its name implies: an organ factory, the first and, at this writing, perhaps the foremost representative of an infant industry that hopes to repair and even overhaul the aging human body. In the process it may be revising and perhaps even revolutionizing the human life span.

Already over a million people a year are fitted with replacement body parts—hips, legs, arms, eyes, ears, toes, tongues, ligaments, cartilage, even genitals. Thousands more are alive thanks to artificial organs: hearts, lungs, kidneys, livers, and stomachs. On the drawing board or already under construction in labs like Organogenesis are artificial skin, pancreases, bones, blood vessels, and blood. In other laboratories bioengineers are conceiving tiny "nanomachines," which, once implanted in human bodies, will help other organs do their jobs. Researchers are also working at a feverish pace on what may become the *pièce de résistance* of the spare parts effort: living "patches" to repair ailing brains. More distant, but out there nonetheless, could be the greatest hope of all—the ability to manipulate tissues so that we can regenerate our own organs at will.

Aging, after all, is to an important degree a matter of sheer wear and tear—like any machine, the human body has a tendency to give in to entropy and simply run down. If we can replace our worn parts as they get tired or diseased, we might be able to stay alive and relatively healthy a good deal longer. "With the appropriate prosthetic devices," says Daniel Schneck, director of the biomedical engineering program at the Virginia Technical Polytechnic Institute and State University in Blacksburg, "we will be able to extend the human life span a minimum of ten years—to one hundred twenty-five—and chances are, it will be even longer than that. When I tell my students that one hundred years from now people will be able to walk into a department store, buy an organ off the shelf, and just replace it themselves," Schneck says, "I'm only *half* joking."

Actually, scientists and surgeons have been partners in the spare body parts business for as long as two hundred years. Probably the first human body parts to come up for replacement were the teeth. But tooth technology has come a long way since the time when George Washington sported a set of ivory dentures. Today's most sophisticated tooth implants use a space-age titanium socket, anchored in a hole in the jawbone as a root for a prosthetic tooth set in place with a gold screw. One tooth costs about $1,500, a full set runs $15,000–$25,000. They don't slip, wobble, or irritate your gums, and you can crunch right down on that carrot or apple.

In this century, some of the first body parts to come up for replacement have been the joints. Artificial plastic hips have been around and in place for more than twenty years. Today, we even have the ability to replace what may be the most complex joint of all: the knee. Although the knee is a marvel of evolutionary design, it's really not built to withstand everything we do to it, especially the high-impact pounding of popular sports like tennis, basketball, running, and skiing. Now, no one is suggesting that a weekend athlete with a sore knee should have the joint replaced; there are other, less drastic treatments that will help put weekend athletes on their feet again. But for some severe accident victims or people whose knees have been extensively damaged by arthritis or tumors, a full replacement can do wonders.

Until recently, replacement knees were artificial knees that restored some of the function of the joint but could never match the natural knee's astounding repertoire of movements. In 1987 the orthopedic surgeon Richard Schmidt of the Graduate Hospital of the University of Pennsylvania in Philadelphia took a whole human knee from a dead donor out of frozen storage and, in a seven-hour operation, transplanted the knee—with its full complement of bone, cartilage, tendons, and ligaments—into the leg of thirty-two-year-old Susan Lazarchick, whose own knee was being destroyed by a grapefruit-sized tumor. Last we heard, Susan was on her feet and walking normally.

The knee bone, as the song goes, is connected to the thigh bone, and further connected in an intricate and marvelous skeletal chain to virtually every other bone in the body. If current lab tests are any indication, there may soon be workable replacements for *all* those bones. At the University of Texas in Austin, researcher Richard Lagow has designed a "bioceramic" bone made of synthetic calcium phosphate hydroxyapatite, one of the natural substances that make up real bone. Because the bioceramic foundation is synthetic, there's no danger of rejection. When transplanted into the thigh bones of rabbits, the bioceramic bone formed a foundation on which natural bone grew, and this, in turn, stimulated the formation of new arteries, which kept the bone supplied with blood. After four years in the rabbits, the bioceramic material has been entirely converted to real bone. Lagow is now gearing up for human clinical trials.

Of course, many joints contain not just bone but cartilage—the connective tissue that lines the surfaces of bones where they come together and keeps the bones from rubbing against each other—and there's now a lab-grown version of that tissue as well. At the University of California at San Diego, Richard Coutts uses a trick that's as old as Adam: he recycles pieces of ribs—rabbit ribs, in this case—to grow substitute cartilage. Coutts culls the stem cells (the basic cells that can grow up to be either bone or cartilage) from the lining of the ribs, places those cells in softened bone, then packs that mixture into tiny holes he drills in the rabbits' own cartilage. So far, new cartilage has grown to fill the holes in 90 percent of the rabbits he's tested. Since natural cartilage can't repair itself, Coutt's work could eventually mean good news not only for sports and fitness buffs (cartilage injuries commonly occur in the knee), but for arthritis sufferers whose own cartilage has been destroyed by the disease. At this writing, human tests are still a few years away.

Further along in development is artificial skin. Here again, Organogenesis is off to a head start—its "Living Skin Equivalent," called "Testskin," hit the market in 1989. Since then, two other companies have entered the race to produce and market replacement skin. Marrow-Tech of La Jolla, California, is testing a version called NeoDerm, which uses human skin cells planted on a synthetic mesh lattice. And Biosurface Technology of Cambridge, Massachusetts, is producing a replacement epidermis made from a patient's own cells. The company has already supplied this replacement epidermis to more than 240 burn and wound victims. Although for the immediate future, replacement skin will probably be limited to healing grafts for burn and wound patients, the day may arrive when it becomes a standard tool for the cosmetic surgeon, to replace old, mottled skin with a fresh and youthful version. But humans won't be the only beneficiaries: there's talk—cheering talk, if you're an animal rights advocate like me—of using these skin replacements instead of lab animals in the testing of drugs, chemicals, and cosmetics.

When bioengineered skin replacements hit the market, they joined an already burgeoning effort to provide replacement parts for the human eye. Cornea replacements have been a fact of medicine since the early 1980s, when surgeons at Tulane University in New Orleans perfected a procedure for transplanting corneas from dead donors into cataract patients. Today, a million Americans a year undergo surgery in which cataracts are removed and artificial lenses implanted.

The next eye part to become replaceable may be the retina. At Wake Forest University in Winston-Salem, North Carolina, James E. Turner and Linxi Li transplanted retinal cells into the eyes of rats whose own outer layer of retinal cells had died. In more than two hundred cases, the transplanted retinal cells survived and prevented the death of the light-receiving cells underneath, thus staving off blindness. Although human tests are still at least five years away, the researchers hope that these retinal transplants will eventually have an impact on senile macular degeneration, which is believed to be caused by the death of cells in the outer layer of the retina, and is one of the leading causes of blindness in people over sixty.

An even more elegant way of replacing defective eye parts would be to stimulate the eye to regrow its own replacement cells. Thanks to the work of Arlene Gwon, that fantasy is now several steps closer to reality. Gwon, an assistant clinical professor of ophthalmology at the University of California at Irvine, works with rabbits who suffer from cataracts. First she breaks up the cataract tissue with ultrasound; then she removes the bad cells with a fine needle. Because she makes a smaller incision than that used in conventional lens replacement surgery, the underlying support system remains intact. (In conventional procedures, that system is party or wholly destroyed.) This allows the animal to regenerate its own lens tissue. At this writing, the newly regenerated lenses are still a bit cloudy, but Gwon hopes to overcome that problem by studying the process of new cell growth itself.

What about artificial blood? The need is great today, but so far progress has been limited. Blood, after all, has a tremendous number of vital jobs to do: it carries nutrients and oxygen to the cells, hauls away the toxic carbon dioxide that cells create as a waste product, and acts as a sort of "police van," transporting the immune system cells that guard against infections and, perhaps, cancer. So far the only adequate replacement for blood has been blood itself; thus the modern transfusion system, with its worldwide network of cooperating blood banks.

Still, scientists continue to search for an artificial blood substitute, a search that has been made much more urgent by the transfusion-borne AIDS infections of the early 1980s. But the quest itself precedes the AIDS epidemic. In 1957, Thomas Chang, then a medical student at McGill University in Montreal, made the first viable artificial red blood cells by surrounding human hemoglobin—the protein in red blood cells that carries oxygen to the body's tissues—with ultrathin membranes made of synthetic polymers and other compounds. Unfortunately, these artificial cells disappear too quickly from the bloodstream. Now the director of McGill's Artificial Cells and Organs Research Center, Chang continues to work on blood substitutes.

In the meantime, other researchers are pursuing a host of alternate approaches to making artificial blood. Some are testing a class of synthetic chemicals known as *perfluorocarbons,* which are known for their ability to carry gases like oxygen and carbon dioxide. But the perfluorocarbon solutions tested thus far have provoked responses from the hosts' immune systems, and those responses have compromised the immune system's ability to fight off invading bacteria and viruses. Earlier researchers tried human hemoglobin that had been "washed" to eliminate fragments of the original red blood cell walls which can cause toxic reactions. Unfortunately, this washed hemoglobin did not stay in the bloodstream long enough to be effective. But washed hemoglobin can now be cross-linked to form polyhemoglobin, which stays in the bloodstream longer than washed hemoglobin alone. Microencapsulated hemoglobin similar to that first developed by Chang can also be made to stay in the bloodstream longer. Clinical trials of these new approaches will begin soon.

The blood substitute of the future, though, may be genetically engineered. Tinkering with hemoglobin genes may change the protein's molecular structure so that the encapsulated version could remain in the bloodstream for days. At the same time, since genetically engineered hemoglobin would not contain fragments of red blood cell walls, it would probably not attract the attention of the host's immune symstem, so that the patient would not be abnormally vulnerable to bacterial or viral infections.

Ironically, it's the immune system—our greatest natural ally in the fight against disease—that becomes our greatest enemy where spare body parts are concerned. The immune system's job is to recognize and then attack any invading agents that it perceives as "foreign." Unfortunately, the category of "foreigner" includes most tissues and cells that are transplanted from sources other than the host's own body. So as soon as the immune system "sees" a transplanted heart or liver, it marshals its forces to try to destroy the organ, which, in its well-meaning but tragically mistaken way, it regards as a dangerous invader.

This means that much of the focus in modern transplantation medicine has been the battle against the host's own immune system. An important step in winning that battle came in the 1970s, when scientists at the Sandoz Pharmaceuticals Laboratories in Switzerland stumbled on *cyclosporin,* a fungus-derived drug that drastically represses the immune system. In fact, many of the headline-making successes in organ transplants over the past twenty years would have been unlikely, if not impossible, without cyclosporin.

The trouble is that cyclosporin does its job too well. It suppresses not only the immune system cells that attack transplanted organs, but also those whose job it is to deal with invading bacteria and viruses. This means that organ transplant patients, who have to continue to take cyclosporin over long time periods to avoid rejection of the new organ, are left with little resistance to disease.

A new drug, FK506, might help. When the transplant pioneer Thomas Starzl of the University of Pittsburgh gave FK506 to ten liver transplant patients after their operations, seven suffered no rejection of the new liver. Two of the remaining three patients were given second liver transplants. Those patients, as well as four new patients, were given FK506. Among those patients, none of the new livers were rejected, and side effects, according to Starzl, were "minor."

The results were equally good with kidney transplants. Starzl's team tried FK506 with thirty-six kidney transplant patients, ten of whom had had previous transplants that failed. Four to thirteen months after the new transplant operations and treatment with FK506, thirty-four of the thirty-six patients were still alive, and most of those had good kidney function. In only one case was the new kidney rejected. Although the patients did suffer some suppression of their immune systems and some infections did occur, the suppression was not as severe as with cyclosporin. Starzl considers the results "encouraging" and hopes to see more trials of FK506.

Drugs like cyclosporin and FK506 have to work very hard to put a damper on the rejection response, because when human tissue is involved, that response is extremely vigorous. Curiously, though—and scientists are still not sure why this is so—if the transplanted tissues are from animals other than humans (this kind of transplant is called a *xenograft,* while human-to-human transplants are known as *allografts*), the response of the immune system is not as strong. That's what led the Loma Linda, California, surgeon Leonard Bailey to attempt the famous "Baby Fay" operation in 1984, in which an infant girl with a fatally damaged heart was given the heart of a baboon. You may remember that the operation itself was a success, but within three weeks the baby's immune system rejected the baboon heart, and the infant died.

The death of Baby Fay put something of a damper on xenograft experiments—at least those involving humans—but the fact remains that rejection responses are less vigorous when donor and recipient are from different species. In 1990, an Australian scientist tried a technique the results of which were so unexpectedly good that interest in xenografts may be revived. Charmaine Simeonovic, an immunologist at the Australian National University in Canberra, was attempting to cure mice of diabetes by transplanting insulin-secreting cells from the pancreases of pigs. Instead of using drugs like cyclosporin or FK506 to suppress the mice's immune responses, she injected the mice with monoclonal antibodies—"magic bullets" that knocked out a set of specific cells in the immune system known as CD4 helper T-cells. (These cells, which are also kayoed by the AIDS virus, are vital in helping to direct immune system responses to a wide variety of invaders.)

Once those cells had been put out of commission, Simeonovic was able to transplant the pancreatic pig cells into the mice without worrying about rejection. In 60 percent of the cases, the transplanted pig cells went straight to work monitoring and churning out insulin, so that those mice were effectively cured of diabetes. The great surprise came after Simeonovic stopped the immune-dampening treatment with monoclonal antibodies. New CD4 cells started to appear. That was to be expected, but the new cells were somehow "tame": that is, they didn't direct an attack against the pig tissues, as they should have.

Simeonovic is still not sure why the new CD4 cells were so cooperative, but she speculates that they might have been "re-taught" to be tame by the mice's thymus glands, the glands that "educate" developing T-cells to do their jobs. In any case, the news of Simeonovic's unexpected discovery has sparked new interest in transplanting animal organs into humans. "We don't know how effective this procedure might be for hearts and other organs," Simeonovic says, "but people are looking into it with lots of interest and excitement." If it works, and animal organs become feasible spare parts for humans, we could go a long way toward solving one of the most important problems in transplantation medicine:

the terribly short supply of compatible human organs. This could even mean that in the future, potential transplant recipients would not have to wait for someone else to die (or sell, as they do in some third world countries, a body part) so that they themselves might live.

Whether by drug or by monoclonal antibody treatment à la Simeonovic, a solution to the rejection problem could eventually pave the way for wholesale medical trafficking in spare organ parts from humans or from other animals. Pancreas transplants, for example, can help cure diabetes, a condition that has been shown to be both age-related and life-shortening. Even with drugs that suppress the immune response, transplanted pancreases are rejected about 40 percent of the time.

The kind of pancreatic cell transplant performed by Simeonovic in mice seems to elicit a milder rejection response, and her monoclonal antibody technique shows promise in reducing rejection even further. In fact, if all goes well, Simeonovic herself hopes within the next few years to begin experimentally transplanting pig pancreatic cells into human diabetics. In the meantime, the Canadian surgeon Dr. Norman Kneteman and his colleagues at the University of Alberta in Edmonton have successfully transplanted pancreatic cells from human cadavers into four diabetic patients. The new cells lodged in the patients' livers, where, as long as six months after the surgery, they were producing enough insulin to significantly reduce the patients' need for insulin injections. At this writing, one of the four patients has been independent of insulin for over nine months since the transplant.

Eliminating or reducing the rejection response could help raise the odds for success not only in pancreas or pancreas cell transplants, but in transplants of kidneys, livers, lungs, and even hearts. Heart transplants have already come a very long way since Christiaan Barnard's dramatic early successes in the 1970s. Today the lifesaving operations have become almost routine: according to the International Society for Heart Transplantation, some 2,437 heart transplants were performed in the United States in 1989.

Still, rejection remains a serious problem in many heart transplant cases. But a new way around that problem—perhaps more promising and certainly more daring than drugs or even monoclonal antibodies—is currently being developed in Lithuania. At the Kaunas Medical Institute, surgeon Yurgis Bredikis took skeletal muscle from the back of a fifty-eight-year-old patient named Vasily Fokin. Bredikis wrapped the back muscle around Fokin's heart and attached blood vessels to it. Then, using an electronic stimulator developed by the Moscow Design Bureau of Precise Machine Building, doctors gave the back muscle pulses of electric current that changed its structure, transforming it from a back muscle into a heart muscle that expanded, contracted, and pumped blood just like the real thing. Because the muscle was from Fokin's own body, there was no danger of rejection.

With this auxiliary "wraparound" heart, Fokin's condition improved dramatically. His legs, which had been so swollen with fluid that he could barely walk (a weakened heart cannot clear fluid from the tissues), regained much of their original size and strength. According to Bredikis, Fokin has gone on to resume a normal life. Bredikis sees a bright future for the wraparound heart in treating a number of heart conditions. Similar experiments are now under way not only in Lithuania but at Hammersmith Hospital in London, the Broussais Institute in Paris, and at a number of research facilities in the United States.

While Bredikis et al. attempt to circumvent the immune system by using spare parts from a patient's own body, others are working at transplanting parts of the immune system itself—not to quell the rejection response but to shore up the body's ability to fight off disease. As I mentioned earlier, the vigor of the immune system tends to decline with age, and part of this decline is believed to be due to shrinkage of the thymus, the immune system's master gland. Takashi Makinodan, a gerontologist at UCLA and the Wadsworth Veterans Administration Medical Center in Los Angeles, thinks that shrinkage might be countered by combined transplants of bone marrow, which manufactures the immune system's antibody-producing B-cells, and thymus. When Makinodan tried this tactic with mice, transplanting bone marrow and thymus from young mice into older mice, the older mice were able to sustain youthful levels of thymic activity for six to ten months.

In humans, Makinodan's idea is to take T-cells from young people, freeze them, and reinsert them later in life, when these people's immune systems may need a boost. The technology for freezing and preserving the cells, he says, already exists. This procedure would be a way of counteracting the shrinkage of the thymus gland. "If we can do that," Makinodan concludes, "I feel very strongly that we would not only sustain the activity of the immune system, but might extend the quality life span as well."

As important as transplants of immune system components, hearts, pancreases, and so on might be, many experts think that the crowning triumph of the spare parts enterprise will be the ability to transplant sections of the human brain. Indeed, surgeons in Sweden startled the world in 1982 when they grafted cells from the adrenal glands into the brains of four patients with Parkinson's disease. (Parkinson's results from a deficiency of the neurotransmitter dopamine, a substance that is secreted in relative abundance by the adrenal glands.) The results of the operations in the Swedish patients were not dramatic, but five years later the surgeon Ignazio Madrazo of Mexico City's Hospital de Especialidades Centro Médico "La Raza" made more headlines when he claimed to have used essentially the same implantation technique to completely cure eight Parkinson's patients.

Although Madrazo raised a storm of controversy—critics maintained that the Mexican patients were not followed carefully, and that many of them remained sick enough to seek treatment at medical centers in the United States—the brain implantation technique itself has continued to excite medical researchers. The neurologist Harold Klawans and the neurosurgeon Richard Penn of the Rush Medical Center in Chicago have tried adrenal implants on four Parkinson's patients, while George Allen and Noel Tulipan of the Vanderbilt University Medical Center in Nashville, Tennessee, have done the same for one patient with a similar ailment, Huntington's disease.

Implanting tissues from the adrenal glands into the brain may one day help cure patients with dopamine-related diseases like Parkinson's and Huntington's. But experts have their eye on a broader range of targets—Alzheimer's disease, for example, and brain damage, or even the common memory loss that can come with aging. For these conditions, probably only brain-to-brain implants will help. There have already been hundreds of brain-to-brain implants in animals, among the most interesting of which was an experiment performed in the mid-1980s by Jeffrey Gray and his colleagues at the Institute of Psychiatry in London, England.

Gray gave a group of rats enough alcohol over a six-month period to produce significant brain damage—so much that the rats' memories were severely impaired. He then "patched" their brains with implants of tissue from the brains of rat fetuses. When he gave the rats tests in which they had to remember where food could be found in a wheel-shaped maze, he found that their memories had, indeed, improved.

By patching their brains with tissue from the hippocampus, Gray had, in effect, given his rats "memory implants." At the University of Rochester in New York State, neurobiologist Timothy Collier has performed a similar operation, this time with aged rats who were suffering from severe memory loss reminiscent of Alzheimer's disease in humans. Collier knew that the memory-impaired rats were deficient in cells that produce the neurotransmitter norepinephrine (NE). So he took NE-producing cells from fetal rats and implanted them in the brains of the senile animals. Sure enough, their memories returned.

Collier and Dr. Joe Springer then did a similar implantation using cells that produce a chemical called nerve growth factor (NGF), hoping that this would repair another set of nerves that are damaged in senility, those that produce the neurotransmitter acetylcholine. Again, the experiment was a rousing success: the NGF-secreting cells did, indeed, begin to repair the rat's damaged nerves. In Collier's mind, the end point is a possible treatment for Alzheimer's. "We would not be curing the disease itself," he says, "but the implants could prevent the memory loss that is often associated with senility."

While Collier goes after Alzheimer's disease, another researcher is using brain implantation to attack a common condition of advancing age: impotence. Henry Huang, a senior research scientist at Mercy Hospital in Chicago, took fetal tissue from an area of the brain known as the anterior hypothalamus and implanted it in the brains of ten elderly, impotent rats. Within a month, seven of the ten codgers had impregnated nine females, siring a grand total of one hundred and six baby rats. Huang hopes the procedure will someday help impotent or infertile humans.

Many of these experiments have depended upon the use of tissue from the brains of fetal animals. This may be fine for experimental rats, but it is a highly controversial and emotional issue when the subjects are human beings. There has been so much outcry against the use of human fetal tissue that in the United States, at least, this sort of experiment is currently banned by the federal government. The ban, and the deeply felt emotions behind it, have led some researchers to look for alternatives to fetal tissue. Don Gash of the University of Rochester has had some early success culturing cells derived from tumor cells that produce some of the same important chemicals that brain cells generate. In the future, Gash hopes to be able to use these cells as a viable substitute for fetal brain cells.

If an acceptable substitute for fetal cells is found—or if the ban on the use of human fetal tissue is lifted—it could pave the way for implant operations that might help treat age-related diseases of the brain like Parkinson,'s, Huntington's, and even Alzheimer's. At least one respectable researcher has an even broader vision: Richard Cutler of the National Institute on Aging foresees a time when fetal brain tissue replacement might be used routinely to keep not only the brain but the entire body in a state of nearly perpetual youth.

One important aspect of aging, explains Cutler, is a process known as *dysdifferentiation,* in which cell types begin to lose the chemical identity that distinguishes one type from another. This blurring compromises the cells' ability to do their jobs. Cutler suggests that when brain cells start to dysdifferentiate, the resulting cellular slowdown might be felt throughout the body. But those losses may be forestalled, he thinks, by removing aging portions of the brain—"10 percent every five years or so," he says—and replacing them with fresh brain cells from fetuses, in a sort of "oil change of the brain." "Perhaps by regenerating the brain in this way," Cutler concludes, "many other body functions might be rejuvenated."

It may be that this ultimate rejuvenation will be achieved with the help of the latter-day version of man's best friend: the machine. Here the idea is to use machinery to take up the work of bodily functions that may be starting to fail with age. Obviously, this idea has been around for quite a while—witness the success of eyeglasses, hearing aids, and, more recently, heart pacemakers.

One researcher is taking the machine idea a bold step further, which is to say, a bold step smaller. The computer scientist Eric Drexler, a visiting scholar at Stanford University and author of the book *Engines of Creation*, foresees a day when tiny computers—some of them no bigger than a single molecule—will rove the body like mobile handymen, repairing age-related damage to the cells and even to individual genes.

Drexler calls his vision *nanotechnology.* (The prefix "nano" means "one-billionth.") In a way, it is the logical extension of the currently popular notion that "small is beautiful." Drexler sees anti-aging nanocomputers coming in two basic models. The first would be a sort of robot blood patrolman—a cell-size computer that would cruise the bloodstream, fighting off bacteria, viruses, cancer cells, even blood clots and artery-clogging plaque. This cruiser in turn might carry a second model, an even smaller computer that could be injected through cell walls to repair damaged and mutated DNA and other chemical compounds. This combined micromechanical fix-it system might, in Drexler's mind, at least, bring "indefinite life extension."

Drexler is the first to admit that designing the proper software for these nanomachines would be a daunting and extraordinarily complex task. Still, he insists, "the hardware of nanomachines is no more complicated than present-day computers, industrial robots, and automated factories." Drexler thinks that the day may not be far off when body repair by nanotechnology becomes a reality. "People now under thirty," he says, "and perhaps those substantially older can tentatively look forward to nanotechnology's overtaking their aging processes and delivering them safely to an era of cell repair, vigor, and indefinite life span."

Drexler's exuberant vision is shared by the biologist Paul Segall, president and CEO of Biotime, Inc., in Berkeley, California, and co-author, with Carol Kahn, of the book *Living Longer, Growing Younger*. While Drexler is betting on nanomachines as spare parts to help extend our lives, Segall thinks we will one day be able to manufacture body parts—including most of our vital organs—by cloning.

Like nanotechnology, cloning has already made its passage from the pages of science fiction to reality. Basically, the technique involves taking an unfertilized egg cell from a female animal, removing the cell's nucleus, and inserting the nucleus from another animal's embryonic stem cells—the early, "mother" cells that will later divide and differentiate into all the varied cells of the animal's body and brain. The egg cell with its new, transplanted nucleus is then implanted in the ovaries of a surrogate mother, whose body nurtures it until the infant animal—a living, breathing clone—is born.

Testimony to the success of this technique can be seen at the home of University of Massachusetts biologist James Robl, where a cloned rabbit named Zeus munches contentedly on a head of lettuce; and on experimental ranches in Texas and Canada, where cloned calves "sired" in the laboratories of the geneticist Steen Willadsen kick up their heels. Segall thinks it's only a matter of time until we can scrape cells from a human's arm and use those cells to custom-grow human organs—hearts, kidneys, whatever the doctor orders—in a lab dish. Segall believes that someday all of us may be able to clone our entire bodies and have them kept in cold storage as personal organ farms, waiting to supply us with rejection-proof livers, lungs, and so on, whenever we might need them.

Although some experts have serious moral and ethical objections to whole-body cloning—"We just don't have the right," says the physiologist and cloning researcher Marie DiBerardino of the Medical College of Pennsylvania in Philadelphia, "to manipulate the gene pool of human individuals"—Segall thinks these objections will be far outweighed by the real needs of real people. "To a mother whose child has debilitating heart or liver disease," he says, "there's no moral question. The question is how can you get the child the organ he or she needs. It would be more unethical," he concludes, "*not* to use cloning to develop transplantable organs for ailing people."

Segall's vision goes even further. In his mind, replacing worn-out body parts through cloning could be the ticket to virtual immortality. "The aging surgeon's dexterity," he says, "the athlete's wind, the construction worker's muscles—all restored. Complexions smooth as a baby's, joints and tendons spry as a teenager's, hearts and lungs of an adult in the prime of life. . . . Cloning will provide the raw materials to put us back together." The benefits, he concludes, will be "so obvious, so ubiquitous, and so life-transforming that we will literally be born again."

Only time will tell if Segall's vision will come to pass. But even if we never see storage facilities full of spare human bodies, many experts think that the day when we'll be able to clone human organs in a lab dish is not far off. Indeed, the laboratories of present-day biotechnology companies like Organogenesis may soon evolve into full-fledged, multipurpose organ factories. As that day draws ever nearer, it becomes more and more apparent that, like the beautiful Mercedes Benz mentioned earlier in this book, we'll be able to extend our lives to the maximum not only through diligent maintenance—diet, exercise, and lifestyle—but by strategically exchanging our worn-out body parts for newer, better replacements.

17

The Fountains of Youth

The dream is as old as recorded history: the magic elixir, the restorer of youth, immortality in a bottle. It haunted the ancient Greeks, motivated the alchemists of the Middle Ages, stirred, and, ironically enough, ultimately killed the sixteenth-century Spanish adventurer Juan Ponce de León. Even today, in our myth-depleted age, we seem to cling hard to the idea that somehow, somewhere, that magic potion exists, and that all we need to do is find it, drink it, and pass it around, and we will, without any further effort, become a race of Methuselahs.

No one has yet found such a potion, but the search goes on. If anything, it has intensified since the days of Ponce de León. The major difference is that today, instead of seeking the elixir in mysterious lands at the edge of the world, we look for it in scientific laboratories, from small biotech companies to mega-universities. The fact that hardheaded scientists have not forsaken the myth, that they continue to look ceaselessly for substances that will restore youth and extend life, is in itself a cause for optimism.

Unfortunately, charlatans have always gotten into the act when it comes to fountains of immortality. Today's snake-oil salesman often wears the white smock of a physician or a scientist. During the past decade there have been a number of stirring proclamations about the youth-giving, life-prolonging properties of this pill, that preparation, or the other hormone. In many cases, including some of the most widely heralded, further examination brought bad news. "Most of these substances," warms Arthur Balin, past president of the American Aging Association, "have significant risks."

There's DMSO (dimethyl sulfoxide), for example. Approved for treatment of cystitis of the bladder, it's been additionally billed as an antioxidant and even an anti-cancer agent. But in some formulations sold in health food stores, DMSO is an industrial solvent, and some experts are concerned that it could cause severe nerve damage. Then there's L-dopa, a prescribed treatment for Parkinson's disease, hailed in some quarters as a rejuvenator and life extender. But L-dopa can cause fatigue, heart problems, hallucinations, blurred vision, and increased risk of some kinds of cancer. DMAE (dimethyl amino ethanol) is another one, once prescribed for some kinds of behavioral problems (discontinued as a drug, it's still available in health food stores as a food supplement), and billed as a potent prolonger of life. But it can provoke hostile behavior and even epileptic seizure.

Does all this mean that a youth potion is nothing but a dangerous fantasy, and that we should give up hope of ever finding substances that might help us live longer and recapture some of our youthful vitality? Not at all. Although it's still too early to single out any one substance and proclaim it an uncontested winner, scientists around the world are currently investigating dozens of candidates, many of which are showing real promise. The trick, of course, is to take everything you hear with healthy skepticism until there's an established consensus among sober scientists. A good rule of thumb might be "the louder the claim, the more suspicious the substance."

In this chapter I've assembled and evaluated a list of substances that seem to offer the most solid hope in terms of life extension and rejuvenation. Because I've already discussed vitamins and dietary supplements earlier in this book, the substances we'll consider now are "extracurricular"—that is, they fall outside the category of essential nutrients.

Many of them come straight from Mother Nature. Columbine, for one. This small blue flower—it's the state flower of Colorado, by the way—produces a potent substance called columbinic acid. William Elliott, an assistant professor of medicine and pharmacological and physiological science at the University of Chicago, tested columbinic acid on rats, and found that it significantly reduced blood pressure and cholesterol. Since high blood pressure and high cholesterol are implicated in the development of heart disease, columbinic acid may someday qualify as a life-extender.

The same may be true of the oil from another flower, the evening primrose. Long used as a folk remedy, primrose oil is holding up well in early scientific testing. Like columbinic acid, it appears to lower cholesterol. It has also relieved some of the symptoms of rheumatoid arthritis and has killed cancer cells in test tubes. The secret of primrose oil's promise may lie in its high content of *gamma linoleic acid* (GLA). Some scientists think that this fatty acid plays an important role in keeping the body's production of hormones up to par, and it's known that our natural levels of GLA tend to decline with age. "That's the reason," says the Lenox, Massachusetts, nutritional biochemist Dr. Neil S. Orenstein, "primrose oil is good for a huge number of biological imbalances." It's something I take every day—twelve pills, in fact. The reason is that it seems to help my eyesight. Now, I don't think you will find any medical opinion on its efficacy in improving eyesight, at least not in the United States. I started taking primrose oil because my aunt, who had glaucoma and had been given it by her doctor, told me that it had really helped her. Maybe it's nonsense, and maybe I'm suggestible. Nevertheless, I find a distinct change for the worse in my sight if I stop taking it for more than a week.

Of all the modern substances that have been billed as life-extenders, perhaps the best known—and certainly one of the most controversial—has been Gerovital. We discussed Gerovital earlier in the book, but here is further information on this widely publicized substance.

Dr. Edward Schneider, dean and executive director of the Andrus Gerontology Center in Los Angeles, summarizes the opinions of the naysayers: "Gerovital," he says, "is a local anesthetic and a mild antidepressant. It does nothing to counter the aging process."

Slightly more upbeat are the results of a study conducted by Michael R. Hall, a professor of geriatric medicine at Southampton General Hospital in England and author of the book *Age and Aging*. Hall gave an oral form of Gerovital known as KH3 to half of the volunteers in a group of 335 people over age sixty-five. The other half got a placebo. While the death rate in the two groups was identical, those in the Gerovital group reported less urinary incontinence, improved grip strength, and better short-term memory. Still, Hall notes, there were disturbing side effects in the Gerovital group, ranging from migraine-like headaches to the autoimmune disease lupus erythematosus.

My father took Gerovital, as I mentioned in Chapter 2, and it certainly seemed to help him. I have given it to my Rhodesian Ridgeback dogs, all of whom have lived well past the average age for the breed, which is between ten and twelve years. One actually made it to seventeen. For those who decide they want to try it, KH3 is available over the counter in Europe and in Nevada, the only state in the United States where it's sold legally. But be forewarned: the majority opinion among medical researchers seems to be in line with Schneider's negative assessment. Michael Colgan, director of the Colgan Institute of Nutritional Science in Encinitas, California, states: "As yet, there is no reliable evidence that Gerovital has any effect in retarding degeneration or preventing disease."

Here's a surprise candidate for a life-extender: good old aspirin. Studies are piling up rapidly, extolling aspirin's unexpected benefits in helping prevent a number of age-related ills. At the Mayo

Clinic in Rochester, Minnesota, the cardiologist James Chesebro found that taking small doses of aspirin daily can help reduce blood clotting, thus dramatically reducing the chances of heart attacks and strokes—even in high-risk patients. Here experts insert a caution: keeping your blood thin has its own risks, in that it can increase your bleeding time in case of accident or hemorrhage. Aspirin is also off-limits for people with ulcers, gout, or a family history of bleeding diseases, and to those taking anticoagulant drugs.

Meanwhile, there's growing interest among medical researchers in a substance that goes by the name of Coenzyme Q-10. Produced by the body and found in a number of foods, especially polyunsaturated oils like corn and soybean, Coenzyme Q-10 plays an important role in the basic chemical reactions that supply the body's energy. It's already been shown to help people with heart problems (in one study, doses of 100 to 150 milligrams a day increased the heart's output in a number of cardiac patients), to increase strength in patients with some kinds of muscle diseases, and to enhance the production of insulin. At the same time, a single shot of CoQ-10 helped restore vigor to the immune systems of elderly animals.

As many as 20 million Japanese take a synthetic version of CoQ-10 every day as a food supplement, and as yet there have been no reports of bad side effects. All this has led UCLA's Roy Walford and Steve Harris to begin testing CoQ-10 as a prolonger of life. "We're going to see if by adding it to the diet," Harris says, "we can get even more life-span extension in animals than we get with dietary restriction." So far, Walford says, early results of lab tests look "very promising."

If CoQ-10 turns out to be a disappointment, there's another entrant in the race, a group of substances that go under the name of *quinones*. Found in many foods, including fruits and vegetables, undistilled vinegar, cheese, yogurt, beer, and wine, and even in drinking water, they've also been detected in the body's adrenal glands and cerebrospinal fluid. One of the quinones, *pyrroloqui-*

noline quinone (PQQ), is manufactured by bacteria in the gut. Scientists are just beginning to learn about how quinones work, but the early indications are that they act as antioxidants and free radical scavengers. Research in Japan indicates that quinones have either helped relieve or prevented oxidative damage to the liver and brain of rats, and to the eyes of chick embryos. When researchers at Marianna School of Medicine in Kawasaki, Japan, and at Dokkyo University School of Medicine in Osaka gave a form of quinone called *idebinone* to human patients with age-related memory and emotional problems, they found that those patients did show a slight improvement.

While the scientific jury is obviously just beginning to deliberate on quinones, at least one highly respected American expert, the Harvard University biological chemist Paul Gallop, thinks they may eventually have impact as a general anti-aging formulation. If so, America may be losing the race to realize that potential. The Japanese pharmaceutical giant Takeda Chemical Industries is already marketing idebinone as a "brain metabolism enhancer." "The Japanese," Gallop notes, "have made a definite commitment to developing quinones as anti-aging drugs."

As a life-extension candidate, quinones are obviously among the newer kids on the block. But they're certainly not alone. At this writing there are a number of substances that are still in early testing, but are so far showing exciting promise. One of these, called AL-721, is derived from egg yolk. Now, we all know that egg yolks are full of cholesterol, but paradoxically enough, AL-721 is a lipid that actually *extracts* cholesterol from cells. By taking out the excess cholesterol that accumulates with age, AL-721 helps restore fluidity to the cell membrane, which, in turn, helps the whole cell function more efficiently.

Testing of AL-721 in humans is still in its early stages, but preliminary results look good. In Israel, the membrane researcher Meir Shinitzky gave AL-721 to ten people over the age of seventy-five. In seven of them, immune responses were boosted, in some cases to the levels of vigorous youth. Shinitzky was so encouraged that he began giving the substance to his seventy-five-year-old father, who, he says, is now "blessing it." In animal tests, there are indications that AL-721 can help cripple viruses and even help cure addiction. "The idea," says Shinitzky, "is to flood the whole system with AL-721 and let it work everywhere it can."

Another substance with intriguing possibilities as an anti-ager —at least for men—is *terazosin*. It's one of a class of compounds known as alpha blockers, which are usually prescribed to treat high blood pressure. But terazosin may have other uses as well— it's currently being tested at ten clinics in the United States as a potential treatment for enlarged prostate glands. So far, the only side effects noted have been mild dizziness and faintness. But these may be outweighed by a substantial bonus: terazosin seems to lower both blood pressure and cholesterol levels. These triple benefits led at least one expert, Perenchery Nareyan, chief of urology at the Veterans Administration Medical Center in San Francisco, to label terazosin a "multipurpose drug for the mid-life male." Given FDA approval, it could be available soon.

Some scientists in New York think there may be a drug with even more sweeping potential than terazosin. They're so excited about the substance that they've set up an entire company, Alteon, to test and eventually market it. It's called *aminoguanidine,* and early preclinical evidence suggests that it works to help prevent one of the basic processes in aging: cross-linking. You may remember that cross-linking occurs when molecules of glucose (sugar) attach themselves to proteins in the body, then bind adjoining proteins to one another. This stiffens the protein fibers, and the stiffening, in turn, is implicated in a wide variety of aging conditions, including diabetes, sagging of the skin, hardening of the arteries, cataracts, and strokes.

Aminoguanidine seems to block this process by reacting with protein-bound glucose before it can form cross-links. Scientists at New York's Picower Institute for Medical Research have shown that aminoguanidine does slow cross-linking in the arteries of diabetic rats. Excited by the early results, the Rockefeller researchers launched Geritech, recruiting as company president Charles Faden, a former president of the pharmaceutical giant E. R. Squibb. Aminoguanidine is now in clinical development for diabetic complications. "The idea that we might be able to prevent the complications of diabetes and aging is extremely exciting," Faden remarks. "And we're not necessarily talking about the distant future."

Somewhat further along the developmental trail (in this country, at least) is *superoxide dismutase* (SOD). This is an enzyme that is naturally produced by the body, and the evidence suggests that it's among the most powerful of the natural antioxidants. In animal tests, SOD has produced some truly amazing results: it helped prevent frostbite in rabbits, and prevented stroke-like brain injury in gerbils whose carotid arteries had been clamped shut for forty minutes. In humans, bovine SOD is already used in Germany, Italy, and Japan to treat people who suffer from osteoarthritis, and a genetically engineered version is currently being tested in the United States and Europe to help victims of strokes and heart attacks.

Could SOD also become an all-purpose anti-aging formula? "Possibly," says Kenneth Munkres, a molecular biologist and geneticist at the University of Wisconsin. While current SOD concoctions are cloned versions of the SOD found inside cells, Munkres thinks researchers on aging would be wise to concentrate on the SOD *outside* the cells, because the extracellular form may have a longer lifetime in the bloodstream and therefore provide longer-lasting protection against free radical damage.

Munkres thinks that SOD research in general could eventually help extend our average life span to as much as one hundred years. In the meantime, though, don't rush out to your health food store to buy SOD pills. Irwin Fridovich, the Duke University biochemist who first isolated SOD in 1968, explains: "SOD is an enzyme, and like other enzymes, if it's taken by mouth it's digested, not absorbed, by the body. To have any effect, it has to be injected. So there's no possible benefit in taking SOD pills, and the people who sell them are really nothing but snake-oil salesmen."

As exciting as SOD and with even more research on its side is a steroid hormone called *dehydroepiandrosterone,* better known as DHEA. Produced by the human body, DHEA is present at exuberantly high levels in youth—in fact, in early life it's the body's most abundant hormone. But after age twenty-five quantities of the hormone tend to fall rapidly. By age seventy it's just about disappeared.

Interestingly, levels of DHEA also tend to be lower than average in women with breast cancer. That's what first tipped off the Temple University researcher Arthur Schwartz to its potential importance. Schwartz has since investigated the role of DHEA in a wide variety of age-related conditions, including cancer ("It inhibits many different kinds of tumors," he says) and obesity ("A very effective anti-obesity agent," he finds). In turn, Schwartz's work has helped inspire what amounts to a flood of DHEA studies, which suggest that in lab animals the hormone and its metabolites can help protect against diabetes, improve memory retention, fight certain infectious diseases, and help extend the lives of mice with systemic lupus erythematosus.

Of course, as with most high-potency substances, there are good reasons to be cautious about DHEA. It's a steroid, and steroids are not to be taken lightly—they can alter our natural production of sex hormones, meaning that men might show signs of femininity while women might find themselves sprouting beards. Schwartz and other researchers are developing chemically altered versions of DHEA that might deliver its benefits without the side effects. When all is said and done, there's a growing number of scientists who agree with Schwartz: "At this stage," he says, "DHEA holds big promise as a practical method of delaying some of the effects of aging."

Meanwhile, researchers in Europe and Japan are having a close look at substances that might extend our lives by helping our cells relax. Known as *potassium channel openers,* these substances create tiny channels in the walls of nerve cells, through which negatively charged potassium ions can escape. As they do, the "excited" cells calm down, and this relaxation can improve blood flow and breathing, and can help reduce high blood pressure. Already patented in Europe and Japan under the names Cromakalin and Nicorandil, potassium channel openers are still being tested in the United States. Eventually, says the pharmacologist Arthur Weston of the University of Manchester in England, "these compounds could improve—as well as lengthen—life for millions."

Ironically, the same may someday be true of a compound now used to abort unwanted pregnancies: RU-486. One of a group of synthetic steroids developed in the early 1980s, RU-486 is legally available in France as an abortion pill, and it's estimated that as many as 44,000 Frenchwomen have used the drug successfully. Up to now, this antiabortion application has made the drug too hot to handle in the United States, where abortion stirs such deep emotions.

But a number of scientists in the United States and Europe are convinced that RU-486 may have enormous potential as an anti-aging formula. First of all, the drug blocks the production of the hormone progesterone, which is necessary to sustain pregnancy (that's how it works to effect abortion), but which also contributes to the spread of certain kinds of cancer tumors. In a 1987 clinical trial in Montpellier, France, in which RU-486 was given to a group of women with advanced breast cancer, as many as 25 percent showed definite improvement, including significant shrinkage of the tumors.

What has some scientists even more excited are tests in which RU-486 has been used to treat a rare hormonal disorder called Cushing's disease. Caused by tumors in the pituitary gland, the disease stimulates the adrenal glands to secrete abnormally large quantities of stress hormones called *glucocorticoids*. These stress hormones, in turn, can produce a wide variety of ailments, including suppression of the immune system, osteoporosis, adult-onset diabetes, hypertension, and loss of muscle mass. If these sound familiar, it's because they're all maladies that are associated with aging. Several experts consider Cushing's disease to be a model for the aging process.

So, what happens when you give RU-486 to people with Cushing's disease? George Chrousos, a senior investigator at the National Institutes of Health in Bethesda, Maryland, tried it on ten patients with a related disorder called Cushing's syndrome, in which glucocorticoid-stimulating tumors appear in parts of the body other than the pituitary. The results were truly remarkable: in six of the ten patients, all the symptoms disappeared.

At the same time, Kalami Mohammed and Willian Regelson of the Medical College of Virginia found that in rats RU-486 reversed another common malady of aging: high blood pressure. Although some experts worry that long-term treatment with the drug may reduce blood pressure so drastically as to produce extreme fatigue—this happened in a few of the patients in the Cushing's syndrome trials—Chrousos says he was able to control these side effects by decreasing the dose or taking the patients off the medication for short periods of time. If you add them up, the potential benefits of RU-486—anticancer effects, blood pressure reduction, and relief of the accelerated aging symptoms of Cushing's syndrome—are impressive indeed, so impressive that Regelson sees RU-486 as "potentially the most potent anti-aging drug currently available."

Tragically, RU-486 continues to be an outcast in the United States because of the machinations of the bigoted religious right. The FDA has placed the drug under "import alert," which effectively bans any use of it outside approved clinical trials. At this writing, no American pharmaceutical company has applied for an FDA license to test RU-486. Apparently worried about the abortion controversy, Roussel-Uclaf, a subsidiary of Hoechst, the French company that manufactures RU-486, will supply it to American researchers who would like to continue testing the drug, but won't pay for research.

Regelson is currently leading an intense campaign to get American research on RU-486 back in motion. He has a political ally in Representative Ron Wyden of Oregon, who plans to conduct congressional hearings on the subject. If Regelson and Wyden are successful, testing of this promising drug could go into high gear. If those tests continue to show the sort of encouraging results already reported by other scientists, RU-486 might become what one of its developers, the French physician and researcher Etienne-Emile Baulieu, calls "a preventive medicine for increasing life span."

RU-486, SOD, DHEA, CoQ-10, AL-721—all this chemical alphanumeric soup may eventually come together to spell life extension. Indeed, at this writing they all look like strong candidates. But there are two substances that may be even more exciting. Both are produced by the human body, and both have garnered an impressive list of experimental accomplishments in humans. One of these is human growth hormone, the other is a class of compounds called *thymosins.*

Let's start with human growth hormone, otherwise known as *somatotropin* or, more simply, hGH. Growth hormones have been arousing hopes—and stirring controversy—since their discovery in plants in the late 1920s. In humans, hGH is an extremely potent substance secreted by the pituitary gland in minuscule amounts (20 to 50 *thousandths* of a gram) during sleep, and these microscopic nightly primings—usually several per night—account for the rapid growth spurts of children and adolescents, who often seem to shoot up overnight. Since 1958 hGH has been used to promote growth in children who are abnormally short, and thousands of children have been treated successfully. By the time they reach their mid-twenties, though, most people are down to about one secretion of hGH per night; and by their mid-thirties many people, especially sedentary people, produce little or no hGH.

The fact that hGH production declines with age has been tantalizing researchers for years. Could "booster shots" of hGH (technically, this kind of treatment is called *replacement therapy*) reverse some of the effects of aging? There have been strong reasons to believe that the answer could be yes. For example: one thing that happens to most of us as we grow older is that we tend to lose muscle and gain fat. When European researchers began to look at children who had been treated with hGH, they found just the opposite effect: the children actually *lost* fat and *gained* muscle. In 1987, a team of scientists at the University of New Mexico School of Medicine showed that what was true for children was also true for a group of normal, healthy adults—in five men and three women aged twenty-two to thirty-three, treatment with hGH trimmed body fat by 1.5 percent and increased muscle mass by an average of three pounds.

All this was impressive enough, but a vital question remained: Could hGH work its apparent magic on older people? In 1990 came the answer, and it sparked headlines all over the world. Dr. Daniel Rudman and his colleagues at the Medical College of Wisconsin in Milwaukee announced that they had given hGH for six months to twelve healthy men, aged sixty-one to eighty-one. Even the oldest of them emerged from the study leaner (the amount of fat in their bodies decreased by an average of 14.4 percent) and more muscular (muscle mass increased by an average of 8.8 percent). At the same time, blood levels of an important hormone, known as insulin-like growth hormone factor 1 (IGF-1), rose to levels that Rudman calls "youthful." As *The New York Times* science reporter Natalie Angier wrote: "Treatment with human growth hormone can significantly reverse many effects of aging."

In the ensuing public clamor, physicians around the country were besieged by calls from patients wanting to know where they could get hGH for themselves. But hGH is approved only for treatment of unusually short children, and its distribution is tightly controlled both by the government and by its manufacturers, Genentech and Eli Lilly. At the same time, experts warned of possible side effects: people whose pituitaries produce too much hGH are prone to arthritis, diabetes, congestive heart failure, and a condition known as *acromegaly*, characterized by a pronounced growth of the bones of the face. Others worried that long-term treatment with hGH might produce as yet undetected side effects—it might, for example, promote the growth of hidden cancer tumors. Rudman himself issued a public disclaimer: "Human growth hormone," he declared, "is not the fountain of youth."

Still, although a great many questions remain to be answered, many scientists remain cautiously enthusiastic about the possibility that human growth hormone will become a key player in the battle against aging. "This work is very important," says the physiologist Douglas Crist, one of the University of New Mexico researchers who tested hGH. "These experiments show that there is some limited age retarding going on."

"It's all very interesting," agrees the National Institute on Aging's Richard Cutler. "Treatment with human growth hormone may enable people to retain a more youthful and vigorous body state as they get older. If we find that it also lengthens life span, that would be icing on the cake."

While human growth hormone offers exciting possibilities in reversing some of the effects of aging, there's another set of substances that may eventually have an even broader impact. These are the *thymosins,* a group of hormones extracted from the thymus gland. You may remember that the thymus is considered to be the "master gland" of the immune system—it's where young, undifferentiated immune cells go to be "educated" in their future specialties—and that with age, it tends to shrink almost into nothingness. For that reason, some scientists think that if we could either restore the gland itself or replace the substances it produces, we might be able to strengthen the immune system so that it could fight off diseases that tend to strike us as we get older.

Chief among these scientists—and the thymosins' biggest booster—is Allan Goldstein, chairman of the biochemistry department at George Washington University in Washington, D.C. It was Goldstein who first isolated the thymic hormones in the mid-1960s. The reason for his enthusiasm is captured in a photograph of a beautiful teenaged girl that hangs on a wall in Goldstein's office. The girl's name is Heather, and in the photo she is a healthy, beaming thirteen-year-old in the uniform of a junior high school cheerleader. But in the early 1970s, when she was five, Heather was near death. She weighed only twenty-six pounds (she should have weighed about sixty) and was prey to a seemingly unending series of life-threatening infections.

Heather was suffering from a condition called *thymic aplasia,* in which the thymus gland fails to issue enough disease-fighting T-cells. "In truth," says Goldstein, "her condition was terminal." The doctor decided to try a radical therapy: he put Heather on thymosins, thinking that the hormone might stimulate the production of T-cells. The results were spectacular. "Five days after we started her on thymosins," Goldstein says, "her T-cells were multiplying, her infections had decreased, and she was gaining weight."

Heather's astounding recovery (she eventually lived into her early twenties, substantially longer than most victims of thymic aplasia) convinced Goldstein that he was on the right track. He has continued to test and develop thymosins ever since, and in 1980 formed his own company, Alpha 1 Biomedicals of Washington, D.C., to pursue the research. Although the thymosins have not yet been approved by the FDA (they are currently in the final stages of FDA testing), not all scientists share Goldstein's enthusiasm. Still, in Europe natural and synthetic thymosin-like substances are routinely prescribed to treat cancer, arthritis, diabetes, asthma, influenza, multiple sclerosis, even gonorrhea and herpes.

But Goldstein's vision goes beyond using thymosins to fight disease: he sees them as having great potential as a broad anti-aging formula. "I think what was true for Heather will be true of the great majority of the aged," he says. "Right now the shriveled thymus glands of the elderly issue only small amounts of T-cells. Instead of suffering from the acute disease that Heather had, they go into gradual decline. But for them and for Heather, the solution will be the same. If we can give them enough thymosin to keep the T-cell level high, we should be able to enhance immunity throughout old age." Enhancing immunity means greater protection not only against infectious diseases but perhaps against many forms of cancer. All in all, Goldstein thinks, it could add up to an extra twelve years of life.

Goldstein foresees an even more sweeping and spectactular range of benefits from thymosins. In the mid-1970s Goldstein and other scientists found evidence that the thymus gland might be part of a chemical pathway that leads directly to the brain. In lab experiments, thymosins stimulated the brain's production of stress chemicals like the "flight or fight" hormone ACTH, sex hormones from the pituitary gland and the hypothalamus, and even the "feel good" neurotransmitter beta endorphin. Equally interesting, there seemed to be a feedback loop between the brain and the thymus: when ACTH is secreted by the brain, the thymus shrinks. This cuts down the production of thymosins, which turns down the secretion of ACTH.

Goldstein thinks that the brain-thymus connection may hold the key to aging itself. "It's possible," he says, "that the whole range of brain hormones falls off from the optimum level as soon as the thymus begins to shrink, before the onset of puberty. The suggestion is that it's the deterioration of the thymus that leads to the deterioration of the brain—and ultimately of the body itself. By adding the thymosins back, much of that decay should be set in reverse."

Goldstein thinks that within the next ten years even healthy people will be taking thymosins on a daily basis. Regular supplements, he states, "should help push the average person's vigorous years upwards of eighty or ninety simply by boosting the immune system. Because we'll also increase the level of vital brain hormones, the impact will probably be greater still."

In this chapter, I've talked about more than a dozen substances —everything from plain, over-the-counter aspirin to still-experimental compounds like growth hormone, aminoguanidine, and thymosins—that may someday qualify as age-fighters. And there are hundreds of others making similar claims. Obviously, the ancient dream remains very much alive.

18

Resetting the Clock

At first glance, there doesn't seem to be much similarity between a human being and a roundworm. We look different. We also live seventy-five years or more while the roundworm lives about three weeks. Yet despite our long lifetimes, we're relative laggards in the reproduction department: in our seven decades we generate at most about a dozen offspring, while the female roundworm cranks out one hundred eggs per day. And it does it all on a genetic dole that seems miserly in comparison: we operate on about 100,000 genes, while the worm has only about 10,000.

When twenty-fifth-century chroniclers write the history of the battle against aging, the roundworm—particularly a species known as *Caenorhabditis elegans*—may turn out to be one of the early heroes. Because among the 10,000 genes that make up the *C. elegans* genome there appear to be one or more that help regulate the clock of aging. In 1988, the molecular geneticist Thomas E. Johnson of the University of Colorado at Boulder isolated one of those genes. When he manipulated the gene, the roundworms turned into tiny Methuselahs—they lived up to five weeks, or 60 percent longer than their normal counterparts.

Johnson came up with a perfectly appropriate name for this apparently vital gene: he called it AGE-1.

The exciting thing about this experiment is that despite their many dissimilarities, humans and roundworms actually have quite a bit in common. Almost every one of the roundworm genes has a counterpart in the human genome. So Johnson thinks there may be a gene or set of genes in humans that correspond to the AGE-1 gene in roundworms. If they do exist, these genes, which Johnson calls "geronto-genes" and other scientists call "longevity determinant genes," may affect the sequence of aging. If we can isolate and then learn to manipulate those genes . . .

"Optimistically," Johnson says, "it could open up avenues for treatments that would significantly slow the aging process."

Johnson is one of a growing number of scientists who believe that the key to aging lies in the genes. True, there is still a lively controversy as to whether or not "gerontogenes" actually exist. Some evolutionary biologists argue that nature has no need to outfit her organisms with a genetic clock of aging, that aging will occur due to wear and tear or internal chemical errors whether you have genes for it or not. Even those scientists who do like the genetic clock idea doubt that the clock is contained in a single gene; some experts think that as many as seven thousand genes may be involved.

Despite these differences of opinion—differences that are undoubtedly healthy and give this fledgling enterprise a lot of its vitality—there is little doubt that increasingly scientists are searching for, and finding, the targets among the segments of DNA that make up our genes. If there is a genetic clock of aging, then our growing ability to reach deep into the interiors of cells and manipulate the genes could mean that we will ultimately be able to reset that clock, with resulting increases in life spans that will make centenarians seem like teenagers.

Even if there turns out to be no clock of aging, no "gerontogenes" in command of the aging process, the ability to add, delete, and modify genes will undoubtedly have a major impact on many diseases that are associated with age. Osteoarthritis is one. Some sixteen million middle-aged and older Americans suffer from this disease, in which the cartilage that acts as a shock absorber in the joints deteriorates, leaving bone grinding painfully against bone. A research team led by the rheumatologist Roland Moskowitz of Case Western Reserve University in Cleveland and the molecular biologist Darwin Prockop of Thomas Jefferson University in Philadelphia have been gene-hunting, looking for a gene that might be implicated in making us more susceptible to osteoarthritis, or even in bringing on the disease.

Moskowitz and Prockop looked at sixteen members of three generations of an Ohio family, nine of whom were victims of osteoarthritis. They found that each of these nine had defective versions of the genes that regulate the production of collagen, the primary building block of cartilage tissue. The other seven family members, who did not have osteoarthritis, had normal versions of the collagen gene. It's a promising lead, and if it pans out in the population at large, doctors might eventually be able to spot the defective gene early in life and urge their patients to take preventive measures—to avoid jobs or forms of exercise, for example, that put strain on the joints. And ultimately therapists may be able to correct the gene itself, or substitute a healthy gene for the defective one, thus staving off the disease.

This would certainly be welcome news. Perhaps even more intriguing, though, is the possibility that the genes hold the key to such major killers as heart disease and cancer. Let's look first at heart disease. Researchers have long wondered why some people with unhealthy lifestyles manage to live into their eighties without a trace of heart trouble, while other people who seem to be paragons of virtue have crippling and even fatal heart attacks before they reach the age of fifty. The British prime minister Winston Churchill drank like a fish, smoked cigars, and slept only two hours a night, yet he managed to live into his nineties; while the tennis champion Arthur Ashe had two heart attacks while still in his thirties. Obviously, if lifestyle were the only factor, Churchill and Ashe would have traded places.

Many experts think that people like Churchill may be genetically protected against heart disease, while others, like Ashe, may have genetic vulnerabilities that predispose them to heart trouble. Which genes are involved? Until relatively recently, no one knew. But now a number of research teams are beginning to come up with at least a partial answer.

Some of the first clues came from a disease called familial hypercholesterolemia (FH), a malady in which people, even young children, have cholesterol levels as much as eight times higher than normal. These people's arteries clog up so mercilessly and so rapidly that if the disease is left untreated they're often dead of heart disease before they reach twenty. No amount of bad diet or lack of exercise could account for a cholesterol profile that is so dramatic and so deadly. Evidently, something in these people's bodies is terribly amiss. Chances are, the experts surmised, that the disease was caused by a genetic defect.

In the 1970s, the medical geneticists Joseph Goldstein and Michael Brown of the University of Texas Health Science Center in Dallas set out to understand what was actually going on in the body to produce FH. To do this, they looked at liver cells, because the liver is the place where much of the cholesterol in the human bloodstream is manufactured. Certain liver cells, Goldstein and Brown discovered, have receptor proteins that constantly monitor the level of LDL—that's the "bad" form of cholesterol—in the blood. If either or both of the two genes that direct the production of those receptors are defective, the LDL detection system is impaired. As a result, the liver manufactures wild excesses of LDL and continually pours it into the bloodstream. The result, proven by Goldstein and Brown's tests with human volunteers, is the potentially fatal FH.

This vital discovery showed that the genes were indeed at the center of at least one form of heart disease, and it eventually brought Goldstein and Brown a Nobel Prize for Medicine. But even though they had shown that genetic defects were responsible for FH, they had not pinned down the specific defect that made those genes go haywire. Meanwhile, at Harvard University and Children's Hospital in Boston, a team of researchers led by the biochemical geneticist Jan Breslow was looking at patients with other forms of the disease that led to abnormally high cholesterol levels. It had long been suspected that some of those abnormalities might result if the liver's ability to clear excess fat and cholesterol from the bloodstream was somehow compromised.

Breslow and his colleagues went fishing for the genes that might be responsible for the liver's failure. By the early 1980s, they and other researchers had found several genes that seemed to be implicated. They were known as *apolipoprotein* genes, and their job was to produce the liver proteins that latch onto cholesterol and clear it from the bloodstream. If certain of those genes are defective, Breslow found, between-meal cholesterol processing lags, and the resulting excess cholesterol is left to build up on artery walls.

What was the nature of the defect itself? This puzzle had Breslow stumped. Then, in June 1982, he read an article in *The New England Journal of Medicine* describing two sisters who though only in their early and mid-twenties already had advanced cases of coronary artery disease. Unlike victims of FH, the sisters had normal cholesterol levels. The author of the article, cardiologist and geneticist Robert Norum of Detroit's Henry Ford Hospital, wrote that the only abnormality his exhaustive tests had turned up was an apparent deficiency in two of their apolipoprotein genes.

This made Breslow sit up and take notice. He immediately asked Norum to send him samples of the sisters' blood. Breslow and his colleagues then fished out the two suspect genes. As they probed those genes, the answer gradually emerged: in some earlier generation, a piece of one of the genes had changed places with a piece of the other, and the abnormal exchange had, in effect, inactivated *both* genes. This meant that neither sister's body could produce the proteins necessary to clear one form of cholesterol from the blood, and this, in turn, led to premature hardening of the arteries.

So Breslow and his colleagues had tracked down one genetic defect that had produced heart disease in two people. While this is only a beginning—there are dozens of genes responsible for cholesterol processing and hundreds of genetic variations that could theoretically account for a predisposition to heart disease— it is still an encouraging sign. It won't be long until scientists and physicians will be able to "read" an individual's genetic profile in such a way that they'll be able to distinguish with great accuracy between the Winston Churchills and the Arthur Ashes among us and use that information to prescribe lifestyle alterations or drugs—or even manipulations of the genes themselves—that will avert the danger of early heart trouble.

What's true for heart disease may someday be true for cancer as well. In an earlier chapter I mentioned Jorge Yunis of Philadelphia's Hahnemann University and his genetic detective work, in which he examines human chromosomes for the "fragile sites" that may be responsible for cancer. Yunis thinks that these fragile sites may be related to *oncogenes*—genes that when activated trigger the cellular processes that lead to the development of malignancies. "It may be," he says, "that when chromosomes break or rearrange themselves in the vicinity of an oncogene, genetic control mechanisms break down, causing an otherwise harmless gene to express itself inappropriately. The cell begins to divide out of control, and cancer is the result."

Yunis is hopeful that the ability to identify fragile sites and track oncogenes will soon lead to a more elegant and more effective arsenal of weapons against cancer. "In a few years," he says, "perhaps it will be possible to deactivate specific oncogenes, eliminating cancer without the dangerous side effects of surgery, radiation, or toxic drugs."

If life-shortening maladies like cancer and heart disease do, indeed, have a genetic basis—and, as we've seen, there's more and more evidence that they do—the approach to treating them will be twofold: first, track down and identify the villain genes; then alter those genes, turn them off, or replace them with healthy versions. Many scientists think that this approach, known as "gene therapy," will eventually have a greater impact on human medicine than anything since the discovery of antibiotics. Gene therapy, says G. Steven Burrill, a consultant to the biotechnology industry at Ernst and Young in San Francisco, "will fundamentally change the way medicine works. Over the next thirty years, we are going to see a revolution."

That revolution is already under way. Its opening shot was fired in September 1990, when a team directed by the hematologist W. French Anderson of the National Institutes of Health removed the white blood cells from a four-year-old girl who was suffering from the genetic disorder *adenosine deaminase* (ADA) *deficiency,* a condition that blunts the immune system's ability to fight disease. Anderson and his colleagues used a custom-made virus to deliver healthy copies of the faulty gene to the cells, then injected the cells back into the girl's bloodstream. At this writing it appears that the girl was helped by the dramatic procedure, but the long-term results are not known. Nonetheless, according to Gerard McGarrity, chairman of the NIH's Recombinant DNA Advisory Board, "it was a truly historic moment. Medicine has been waiting for this kind of therapy for thousands of years."

Of course, ADA is nowhere near the top of the list of killer diseases—there are only about ten cases reported in the United States per year. But the gene therapy front is broadening rapidly. On January 29, 1991, Dr. Steven A. Rosenberg of the National Cancer Institute in Bethesda, Maryland, performed a dramatic and historic operation to try to save the lives of two cancer patients. The patients, a twenty-nine-year-old woman and a forty-two-year-old man, were both suffering from metastatic melanoma, a lethal variety of skin cancer that affects eight to ten thousand Americans a year. In a procedure that lasted only twenty minutes, Rosenberg injected the two patients with up to 100 million white blood cells that had been genetically altered to produce a potent anticancer substance called *tumor necrosis factor* (TNF). Rosenberg's hope is that those cells will home in on the patients' tumors, releasing the cancer-destroying TNF.

At this writing it is too early to tell whether or not Rosenberg's operation has succeeded, but it is a sign that gene therapy is beginning to come into its own. Already scientists have identified the genes that cause cystic fibrosis, one form of muscular dystrophy, and, as we've seen, some of the genes involved in high cholesterol and some varieties of cancer. They're currently hot on the trail of the genes responsible for other forms of muscular dystrophy and cancer. Eventually, many of them believe, they'll identify and treat the genes that cause most of the diseases that prevent us from living out our natural life span.

At this point, the technique for replacing defective genes is still imprecise—researchers like Anderson can only hope that the viruses they use to deliver the new genes will get them to the right spot in the cells' DNA. Many experts are confident that this problem will be overcome in the next few years, and that within the next ten years replacement therapy for diseases in which only one or two defective genes are responsible, like muscular dystrophy and some kinds of liver and skin cancers, will be widely available.

The ability to treat killer diseases by rooting out and replacing bad genes will undoubtedly have an impact on human longevity. One study has shown that eliminating cancer and heart disease would increase our average life span by about three years—in other words, into the late seventies and early eighties. Making the leap to a hundred-plus, though, may well depend on a far more complicated and daunting task: finding the genes responsible not only for disease but for aging itself.

If genes for aging do exist, then researchers have already taken a giant step toward finding them. That step is the Human Genome Initiative, an immense cooperative scientific project with an audacious goal. For the object of the Human Genome Initiative is nothing less than identifying and mapping every one of the genes that make up the human genome—more than 100,000 of them.

Funded to the tune of $3 billion by the federal government, the project is expected to take at least fifteen years and occupy the efforts of an estimated 3,000 scientists. When completed, says Dr. Walter Gilbert of Harvard University, "it will change the way we do biology. We'll have total knowledge of the genetic blueprint of a human being."

Many scientists are confident that this knowledge will include a schematic diagram of the clock of aging. Although, as we mentioned earlier, not all scientists believe that "gerontogenes" exist, there are already tantalizing early indications that they do. Genes are, in effect, blueprints for proteins; and as researchers peer deeper and deeper inside human cells, increasingly they're finding proteins that seem to be implicated in the process that makes those cells age and die.

One of these proteins goes by the name of *fibronectin*. Ordinarily, fibronectin anchors cells in position and helps young cells retain their shape. But Mary Beth Porter of the Baylor College of Medicine in Houston has found that fibronectin interacts with old cells in a different way than with young cells. This changed mode of interaction, she thinks, may be involved in the process of aging.

The University of Arizona geneticist and physician Marguerite M. B. Kay has found another protein that seems to act as a "death marker." For more than fifteen years, Kay has been looking at human red blood cells and, in particular, at a protein in the membranes of those cells. Known as *band 3*, this protein is truly a jack-of-all-trades: among other things, it supports the cell membrane, patches and repairs damage to cell membranes, helps maintain the membranes' acid-base balance, and acts as a binding site for a number of enzymes, including the vital oxygen transporter hemoglobin.

But Kay has found that as red blood cells grow older, band 3 begins to change into another protein, which she calls *senescent cell antigen*. Senescent cell antigen seems to mark old cells for death—once it appears on the surface of the cell membrane, it acts as a flag, initiating a process that eventually attracts immune system cells called macrophages, which destroy the marked old cells and "eat" them.

The exciting thing about Kay's work is that band 3 and senescent cell antigen are found not only in red blood cells but in liver cells, kidney cells, cells of the immune system, and brain and central nervous system cells. Kay says that if senescent cell antigen appears too early on the membranes of certain red blood cells, the result can be anemia. Perhaps even more interesting is her notion that the appearance of senescent cell antigen on the membranes suggests its involvement with Alzheimer's and other neurological diseases. Ultimately, Kay thinks, the degradation of the band 3 protein into senescent cell antigen may prove to be one of the key processes in aging as a whole.

If senescent cell antigen, ubiquitin, fibronectin, and other proteins do turn out to be central to the aging process, that will amount to a flaming arrow pointing directly to the genes, for behind every protein is a gene that "designs" it. The protein connection is not the only evidence linking aging to the genes. Another indication is Thomas Johnson's discovery of the AGE-1 gene in the roundworm. Also, the biologist H. R. Horvitz of MIT's Howard Hughes Medical Institute has studied eleven genes that contribute to cell death in *C. elegans*—three that control the onset of the death process, seven that act in the engulfment of the dying cells by their neighbors, and one that helps break down the cell "corpses." "It's possible," says Horvitz, "that genes like those that act in programmed cell death in *C. elegans* cause cells to die during the aging process in humans."

Elsewhere, scientists are homing in on what may be a set of longevity genes in the fruit fly. Biologist Robert Arking of Wayne State University in Detroit has looked at two different strains of fruit flies, one of which lives significantly longer than the other. By systematically deleting certain chromosomes from the long-lived flies, he found the location of the genes that seemed to determine their longevity—two or three areas on the left arm of chromosome 3. The shorter-lived flies were without these two areas. Arking is now tying to find the specific genes responsible for the flies' extended longevity.

Roundworms and fruit flies are one thing and human beings quite another. At the National Institutes of Health, the molecular biologist J. Carl Barrett and his colleagues are trying to unlock the key to cellular aging in the chromosomes of humans. That key, Barrett thinks, may lie in the difference between normal cells and cancer cells. As we've seen, most human cells seem to divide and replicate a certain number of times, then grow old, stop dividing, and die. Some kinds of cancer cells grow and replicate far beyond normal limits—so much so that scientists call those cells "immortal." Are there genes inside cells that turn on the aging process in normal cells and turn it off when cells become cancerous? That's the question Barrett's team is asking.

To answer it, they made a group of hybrid cells by fusing "immortal" cells from hamsters with normal cells taken from human lungs. Most of those hybrid cells grow old normally and died normal deaths. The researchers found that the few cells that turned immortal were all missing a specific chromosome, human chromosome 1. When the scientists introduced copies of human chromosome 1 into the immortal cells, the aging process was turned on again, and the cells ultimately grew old and died.

The next step is to find the specific genes on human chromosome 1 that may be responsible for turning on the process of cellular aging. Helping Barrett take that step is another Baylor team, this one led by James R. Smith and Olivia Pereira-Smith. Like Barrett, the Smiths have worked with fused cells, in their case combining several strains of immortal cells. In a sort of mirror image of Barrett's results, the Baylor team found that some of their hybrid cells turned mortal again—that is, they stopped dividing and eventually died. They think that changes in as few as four genes could have made the difference between mortality and immortality. At this writing, the Smiths have not yet identified the crucial genes.

We can hope that all these experiments will represent the first steps in a grand effort: to reset our genetic clocks to yield life expectancies of up to 120. Combining genetic life extension with the kind of lifestyle strategies we talked about earlier could help ensure that those extra years would be not just more life, but better life: healthy, happy, and hearty, full of the vitality and enthusiasm that characterize youth.

The message is clear: making changes in your lifestyle *right now*—in diet, in physical and mental exercise, stress reduction, and healthy doses of love and friendship—can help each of us live out our maximum life span with vigor and in great good health. On the horizon may be scientific discoveries which promise to increase that capability and stretch active life far further than anyone would ever have thought possible.

The secrets of the aging process—in the hormones, in the cells, in the genes themselves—are steadily being revealed. Gradually, inexorably, perhaps inevitably, the battle against aging is being waged and won.

Appendix I

LOCATING, SELECTING, AND EVALUATING PROFESSIONAL SERVICES

The purpose of this section is to help you find professionals in all fields, and specifically those who have been trained to make discussing sensitive personal problems easier and more comfortable to you. It also explains how to find medical specialists who are trained to assess physical problems that can affect the sexual or reproductive aspects of your life, as well as other health-care professionals. Also included are suggestions to help you get the most information possible from interactions with these professionals so that you can then make informed decisions about your health care.

Remember, as a patient or client you are entitled to get the information you need, to choose the medication, therapy, treatment, or surgery that is best for your particular needs and lifestyle. You also have the responsibility to ask questions about how a medication or treatment will affect your general health and well-being.

Appendix I is reprinted in part from *The Kinsey Institute New Report on Sex*, by June M. Reinisch, Ph.D., with Ruth Beasley. © 1990 by the Kinsey Institute for Research in Sex, Gender, and Reproduction. St. Martin's Press, Inc., New York.

DIFFICULTIES WITH YOUR SEX LIFE

Steps to Locate a Sex Therapist or Marriage Counselor:

1. If you are comfortable doing so, ask friends, family members, or co-workers who have gone to a counselor whether they can recommend someone, or ask your family physician for a recommendation.
2. Look in the yellow pages of your telephone book under Human Services Organizations; Marriage, Family, Child and Individual Counselors; Mental Health Services; Psychologists; Psychiatrists (may be listed under Physicians & Surgeons—Medical—M.D. or separately under Psychiatrists); or Social Service Organizations. Such listings often state specialties, certification status, and qualifications.
3. Call your local Community Mental Health Center and ask for recommendations, or call the nearest medical school or large hospital and ask if they have a sex dysfunctions clinic.
4. When you suspect your sexual or relationship problems may include medical or physical factors, locate a sex therapist who works closely with medical professionals or a physician with special training in sexual medicine and experience in diagnosing problems with sexual functioning.

Steps to Locate a Medical Sex Dysfunctions Specialist:

1. If you are comfortable doing so, ask your family physician, friends, family members, or co-workers to recommend a clinic or therapist.
2. Look in the yellow pages of your telephone book under Marriage, Family, Child and Individual Counselors; Mental Health Services; Physicians & Surgeons—Medical—M.D.; Psychologists; or Psychiatrists (may be listed under Physicians & Surgeons—Medical—M.D. or separately under Psychiatrists); Such listings often state specialties and qualifications.
3. Write to the American Association of Sex Educators, Counselors and Therapists and the American Association for Marriage and Family Therapy (see page 292) and ask for referrals near you.
4. Call the nearest medical school, university, or large hospital and ask if they have a special clinic for diagnosing and treating sexual problems (dysfunctions). If your town does not have such a facility, most libraries have telephone directories of nearby large cities and

will help you find the telephone number. Or call your county or state medical society and ask for the telephone numbers of qualified clinics or physicians.

HOW TO GATHER INFORMATION ABOUT HEALTH CARE PROFESSIONALS AND SERVICES YOU HAVE LOCATED

1. Call these counselors, therapists, physicians. Try more than one.
2. Be prepared with a pen and paper so you are ready to take notes during the telephone conversation.
3. Briefly state what you think the problem is and/or any symptoms.
4. Ask if the professional or clinic has experience treating problems like yours.
5. Ask the fee for an initial appointment.
6. Ask if the professional or clinic can provide information about their qualifications, the services available, and standard fees.
7. Ask if they are certified by any government agency or national organization.
8. Select one professional or clinic and call to make an appointment for an initial meeting.
9. State that you are looking for help but do not want to begin the diagnostic or therapy process until you make a final decision on whom to hire. If you want to have your spouse or partner accompany you to the meeting, ask about that.

EVALUATE THE HEALTH CARE PROFESSIONAL OR SERVICE AT YOUR FIRST APPOINTMENT

1. Write down any medical or scientific words you may hear. Ask the professional to spell them out for you and define them. You can read more about your diagnosis, tests, and treatments later.
2. Notice whether there are diplomas and certificates displayed on the office walls. If there are, read them.
3. When you meet the professional, briefly state what you think the problem is or what symptoms you have.
4. Ask what special training the person has had to qualify him or her to treat your problem. This information, combined with any diplomas and certificates displayed, should give the impression that the person

is well educated and has kept up to date by attending educational seminars and training programs in his or her specialty. Ask about membership in state and national professional organizations and whether the person is licensed by your state. Some professionals are not accustomed to being asked such questions, but a reputable professional will not mind providing this information. Moreover, giving informative answers to questions like these in a patient manner can be an early clue that the person will be easy to work with and supportive of your concerns.

5. Ask if the person regularly does referrals to other professionals if special tests are needed and who those specialists are. Good working relationships with specialists such as endocrinologists, psychiatrists, psychologists, urologists, dermatologists, nutritionists, gynecologists, surgeons, and plastic surgeons are often necessary for adequate diagnosis and treatment.

6. Ask how many cases similar to yours the person has diagnosed and treated and what the outcomes were for these other cases.

7. Ask what the person might recommend as diagnostic tests and typical treatment for problems such as yours. In many cases an exact answer may not be possible, but the person should at least try to explain what may be involved.

8. Ask what you might expect in the way of number of appointments, length of treatment, and fees.

You Have the Right to Full and Clear Answers to All Your Questions. If You Don't Get Them, Select Another Professional.

1. Your final selection of a professional should be based on whether you feel comfortable with the person and with the treatment methods and goals proposed.

2. If you are not sure about the first professional you see, make an appointment and interview another. If after several appointments you find yourself disappointed with the professional you've selected, think about changing to someone else. Even competent professionals vary greatly in their personalities, treatment methods, and style of interactions with clients. It is not unusual for mismatches to occur. For example, you may prefer someone whose interactions with you are either more reserved or more informal.

3. The relationship between doctor or therapist and patient needs to be a working partnership. A particular professional may be exactly right for one person and wrong for another.
4. Ask to have copies of your records and test results to give to the new professional. (Unfortunately, in some states such records must be transferred directly to the new therapist or physician without the patient's seeing them.)

HOW TO FIND A MEDICAL SPECIALIST

At various points this book has suggested seeing a specialist in particular fields of medicine such as endocrinology, nutrition, dermatology, or plastic surgery, or a physician who has specialized expertise in dealing with a particular problem, such as surgery for varicose veins.

Steps That Will Help You
Locate a Specific Medical Specialist:
1. If you are comfortable doing so, ask your family physician for a referral.
2. Look in the yellow pages of your telephone book under Physicians & Surgeons—Medical—M.D. to see if there are such specialists in your area. Call the nearest medical school or large hospital and ask if there is such a specialist on staff and how to make an appointment. (For example, you might say, "Do you have a gynecological endocrinologist on staff who specializes in menopause? How do I make an appointment?") Public libraries will help you find these telephone numbers.
3. Look in the Marquis *Directory of Medical Specialists*. This reference book is updated every two years and should be available at your local public library.
4. Call your county or state medical society and ask for telephone numbers of the particular type of specialists you are looking for.

Call the Specialists You've Located:
1. Have a pen and paper ready to write down the answers to your questions. Briefly state to the person answering the telephone what you think your problem is and any symptoms. (You will probably not be speaking directly to the specialist at this point.)
2. Ask if the specialist has experience in treating problems such as yours.

3. Ask what the fee is for the first appointment.
4. Ask about the specialist's credentials. Most specialized fields of medicine require training beyond medical school and/or special examinations for professional certification. These are often referred to as "Boards"; for example, in urology a physician who has satisfactorily completed advanced training and passed special written and oral examinations is called a diplomate of the American Society of Urology, or, in gynecology, a fellow of the American College of Obstetrics and Gynecology. Only after meeting such criteria is the physician certified as belonging to the specialty.

   In the United States any M.D. is permitted to practice any specialty without specialized training, and this is why it is important to determine a physician's training and certification.
5. When you decide on a specialist, call to make an appointment.
6. Ask what records or other information you should bring with you or have sent from other doctors you have seen.

Before Your Appointment:

1. Collect any records you have been asked to bring.
2. Make a list of all prescription and nonprescription (over-the-counter) medications you take, the dosages, and how often you take them—even aspirin, vitamins, or ordinary cold medications.
3. Write down everything you recall about your problem (what the symptoms are, when you first noticed symptoms, how long you've had the problem, whether symptoms are worse with any particular activity or at different times of the day or month).
4. Write down anything you don't want to forget to tell the doctor.
5. Make a list of all the questions you want to ask the doctor.

When You Go the the Appointment:

It is common to be upset or anxious about seeing a physician, especially if a frightening or embarrassing condition is involved or you do not feel well. Below are some suggestions to help make visiting a physician more reassuring and informative.

1. If you feel comfortable, bring a relative, friend, or partner with you. They are likely to be less anxious and may help you remember to ask questions and get information.

2. Take along your records and lists.
3. Also take along a pen and paper so you can write down what the doctor says.
4. Ask to have words spelled out, so you can look them up later at the library if you want to find out more about your diagnosis, proposed treatments, or medications.
5. When a professional suggests tests, ask for their names, costs, and what each is designed to determine.
6. Before you leave the office, check your list of questions to make sure they have all been answered in a way you can understand.

If a Diagnosis Is Made (The Doctor Says What Is Wrong and What May Have Caused the Problem):

1. Ask what led him or her to decide on that particular diagnosis. Especially ask what the results were of any tests you had. Write them down or get copies.
2. Ask how certain he or she is of the diagnosis and whether any of the test results are questionable or borderline.
3. Ask if there are any other possible causes of your problem.

If Recommendations for Medication Are Made:

1. Write down the name of each medication, the dosage, and the schedule you are to follow for taking it.
2. Ask if there are any side effects you should watch for, including changes in your sex life and in your looks, if this is important to you.
3. Ask what might happen if you decide not to take the medication.
4. Make sure you clearly understand how and when to take the medication and what might happen if you forget to take it.
5. Keep track of any changes you notice while you take the medication on a calendar or date book and report them to your doctor. This is essential for your physician to evaluate the effectiveness of treatment and to spot side effects early.

If Treatment or Surgery Is Recommended:

1. Ask for a description of the procedure, how long it will take, the costs involved, and the recovery time.

2. Ask about any side effects (including those which might affect your looks or your sex life) and if any risks are involved.
3. Ask how many other treatments or surgeries like the one proposed for you the doctor has performed and his or her success rate.
4. Ask to speak with other patients to see if they are pleased with the results of their procedures.
5. Ask what other options are available to treat the problem, and the side effects, costs, and other details about those other options.
6. Ask what will happen if you decide not to have the treatment or surgery.
7. Say that you will need time to make a decision about the recommendations, then really do take the time to go home, calm down, and honestly consider your choices.
8. In the case of surgery, radiation treatments, experimental treatments, or any other recommendations that appear to involve a degree of risk, seek a second medical opinion. Responsible professionals will not discourage you from doing this.

GETTING A SECOND MEDICAL OPINION

This means locating a different, similarly qualified physician to assess your situation. However, the second physician should usually not be in practice with or specifically recommended by the first physician or specialist you've seen. For example, when surgery has been recommended, do not seek your second opinion from a surgeon unless you know surgery is absolutely necessary and you are trying to compare surgical techniques or success rates. The same is true for other types of specialized treatments, such as radiation therapy. This is because a surgeon is likely to recommend surgery and a radiation specialist will recommend that treatment, not necessarily because one or the other is best, but because that's what they are most familiar with.

Most health insurance plans will pay for second opinions, and, in fact, many insist on having a second opinion before authorizing payment for surgery or other costly medical treatments. If you have health insurance, call your company and ask for suggestions as to how to proceed with getting a qualified second opinion.

Go through the steps outlined above to locate a specialist for a second opinion. Or if you happen to know a nurse or other person who works in health care, ask about the reputation of the physician who recommended a particular treatment or surgery and ask if he or she can suggest competent physicians for a second opinion.

When You Select a Physician for the Second Opinion:
Call and state what the first doctor said your problem was and that you are seeking a second opinion.

If you had tests or X rays done by the first physician, mention this and ask how to arrange for copies of the results to be sent for review before your appointment.

ONCE YOU'VE MADE A DECISION

It is essential that you keep your physician informed about the effects of any treatment, medication, or surgery—even long after it has been completed. There is no way your physician can know how effective any treatment has been or if you need additional treatment if you don't keep him or her informed.

IF PROBLEMS ARISE

Regardless of which type of professional you see or the person's stated credentials and qualifications, you are the best judge of whether you have been helped or not. If at any time during the diagnostic and treatment process you are not satisfied with the treatment you are receiving, discuss your feelings with the professional involved. Some medications and treatments do take a while before you will be able to notice progress. Although you need to give the professional a chance to explain, if the situation does not improve in a reasonable amount of time, see someone else. Sometimes it is necessary to try a series of treatments or medications before the right one for you is found. If you have confidence in the health professional you have chosen, stick with him or her.

HOW TO GET THE LATEST MEDICAL INFORMATION
ON HEALTH, SEX, LONGEVITY, AND COSMETIC SURGERY

Alliance for Aging Research
2021 K Street N.W., Suite 305C
Washington, D.C. 20006
202-293-2856
Private, nonprofit. Publishes a quarterly newsletter called *Alliance Reports*.

American Academy of Cosmetic Surgery
159 E. Live Oak Ave
Suite 204
Arcadia, Calif. 91006
818-447-1579
Professional association. Publishes *American Journal of Cosmetic Surgery*, quarterly, in conjunction with the American Society of Lipo-Suction Surgery.

American Academy of
Facial Plastic and Reconstructive Surgery
1110 Vermont Ave N.W., Suite 220
Washington, D.C. 20005
202-842-4500
Toll-free telephone referral service for patients: 800-332-FACE, and 800-523-FACE in Canada.

The American Aging Association
University of Nebraska Medical Center
600 South 42nd Street
Omaha, Neb. 68198-4635
402-559-4416
Publishes *AGE: The Journal of the American Aging Association*. Annual subscription $30—U.S. and Canada, $35—Foreign.

American Association for Marriage and Family Therapy (AAMFT)
1100 17th Street, N.W.
Washington, D.C. 20036
202-452-0109

American Board of Plastic Surgery
7 Penn Center, Suite 400
1635 Market Street
Philadelphia, Pa. 19103
215-587-9322
Certification board.

American Federation for Aging Research
725 Park Avenue
New York, N.Y. 10021
212-570-2090
Private, nonprofit. Publishes *AFAR Newsletter* three or four times a
year.

Center for Drug Evaluation Research (CDER)
(HFD-8) Food and Drug Administration
5600 Fishers Lane
Rockville, Md. 20857
301-295-8012
Answers inquiries on the use and safety of drugs.

Center for Science in the Public Interest
1875 Connecticut Avenue N.W., Suite 300
Washington, D.C. 20009
202-332-9110
Consumer watchdog. Widely respected. Nonprofit. Publishes *Nutrition
Action Health Letter*: $19.95 for 10 issues.

Colgan Institute of Nutritional Science
531 Encinitas Boulevard, Suite 101
Encinitas, Calif. 92024
619-632-7722; Fax 619-632-7375
Specializes in nutrition. Publishes nutrition and fitness magazine for
clients.

Huxley Institute for Biosocial Research
900 North Federal Highway
Boca Raton, Fla. 33432
407-393-6167

Publishes a newsletter dealing with biochemical disorders such as senility, nutrition, etc. Will send national referral packet.

The Life Extension Foundation
Box 229120
Hollywood, Fla. 33022
800-841-LIFE
Nonprofit. Membership $50, entitles you to *The Life Extension Report* and *The Life Extension Update* monthly newsletters. Toll-free number answers questions on aging, nutrition, etc. Will refer you to nutritionists, M.D.s worldwide.

The Linus Pauling Institute of Science and Medicine
440 Page Mill Road
Palo Alto, Calif. 94306
415-327-4064
Publishes newsletter detailing research on vitamin C about once a year.

Longevity **Magazine**
General Media Company
1965 Broadway
New York, N.Y. 10023
212-496-6100
Subscriptions: 800-333-2782
Consumer magazine specializing in the latest news, research reports, and information on health, fitness, nutrition, cosmetic surgery, and life extension for the layman. Subscription: $17.97 for 12 issues.

National Institute on Aging
Public Information Office
9000 Rockville Pike
Federal Building, Room 6C12
Bethesda, Md. 20892
301-496-1752
Part of the National Institutes of Health. Offers publications and materials on a variety of topics.

Orentreich Biomedical Research Station
R.D. 2, Box 375
Cold Spring–on–Hudson, N.Y. 10516
914-265-4200
Private foundation. Develops interventions that increase the quality
and length of life. Contributors receive information reports from the
foundation's director.

World Health Foundation
360 San Miguel Drive, Suite 208
Newport Beach, Calif. 92660
714-720-9022
Nonprofit. Researches causes and prevention of accelerated aging.
Publishes *The World Health Foundation News and Report* newsletter
for members.

Appendix II

RESOURCES TO HELP YOU
STAY YOUNGER LONGER

BOOKS

Andrews, Elizabeth. *Muscle Management: A New and Revolutionary Technique for Maximizing Potential and Dealing with Sports Injuries.* Harper San Francisco, 1991.
A self-help approach offering more than three hundred sage, simple, and effective techniques for treating injuries and enhancing athletic performance. $34.95.

Auckett, Amelia D. *Baby Massage: Parent-Child Bonding Through Touch.* **Introduction by Tiffany Field, Ph.D.** New York: Newmarket Press, 1989.
"Touch is a means of communication so critical that its absence retards growth in infants," according to a recent article in *The New York Times* summarizing research by Dr. Field. This book covers bonding, body contact, massage as an alternative to drugs, healing the effects of birth trauma, and massage as an expression of love, and gives complete instructions on the techniques of massage for infants. $9.95

Biermann, June, and Barbara Toohey. *The Diabetic's Book: All Your*

Questions Answered. **Revised and Expanded Edition.** Los Angeles: Jeremy P. Tarcher, 1990.

Whether you have just been diagnosed or have had the disease for years, this book is for you. The authors answer more than 130 of the most frequently asked questions about diabetes. Topics included are the causes of diabetes, the effects on your body, lifestyle changes you need and don't need to make, the diabetes exam and what to expect from your doctor, the latest technology in home care, the prevention of complications, and the care of diabetic children. With encouragement and understanding, Biermann and Toohey teach you how changes in diet, exercise, and attitude can make significant contributions to controlling the disease. $10.95.

Bounds, Sarah. *Thorsons Green Cookbook: Food for a Future, for You and the Planet.* Harper San Francisco, 1991.

How to eat food that is healthy for you and the planet, with a hundred green recipes and advice on buying organic foods. $9.95.

Chaitow, Leon, and Simon Martin. *Chelation Therapy: The Revolutionary Alternative to Heart Surgery.* New York: HarperCollins, 1989.

Hardening and narrowing of the arteries is one of the main causes of heart failure. Here is a guide to this still highly controversial therapy. $12.95.

Chaitow, Leon. *Thorsons Guide to Amino Acids.* Harper San Francisco, 1991.

A complete guide to the healthful properties of amino acids. $8.95.

Colen, B. D. *The Essential Guide to a Living Will.* Englewood Cliffs, N.J.: Prentice Hall, 1991.

If you are horrified by the idea of existing in a persistent vegetative state while medical technology keeps your vital organs functioning, then read this book. Colen has written an up-to-date synthesis of all you need to know to protect yourself and your survivors from someday possibly undergoing a terminal nightmare. $7.95.

Gollub, James O. *The Decade Matrix: Why the Decade You Were Born Into Made You What You Are Today.* Reading, Mass.: Addison-Wesley, 1991.

Director of the Life Span Program at SRI International, Gollub thinks that at any point in time your values are shaped by four things: the "time signature" of the decade you were born in, the "birthmarks" that are the personality characteristics you developed early on, the "rites of passage" you're going through developmentally at this stage of your life, and the "weather report," which includes external factors such as a recession or a boom economy. $24.95.

Lacroix, Nitya. *Massage for Total Stress Relief.* New York: Random House, 1991.

A journalist and massage therapist, Lacroix believes that the most powerful way to heal the mind is to work on the body. She identifies six body types and prescribes remedies for each. With massage, she believes, you can free your body, calm your mind, and perhaps even improve your character. $15.95.

Logue, A. W. *The Psychology of Eating and Drinking: An Introduction.* **Second edition.** New York: W. H. Freeman, 1991.

This book is a scholarly look at such questions as why we eat and drink, how we choose what and how much to consume, the origins and treatments of eating and drinking disorders, how eating and drinking habits are genetically or environmentally determined, and how they are affected by pregnancy, smoking, and menstrual cycles. Provides a good informative overview for the general reader. $17.95.

Pannell, Maggie. *High Blood Pressure Special Diet Cookbook.* Harper San Francisco, 1991.

Provides healthy versions of favorite classic and ethnic dishes and offers readers advice on how to improve their diets without sacrificing flavor. $7.95.

Peikin, Steven R., M.D. *Gastrointestinal Health.* New York: HarperCollins, 1991.

Self-help advice to people with anything from heartburn to ulcers. Peikin is director of gastrointestinal nutrition at Thomas Jefferson University Hospital in Philadelphia. The book includes a self-test to find your Gut Reaction Quotient, descriptions of diagnostic tests, a rundown of the best over-the-counter drugs, and a sometimes surprising list of problem foods. $19.95.

Reinisch, June, Ph.D., with Ruth Beasley, M.L.S. *The Kinsey Institute New Report on Sex.* New York: St. Martin's Press, 1990.

Containing everything you need to know to be sexually literate, this book answers the most frequently asked questions about sex and reproduction, including sex and aging, sexual dysfunction, and sexually transmitted diseases and reproductive health. $22.95.

Sarno, John, M.D. *Healing Back Pain: The Mind-Body Connection.*
New York: Warner Books, 1991.
Where other doctors see troubled vertebrae and slipped discs, Sarno,
a physician at New York University's Rusk Institute of Rehabilitation
Medicine, sees what he calls TMS (tension myositis syndrome). His
theory, developed over nearly two decades, is that repressed emotions,
particularly anger, are the cause of back pain. $9.95.

Stressmap—Personal Diary Edition: The Ultimate Stress Management,
Self-Assessment and Coping Guide Developed by Essi Systems. **Ex-**
panded ed., Rev. by Esther M. Orioli, M.S. Foreword by Robert K.
Cooper, Ph.D. New York: Newmarket Press, 1991.
The only measurement tool that integrates all major stress research,
medical, psychological, and interpersonal, *Stressmap* gives you a revealing self-portrait of the state of your stress health. A self-help section, Action Planning Guide, gives more than a hundred simply
written, effective counseling tips on how to handle pressure on the
job and at home. $14.95.

Verny, Thomas, M.D., and Pamela Weintraub. *Nurturing the Unborn*
Child. New York: Delacorte Press, 1991.
A nine-month program for soothing, stimulating, and communicating
with your baby. Scientists have recently learned that the unborn child
is a deeply sensitive individual who forms a powerful relationship with
his or her parents while still in the womb. Using the techniques in
this book, parents can communicate with the developing baby,
strengthening the lifelong parent-child bond. $18.00.

The Wellness Encyclopedia: The Comprehensive Family Resource for
Safeguarding Health and Preventing Illness, the Editors of the Uni-
versity of California, Berkeley, Wellness Letter. Boston: Houghton
Mifflin, 1991.
Written for aging but still healthy baby boomers who want to enjoy
a long life in top shape. Unlike traditional, disease-oriented medical
encyclopedias, this one focuses on what to do to avoid getting sick,
with long sections on nutrition, exercise, and environmental safety.
Especially useful is "The Wellness Food Guide," a sixty-one-page
review of best bets for healthy eating. $29.95.

Witkin, Georgia, Ph.D. *The Female Stress Syndrome: How to Become*
Stresswise in the 90's. **Revised and expanded second edition.** New
York: Newmarket Press, 1991.

Witkin was the first to document how and why women experience stress differently from men. Written with candor and simplicity, and laced with case studies, checklists, and quizzes, the book provides practical solutions to short- and long-term stress situations, and proven coping strategies, gleaned from Witkin's more than fifteen years as a clinician and educator. $12.95.

STRESS REDUCTION AUDIO TAPES

Rather than letting stress wear you down mentally and physically, consider listening to a tape that relaxes you and restores your energy.

Deep Relaxation 40 minutes; a lesson in visualizing techniques that help you enter a tension-free state. HarperCollins, $9.95. 212-313-3761.

Interludes 60 minutes; sounds of a tropical beach, babbling brook, thunderstorm, and crackling fireplace. Great American Audio, $9.95. 914-576-7660.

Machu Picchu Impressions 43 minutes; birds and insects recorded at dawn in this ancient Incan city in the Peruvian Andes. Vital Body Marketing, $9.95. 516-759-5200.

The Rush Hour Refresher 30 minutes; breathing techniques for drivers to relieve tension and restore energy. Enhanced Audio Systems, $9.95. 510-652-4009.

Sounds of Nature Four cassettes, 90 minutes each: ocean waves, forest sounds, gentle rain, creek in the forest. Center for Marine Conservation, $36 the set. 800-227-1929.

COMPUTER SOFTWARE AND ON-LINE SERVICES

Even if you are a life-extension devotee, you probably don't know everything about the food you eat: calories, fat, fiber, carbohydrates, vitamins, and minerals. Books that list common foods and their component nutrients are of necessity limited in scope and clumsy to use. On the other hand, a computer database is a perfect way to organize and present this information.

Diet Wise/Energy Wise Provides information on sodium, sugar, and cholesterol content of foods. Toll-free assistance is available from a registered dietitian. Nutritional Data Resources, $159. For IBM and compatibles. 800-637-3438.

The Dieter's Edge A comprehensive system of measuring personal metabolism rates, eating habits, and exercise regimes. Takes time, but if you are serious about nutrition, worth the effort. Training Table Systems, $49.95. For IBM and compatibles. 800-336-6644.

DINE Windows Comprehensive diet and nutrition information. DINE Systems, $295. For IBM and Mac. 716-688-2492.

Fitness Profile Scores your current fitness from several tests, most of which can be done at home. Wellsource Clackamas, $395. For IBM and compatibles. 800-533-9355.

The Food Processor II One of the most complete nutrition and dietary data bases and analyzers around. The program includes 2,400 foods, each analyzed for thirty different nutrients. ESHA Research, $295. For IBM, Mac, and Apple II. 503-585-6242.

Home Doctor A rudimentary self-diagnostic tool that can help answer questions about simple ailments. Dynacomp, $39.95. For IBM and compatibles. 716-671-6180.

Life and Death II: The Brain Lets you play doctor and diagnose a variety of ailments, call for CAT, MRI, X rays, or angiograms, and actually "operate" on a patient. Fun to use. Software Toolworks, $49.95. For IBM and Mac. 415-883-3000.

Sante Computerized meal and recipe analysis. Reports cover cholesterol, fat, calories, essential vitamins, minerals, and twenty-nine nutrients from 3,000 possible foods. Hopkins Technology, $59.95. For IBM and compatibles. 612-931-9376.

Vision Aerobics Eye exercises for people whose eyes need to withstand all-day punishment. Vision Aerobics, Inc., $99. For IBM and compatibles. 908-219-1916.

COMPUTER ON-LINE SERVICES

CompuServe Although most, if not all, on-line services offer health information, none is equal to CompuServe. Expect to find *Longevity* magazine on-line by late 1992. It offers:

1. **The Health Database Plus,** which allows you to keep up with the latest-breaking medical news in the form of short summaries of articles from leading medical journals.

2. **Health Net,** an on-line medical reference library which you can consult at any hour to learn about symptoms, diseases, home health care, drugs, and more.
3. **Court Pharmacy,** an on-line drugstore that files prescriptions.
4. **Health Forums,** which gather together people with common interests, allowing them to discuss their illness, share advice, and offer support.

SPAS AND RETREATS

Which is the best for you? Simple: the place that does best what you want most, like serious weight loss, tough shape-ups, no-nonsense stress relief, peace and quiet, or blissful pampering.

The Aerobics Center
12200 Preston Road
Dallas, Texas 75230
800-444-5187

Headed by Dr. Kenneth Cooper and the Aerobic Institute, the institute emphasizes preventive health care, health, nutrition, exercise, and an improvement in quality of life. It is a "practical application" approach with no pampering. There are outstanding medical resources and facilities. Each individual receives a comprehensive program. The minimum stay is four days. Cost includes a physical examination, lodging, meals, nutrition consultation, stress management, exercise program, behavior modification, and lifestyle analysis.

SPECIALIZATIONS: health, nutrition, and exercise.

Bon Reussite Resort
43019 North Sierra Highway
Lancaster, Calif. 93534
800-432-5847

The program aims at health improvement and weight reduction. There is a supervised fitness program in conjunction with diet. No smoking, no alcohol! Facilities include tennis courts, pool, sauna, gym, walking track, and lectures beginning at 7:00 a.m. Nightly entertainment (magic shows,

music, dancing) is provided. The meals are 900 calories of complex carbohydrates per day. No pampering.
SPECIALIZATIONS: weight reduction, health improvement.

Bonaventure Resort and Spa
250 Racquet Club Road
Fort Lauderdale, Fla. 33326
800-327-8090

Rooms are decorated in southwestern style; services include massage, a full-service salon, herbal wraps, therapy baths, loofah, individual fitness, and three nutritionally balanced meals a day.
SPECIALIZATIONS: combination of pampering and fitness.

Canyon Ranch
Bellefontaine and Kemble Streets
Lenox, Mass. 01240
413-637-4400
and
8600 East Rockcliff Road
Tucson, Ariz. 85715
800-742-9000

This spa vacation is a complete experience including gourmet meals, fitness classes, sports, health and fitness assessment, presentations, and recipe demonstrations. Packages include massage, herbal wraps, hydrotherapy, facials, sports lesson, haircut, manicure, and pedicure.
SPECIALIZATIONS: fitness, sports, beauty, healthy living.

The Claremont Resort
Ashby and Domingo Avenues
Box 23363
Oakland, Calif. 94623
415-843-3000

The San Francisco Bay Area's newest spa, situated on twenty-two acres of landscaped grounds in the hills of Oakland and Berkeley. The Claremont's spa programs include aerobics, weight training, swimming, and tennis. Hydrotherapy, body wraps, and massage are major features here. Aromatherapy is used to detoxify the food. Spa cuisine is low-calorie, low-cholesterol, low-salt.
SPECIALIZATIONS: hydrotherapy, aromatherapy.

The Cliff Spa
Snowbird Ski and Summer Resort
Snowbird, Utah 84092
801-742-2222

Located near Salt Lake City, the facilities operate year-round. During the summer, hiking and swimming (indoor and out) are available, in addition to regular spa amenities such as massage, whirlpool, hydrotherapy, herbal wraps, and facials. In the winter, aerobics are offered, in addition to the main draw of fabulous downhill skiing.

SPECIALIZATIONS: spa pampering as adjunct to downhill skiing.

Coolfront Resort
Rt. 1, Box 710
Berkeley Springs, W.Va. 25411
304-258-4500

Coolfront offers different types of accommodations, including chalets and lodges, for a diverse clientele. It is a corporate retreat and conference center that also caters to families. Children are welcome and get a price break if they are between the ages of three and twelve. Babysitting is provided.

SPECIALIZATIONS: health retreats, spa facilities.

Cosmyl Spa and Beauty Institute
4401 Ponce de Leon Boulevard
Coral Gables, Fla. 33146
305-442-9305

Primarily a day spa; however, packages are available in conjunction with the Mayfair House Hotel. Services include hydrotherapy, facials, massage, sea herbal wrap, body waxing, makeup lessons, fitness room, low-impact aerobics, and strength exercises.

SPECIALIZATIONS: skin care (the spa also manufactures its own skin care line).

Deerfield Manor Spa
R.D. 1, Route 402
East Stroudsburg, Pa. 18301
717-223-0160

Deerfield Manor is a small coed spa for only thirty-three guests which specializes in a hiking program. The minimum stay is a weekend, and the costs include room, meals, exercise program, and evening entertainment. Seasonal.

SPECIALIZATIONS: fitness and diet with strong hiking program.

Desert Hot Springs Hotel and Spa
10805 Palm Drive
Desert Hot Springs, Calif. 92240
619-329-6495

This tropical spa offers massages, facials, body wraps, and an Olympic-size pool. Stays can range from daily to monthly.

SPECIALIZATIONS: natural hot mineral water with eight minerals, pampering, rejuvenation.

Doral Saturnia International Spa and Resort
8755 N.W. 36th Street
Miami, Fla. 33178
305-593-6030

A casually elegant spa with services including pickup at the airport by limousine, three spa meals a day, weight room, three pools, massages, facials, hydrotherapy, computerized health profile, and cooking demonstrations.

SPECIALIZATIONS: you choose an emphasis—e.g., stress management, cellulite program, health and fitness, diet, sports (golf and tennis), total image (pampering).

The Four Seasons Resort Club at Las Colinas
4150 North MacArthur Blvd.
Irving, Tex. 75038
214-717-0700

A European spa and salon, this club is open to the public for individual treatments. Considered one of the most comprehensive clubs in North America.

SPECIALIZATIONS: hosts several televised celebrity golf and tennis tournaments.

Garden Spa Inn
92 Highway 34 South
Colt's Neck, N.J. 07722
908-303-0717

Garden Spa Inn offers a complete pampering package for the individual who needs to be rejuvenated and de-stressed. It does not ordinarily accept anyone under the age of eighteen but has made some special exceptions. *SPECIALIZATIONS:* weight loss and rejuvenation (pampering). Closed in December.

The Ghost Ranch
Abiquiu, N.M. 87510
505-685-4333
A Spartan Presbyterian-run facility located on 20,000 acres, ninety minutes north of Santa Fe. The focus here is on solitude and time for inner reflection. Ghost Ranch primarily serves as a site for group meetings and seminars, but individuals are welcome if space is available. Spectacular scenery, mountainous terrain, and vast pasturelands for hiking. *SPECIALIZATIONS:* solitude, spectacular New Mexico scenery.

The Golden Door
P.O. Box 463077
Escondido, Calif. 92046-3077
619-744-5777
Located on 177 acres of beautifully landscaped grounds, The Golden Door provides a serene atmosphere. Facilities include four gyms, two pools, four tennis courts, and a weight room. There are only thirty-nine guests per week. Guests can choose from several activities including weight training, yoga, hikes, water exercises, and aerobics. Spa cuisine is low-fat, low-salt, low-sugar, with organic vegetables grown on the premises. The minimum stay is one week. Rates include all beauty treatments and personalized programs.
SPECIALIZATIONS: fitness, beauty, relaxation, stress reduction.

The Greenbrier
White Sulphur Springs, W.Va. 24986
800-624-6070
A beautiful hotel-connected spa with superlative service and luxurious accommodations. Many of the staff proudly claim two and three generations of family service and guests return year after year. The flavor is Old South, while the spa treatments available are European-style with

revitalizing mineral waters. The Jack Nicklaus–designed golf course and the twenty championship tennis courts are renowned. Unique "extras" include afternoon tea and chamber music concerts.
SPECIALIZATIONS: mineral-water treatments in a luxurious setting.

The Greenhouse
P.O. Box 1144
Arlington, Tex. 76004
817-640-4000

The Greenhouse offers many different and beneficial services for the body. Included in the cost for a day are: a one-hour massage, one-hour facial, hair/scalp treatment, pedicure or manicure, beauty class and makeover, three or four hours of exercise, lunch, fitness consultation, and nutrition consultation.
SPECIALIZATIONS: red-carpet treatment, ultimate pampering, and individual attention.

Green Mountain at Fox Run
P.O. Box 164
Ludlow, Vt. 05149
802-228-8885

Green Mountain at Fox Run offers many different and beneficial services for maintaining good health. The spa is for women only and guests must be seventeen or older. No alcohol is permitted.
SPECIALIZATIONS: weight and health, lifestyle management. The spa has the oldest "anti-diet" program in the country, and offers continuing-education programs to the medical and scientific communities in January and February.

Green Valley Spa Resort
1515 West Canyon View Drive
St. George, Utah 84770
801-628-8060

Located in Utah's red rock country, Green Valley specializes in creating one-on-one exercise programs to meet and challenge the fitness level of each guest. Running, hiking, and weight training are scheduled at beginner through advanced levels. Pampering services including massage and sauna are available, and careful attention is paid to how the color, smell, sound, and ambience of each room affect the senses. Diet is salt-free, caffeine-free, and low-fat. Guests learn to cook delicious low-fat meals. No one under sixteen allowed.

SPECIALIZATIONS: one-on-one fitness and exercise programs.

Gurney's Inn
Box UUU, Old Montauk Highway
Montauk, N.Y. 11954
516-668-2345

Located on the shore, Gurney's is a full-service spa offering a comprehensive range of targeted programs. The special "five-day plan" is a program for top corporate executives that utilizes exercise, nutrition counseling, and stress reduction to improve productivity and prolong life. The "four-day marine renewal" utilizes hydro-relaxation, seaweed wraps, Roman baths, and aerobic beach walks for stress relief. There are many other programs available, all of which emphasize the healing and restorative powers of the sea. Meals are gourmet, low-calorie.

SPECIALIZATION: executive longevity program.

The Heartland Health and Fitness Retreat and Spa
20 East Jackson Blvd.
Suite 300
Chicago, Ill. 60604
800-545-4853

Located 90 miles south of Chicago, this is a peaceful country estate on a private lake. Year-round, it offers a wide range of exercise activities and information on nutrition, fitness, and stress management. The minimum stay is two days. Costs include room, meals, exercise classes, and one massage. No smoking is allowed.

SPECIALIZATIONS: relaxed environment, personalized programs.

The Himalayan Institute
R.R. 1, Box 400
Honesdale, Pa. 18431
800-822-4547

Located on 400 acres in the Poconos, this retreat focuses on teaching yoga, diet, nutrition, and Eastern and Western philosophy. First-timers

are encouraged to attend weekend seminars. No TV or spa facilities.
SPECIALIZATION: yoga.

Holy Cross Monastery
P.O. Box 99
West Park, N.Y. 12493
914-384-6660

This retreat, located on the banks of the Hudson, offers a peaceful coun-trified environment in which to get away from it all. Guests are welcome for weekend stays in a small facility with no private bathrooms, TV, or spa facilities. A complete retreat where silence is observed from evening until after breakfast.
SPECIALIZATIONS: monastic retreat, reflection.

Insight Meditation Society
1230 Pleasant Street
Barre, Mass. 01005
508-355-4378
and
P.O. Box 909
Woodacre, Calif. 94973
415-488-0164

This retreat center has been attracting increasing numbers of people over the years, including therapists and physicists. First-timers are encouraged to participate in retreats, which can last from two to nine days. The technique, "mindfulness" (a 2,500-year-old Buddhist form of meditation), is an integral part of the Stress Relaxation Pro-gram at the University of Massachusetts Medical Center in Worcester. During the retreats, as many as a hundred people sleep on mats and eat vegetarian meals. Silence is observed twenty-four hours a day. No spa facilities.
SPECIALIZATION: Buddhist retreat.

The Kerr House
17777 Beaver Street
P.O. Box 363
Grand Rapids, Ohio 43522
419-832-1733

The Kerr House is a Victorian mansion that accommodates no more than eight guests. A coed spa, it specializes in natural eating and total relaxation. Cost includes everything except gratuities.
SPECIALIZATIONS: total relaxation, natural eating.

La Costa Resort
2100 Costa del Mar Road
Carlsbad, Calif. 92009
619-438-9111

Located 90 minutes from downtown Los Angeles on 400 acres, La Costa is generally acknowledged to be the world's preeminent spa. It specializes in medical/fitness evaluation and nutritional analysis. With a minimum stay of seven days, one can attend the longevity center, where a personalized health plan is created. Superb golf and tennis are available, as are all spa amenities. Smoking and alcohol are permitted, and there are even bars on the premises.
SPECIALIZATIONS: medical/fitness evaluation, nutritional analysis.

Le Meridien Spa
2000 Second Street
Coronado, Calif. 92118
619-435-3000

Spread over 17 acres in Southern California, this San Diego spa specializes in pampering! There is a total fitness program combined with a European-style Clarins beauty program. A typical day includes a mixture of massages, facial and herbal wraps, fitness cuisine, and a minimum of two fitness activities. The emphasis here is not on weight loss but on fitness and beauty. Guests must be at least sixteen years old.
SPECIALIZATIONS: beauty and pampering combined with fitness via Clarins method.

Mario's International Spa
35 East Garfield Road
Aurora, Ohio 44202
216-562-9171

Mario's International Spa has only fourteen guest rooms, each with a private Jacuzzi. The decor is antiques and white wicker, and spa cuisine is approved by the Cleveland Clinic Foundation. It also specializes in skin care. Three packages are available: Day Retreat, Shape Escape, and Complete Retreat.

SPECIALIZATIONS: skin care, facials.

The Mountain
Highlands Camp and Conference Center
841 Highway 106
Highlands, N.C. 28741
704-526-5838

Located on the top of Mount Scaley, this retreat provides a 70-mile vista—you can see both Georgia and South Carolina on clear days. The lodge overlooks the Blue Valley and is surrounded by the lush vegetation of a temperate rain forest. Three main programs are available: summer youth camps, an elderhostel which provides education for people over sixty, and Mountain Magic, which includes nature walks, hiking, and rafting.

SPECIALIZATIONS: hiking, outdoor activities.

National Institute of Fitness
202 North Snow Canyon Road
Ivins, Utah 84738
801-673-4905

Located in the heart of canyon country at an altitude of 3,000 feet. The atmosphere here is decidedly high desert. Stays are for one week minimum, with the focus on education and permanent lifestyle change through correct nutrition and exercise. Lowering cholesterol and blood pressure are targeted goals. In addition to the daily lectures, swimming, tennis, racquetball, and hiking are available. Smoking, caffeine, and soda are forbidden.

SPECIALIZATIONS: education and permanent lifestyle change.

New Age Health Spa
Route 5
Neversink, N.Y. 12765
914-985-7601

Located in picturesque upstate New York. The emphasis here is holistic: healthy unity of mind, body, and spirit. Exercise, hiking, meditation, and other New Age activities are available. No smoking or alcohol.
SPECIALIZATION: holistic.

The Oaks at Ojai
122 East Ojai Avenue
Ojai, Calif. 93023
800-753-6257

The No Pain Total Fitness Program is the attraction here. Guests put together their own programs from the sixteen fitness classes available. Food is all natural, and all unnatural substances are banned. Nature walks, aqua-toning, and body scrubs are available, in addition to swimming, sauna, and aerobics.
SPECIALIZATION: No Pain Total Fitness Program.

Omega Institute
R.D. 2, Box 377
Rhinebeck, N.Y. 12572
914-266-8049

New Age in approach, with an emphasis on personal development. The setting is rustic, often described as "old scout camp." Weekly and week-end workshops are organized around such topics as healing, relationships, dance and music therapy. Massage, sauna, swimming, and hiking are available but are not part of the organized activities. All meals are vegetarian, and fish is served only once weekly. Seasonal.
SPECIALIZATION: self-development.

Palm Aire Spa Resort and Club
2501 Palm Aire Drive North
Pompano Beach, Fla. 33069
305-972-3300

In a celebrity atmosphere, spa services include three meals, medical and fitness evaluation, massages, facials, herbal wraps, whirlpools, fitness classes, and airport transportation. No children are allowed.
SPECIALIZATIONS: weight loss, beauty treatments.

The Palms
572 North Indian Canyon Drive
Palm Springs, Calif. 92262
800-327-0867

The Palms is not a pampering spa. Smoking and alcohol are banned, and guests are restricted to 1,000 calories a day. Exercise, including mountain hikes, aerobics, swimming, and yoga, is emphasized. Guests are usually mothers and daughters. This is a small spa, with only thirty-three rooms.
SPECIALIZATIONS: fitness and weight loss.

The Phoenix Fitness Resort
111 North Post Oak Lane
Houston, Tex. 77024
800-548-4700

The Phoenix Fitness Resort offers many different and beneficial services for the mind and body. Services included in the cost are three meals a day, exercise classes, two choices of massage, pedicure, manicure, a facial, or reflexology. In the evening there are workshops on everything from gift wrapping to self-image. There are no restrictions.
SPECIALIZATIONS: fitness and exercise programs.

Plantation Spa
51-550 Kam Highway
Kaawa, Hawaii 96730
800-422-0307

Located on an old estate in the mountains of Hawaii, this is the place to come to develop new habits. The Hawaiian experience includes gourmet vegetarian cuisine, waterfall setting, jogging, sauna, gym exercise. There are daily programs, mini-retreats, weekly stays. No children are allowed.
SPECIALIZATION: lifestyle changes through positive thinking, healthy eating, and regular exercise.

Ponte Vedra Inn and Club
200 Ponte Vedra Boulevard
Ponte Vedra Beach, Fla. 32082
904-285-1111

A four-star resort hotel and spa. Programs are individually designed as the guest desires—whether pampering or weight loss. There are no spa

packages; after you make hotel reservations, you set up your spa appointments. Facilities include Jacuzzi, lap pool, aerobics, Nautilus, free weights, and Aquasize. There is no smoking permitted in the spa and there is an age limit for children (over fourteen). A nursery is available.
SPECIALIZATIONS: pampering, weight loss, and any individualized program requested.

Pritikin Longevity Center
5875 Collins Avenue
Miami Beach, Fla. 33140
305-866-2237

Set up as a residential program, this spa is designed to teach you a new lifestyle. Services include massages, facials, lectures, exercise, and cooking classes. The program is designed to get you on track with the Pritikin lifestyle. There are usually no more than fifty people in a group.
SPECIALIZATIONS: diabetes, heart disease, high blood pressure patients; weight loss through proper nutrition and lifestyle management.

Regency Health Resort and Spa
2000 South Ocean Drive
Hallandale, Fla. 33009
305-454-2220

The Regency offers a very relaxed, friendly, family feeling. It is on the ocean, just north of Miami. All meals are vegetarian. Exercise classes and equipment are available, including yoga, walking classes, and Nautilus machines. The health director sets up a dietary program for each individual and gives daily lectures. The emphasis is on a healthy lifestyle, which includes stress reduction and weight loss. Special classes are given in food preparation. The minimum stay is one week. There is no smoking or drinking allowed.
SPECIALIZATIONS: healthy lifestyle, stress management, meditation, behavior modification, weight loss.

Russell House
611 Truman Avenue
Key West, Fla. 33040
305-294-8787

A European-style health resort in quaint and historic Key West. Holistic meals and juice fasting are specialties. The environment is totally relaxed and all you need to bring is your bathing suit. It accommodates only twenty to twenty-five guests. No children are allowed.

SPECIALIZATIONS: weight loss, beauty, individual attention.

Safety Harbor Spa
105 North Bayshore Drive
Safety Harbor, Fla. 34695
813-726-1161

Safety Harbor offers a little of everything, with an emphasis on fitness. It has a full exercise room and thirty-five classes a day. The spa's salon uses only Lancôme products, and services include makeup, skin care, hair, and sun care. It offers facials, manicures, pedicures, loofah, herbal and hair treatments. All meals are nutritionally balanced for a total calorie count of 900. It has numerous packages including stays of four nights and five days, seven nights and eight days, a weekend special, a four-day fitness program, a four-day tennis program, and à la carte services with hotel rates only.

SPECIALIZATIONS: fitness, beauty.

Sans Souci Spa
3745 Route 725
Bellbrook, Ohio 45305
513-848-4851

This spa offers a personalized program of fitness and nutrition, as well as weight control classes. There is no age restriction, and smoking is permitted outside only. The minimum stay is one day.

SPECIALIZATION: overall wellness program.

Shangri-La Natural Health Resort
P.O. Box 2328
Bonita Springs, Fla. 33959-2328
813-992-3811

Shangri-La is located on more than eight acres, 26 miles south of the Fort Myers airport. Meals are completely vegetarian and consist of mostly raw fruits and steamed vegetables. Hot food is served only four times a week. There is a health director on staff who gives lectures three times a week. The only liquid served is distilled water. The spa also offers a distilled-water fast or a watermelon fast for those who want more energy.

Low-impact aerobics, yoga, and relaxation classes are offered. On Thursdays and Saturdays, special trips are arranged to local malls and shopping centers. Every Tuesday night is a square dance. Shuffleboard and paddleboating are popular recreations. No smoking or drinking is allowed. The atmosphere is old Florida, restful and peaceful. Many come to stay for months.

SPECIALIZATIONS: total vegetarian program, rest.

Sivananda Ashram Yoga Farm
14651 Ballantree Lane
Grass Valley, Calif. 95949
916-272-9322

Spiritual, rural, simple, located on 80 acres in the foothills of the Sierras. A stay at this rustic spa begins and ends with silent meditation. Facilities include a pond for swimming; walking and cross-country skiing are other activities. There is a minimum stay of one week. Rates include two meals and two yoga classes.

SPECIALIZATIONS: yoga, diet, general health.

Sonesta Sanibel Harbour Spa
17260 Harbour Pointe Drive
Fort Myers, Fla. 33908
813-466-2156

Located on 45 beautiful and private acres fifteen minutes from the Fort Myers airport, the spa specializes in everything and the staff boasts that "all our guests want to move in and never leave." It has three restaurants that offer low-fat, diet, and vegetarian meals. Tennis and beauty treatments are popular packages.

SPECIALIZATIONS: all programs available, from tennis to beauty and weight loss.

Sonoma Mission Inn and Spa
P.O. Box 1447
Sonoma, Calif. 95476
707-938-9000

Located in the heart of Northern California's wine country, this spa mixes pretty surroundings, canopy beds in bedrooms with fireplaces, and landscaped grounds with traditional spa amenities. Hydrotherapy is an important aspect of the spa program, with swimming, weights, tennis, and hiking. Meals are low-calorie and gourmet. Horseback riding and golf are available nearby.

SPECIALIZATION: hydrotherapy.

The Spa at Grand Lake
1667 Exeter Road
Lebanon, Conn. 06249
203-642-4306

Located near Hartford, this is a full-service spa. Its style is conservative, traditional, low-key, and not glitzy at all. The setting is akin to an estate, with 75 acres of grounds. Services available include massage, water aerobics, calisthenics, yoga, tennis, swimming. Meals are sugar- and fat-free.

SPECIALIZATIONS: weight loss, stress reduction.

The Spa at the Crescent
400 Crescent, Suite 100
Dallas, Tex. 75201
214-871-3232

The Spa at the Crescent is a club but does allow hotel guests to use the facilities. It offers many different and beneficial services for the body. Services for the day include: facial, massage, aroma bath, manicure, paraffin treatment, lunch, sauna/whirlpool, a Chanel makeover, and a bouquet of flowers for ladies. Benefits included for members are fitness classes, cardiovascular workouts, weight machines, workout clothes, and a discount on beauty and spa facilities. No children under seventeen are permitted.

SPECIALIZATION: rated one of the best hotel, beauty and aerobics spas.

Sufi Summer Workshop
P.O. Box 75
Torreon, N.M. 87061
505-384-5135

The Sufi Summer Workshop combines movement, mystical dance, and meditation for a unique summer experience to rejuvenate the mind and body. The workshop begins July 7 and closes for new participants after August 7. Lodgings are in modest cubicles, and vegetarian food is served.

SPECIALIZATIONS: movement, mystical dance, and meditation.

Tassajara
39171 Tassajara Road
Carmel Valley, Calif. 93924
415-431-3771

This is a monastic community turned summer resort set in the mountains of Monterey. The area is rustic and beautiful. Guests can practice meditation with the Buddhist monks who live there or they can just sit by the pool.

SPECIALIZATIONS: Zen retreat, relaxation.

Topnotch Resort and Spa
P.O. Box 1458
Stowe, Vt. 05672
802-253-8585

Set in beautiful Stowe, in the heart of the Green Mountains, the Spa at Topnotch offers a retreat for the health conscious with the added benefits of its beautiful setting. Only one restriction applies—no one under the age of fourteen is admitted.

SPECIALIZATIONS: new perspectives on eating and exercising; fitness and exercise classes with complete individual attention.

Dr. Wilkinson's Hot Springs
1507 Lincoln Avenue
Calistoga, Calif. 94515
707-942-4102

Mud, mineral water, and massage are the three reasons for visiting this historic Napa Valley spa. The clientele is young and includes many European visitors, who find Dr. Wilkinson's Hot Springs a bargain compared with Termi di Saturnia in Italy. The focus is very specific: mudbaths, followed by a cooling plunge, then whirlpool or steam. Meals are *not* available, but rooms in the hotel are furnished with refrigerators and coffee-makers.

SPECIALIZATIONS: mud baths, mineral water.

Zen Mountain Monastery
P.O. Box 197
Mt. Tremper, N.Y. 12457
914-688-2228

Located 100 miles north of New York City, Zen Mountain Monastery exposes visitors to and lets them participate in the everyday activities of a monk. Visitors use their hands as well as their minds, which provides for an exceptional retreat with hard work.

SPECIALIZATIONS: reading up on topics ranging from martial arts to Chinese healing techniques, self-exploration, meditation.

If none of the above spas is to your liking, you can contact Frank Van Putton, President, Spa Finders, at 212-924-6800 or 800-ALL-SPAS.

Index

accident control, 96–97
acne, dermabrasion and, 215
aerobic exercises, 155–61
  balancing between anaerobic and, 155–56, 160–61
  high-impact, 157–59
  low-impact, 157–58
  moderate-impact, 158–59
  selection of, 156–59
aflatoxin, 140–41
AGE-1, 60–61, 272, 280
aging:
  charlatans on, 16–17, 22–25, 255–56
  common picture of, 1
  definition of, 1
  launching battle against, 1–2, 8–9
  as loss of innate heat, 17–18, 20
  pluses and minuses of, 2–8
  rates of, 10–11, 80–99
Aging Potential Test, 81–86
alcohol use, 81, 90
Allen, George, 248–49
aloe vera gel, 209
AL-721, 260–61

altruism, 188–89
Alzheimer's disease:
  antioxidant treatment of, 45
  brain transplants for, 249–50
American Cancer Society, 119, 152
American Heart Association, 103, 110, 119
aminoguanidine, 261–62
anaerobic exercises, 159–61
  balancing between aerobic and, 155–156, 160–61
  benefits of, 159
  fitness trainers for, 159–60
anorexia, dietary restriction and, 136
antioxidants, 43–47
  in prolonging life, 47
  for skin, 216
  sources of, 43–46
Aristotle, 17–18, 20
Arking, Robert, 280–81
aspirin, 258–59
atherosclerosis, 103
autoimmunity, 56–57

321